The 1973 Arab-Israeli War

The 1973
Arab-Israeli War

William B. Quandt, Yigal Kipnis, Risa
Brooks, Galen Jackson, Marc Trachtenberg,
Raymond Hinnebusch, Khaled Elgindy,
Jeremy Pressman, Jerome Slater

ROWMAN & LITTLEFIELD
Lanham • Boulder • New York • London

Published by Rowman & Littlefield
An imprint of The Rowman & Littlefield Publishing Group, Inc.
4501 Forbes Boulevard, Suite 200, Lanham, Maryland 20706
www.rowman.com

86-90 Paul Street, London EC2A 4NE, United Kingdom

Copyright © 2023 by The Rowman & Littlefield Publishing Group, Inc.

All rights reserved. No part of this book may be reproduced in any form or by any electronic or mechanical means, including information storage and retrieval systems, without written permission from the publisher, except by a reviewer who may quote passages in a review.

British Library Cataloguing in Publication Information Available

Library of Congress Cataloging-in-Publication Data

Names: Quandt, William B., author. | Brooks, Risa, author. | Jackson, Galen, 1987– author. | Hinnebusch, Raymond A., author. | Pressman, Jeremy, 1969– author. | Slater, Jerome, author.
Title: The 1973 Arab-Israeli war / William B. Quandt, Yigal Kipnis, Risa Brooks, Galen Jackson., Marc Trachtenberg, Raymond Hinnebusch, Khlaed Elgindy, Jeremy Pressman, Jerome Slater.
Description: Lanham : Rowman & Littlefield, [2023] | Includes bibliographical references and index. | Summary: "The October 1973 Middle East War transformed the region's politics and had a huge impact on the international political system as a whole. For the 50th anniversary of the war, this book grapples with these issues in an objective way by using the mass of declassified material that has recently become available"— Provided by publisher.
Identifiers: LCCN 2023036238 (print) | LCCN 2023036239 (ebook) | ISBN 9781538172025 (cloth ; alk. paper) | ISBN 9781538172032 (electronic)
Subjects: LCSH: Israel-Arab War, 1973.
Classification: LCC DS128.1 .Q36 2023 (print) | LCC DS128.1 (ebook) | DDC 956.04/8—dc23/eng/20230808
LC record available at https://lccn.loc.gov/2023036238
LC ebook record available at https://lccn.loc.gov/202303623

∞™ The paper used in this publication meets the minimum requirements of American National Standard for Information Sciences—Permanence of Paper for Printed Library Materials, ANSI/NISO Z39.48-1992.

Contents

Introduction: The October 1973 Arab-Israeli War: Looking Back Fifty Years Later   vii

Chapter 1: The October 1973 War: Culmination of the Failure of Political Analysis   1
Yigal Kipnis

Chapter 2: Egypt's Military Effectiveness in the October War   35
Risa Brooks

Chapter 3: A Self-Inflicted Wound?: Henry Kissinger and the Ending of the October 1973 Arab-Israeli War   57
Galen Jackson and Marc Trachtenberg

Chapter 4: Syria and the 1973 Arab-Israeli War   93
Raymond Hinnebusch

Chapter 5: The Impact of the October 1973 War on the Palestinians   123
Khaled Elgindy

Chapter 6: The Cold War and Oil: Paving the Way to a US-Led Peace Process   151
Jeremy Pressman

Conclusion   165
Jerome Slater

Index   171

About the Authors   181

Introduction

The October 1973 Arab-Israeli War: Looking Back Fifty Years Later

William B. Quandt

One might expect that after nearly five decades a relatively clear picture of the causes and consequences of the October 1973 Arab-Israeli War would have emerged. After all, another international crisis, of even greater severity and equal complexity, the Cuban missile crisis of 1962, has been the subject of a fairly broad and very well documented understanding for many years. But that is not the case with the October 1973 war—also known as the Yom Kippur War or the Ramadan War, depending on whose perspective is being emphasized.

Part of the difference between the two crises may stem from the fact that there were essentially two key parties to the Cuban missile crisis—Soviet leader Nikita Khrushchev and the American president John F. Kennedy— each of whom could claim at least some degree of success from the way the crisis was resolved. By contrast, in 1973 the number of key actors was greater. There was Egyptian president Anwar Sadat, who essentially made the decision for war; Israeli prime minister Golda Meir, who refused to consider the political alternative to war, since she was convinced Israel could easily defeat Egypt on the battlefield, as it had in June 1967; Soviet leader Leonid

Brezhnev, who ineffectually tried to warn against the war, but then decided to provide political and military support to his Arab allies once it was underway; and, finally, US president Richard Nixon, who presciently warned in early 1973 that the conflict was about to erupt, but then became distracted by his own collapsing political position, leaving his national security adviser and secretary of state, Henry Kissinger, as the key American decision-maker having to deal with a region of the world that was relatively unknown to him. And there were others who played significant roles in the 1973 crisis as well, most notably Syrian president Hafiz al-Asad and Saudi Arabia's King Faisal.

One similarity in the two crises on the American side is the unusually rich documentation of key moments of decision. After all, both Kennedy and Nixon kept tape recordings of many of the most important meetings and phone calls, and those have been available to scholars for years. In addition, many of the American participants have written revealing memoirs with detailed accounts of these crises. But the abundance of source material for both crises has not been enough to provide an entirely clear picture of what happened at key moments in 1973. In part, as the chapters in this volume emphasize, the key actors have had strong motives to spin their respective versions of what actually occurred for political reasons. If both parties to the Cuban missile crisis could take some satisfaction in successfully managing a truly unprecedented nuclear crisis, the same was not true in October 1973. The Israelis, while ultimately prevailing on the battlefield, suffered serious losses, were caught by surprise, required massive American military help, and were denied a decisive victory on the Egyptian front by their own American ally. For most Israelis, someone had to be blamed for this startling and disappointing outcome.

For Egyptians, the story was just the opposite. Sadat, who had taken the gamble of launching the limited war, had no interest in revealing how close he had come to defeat. For him and most Egyptians, the war was a success, one that helped to erase the shame of the 1967 failure. For Kissinger, who has written extensively about the war, this was a crisis that established his "Super K" reputation, and he has doggedly defended his record, while soft-peddling some of his more questionable judgments, such as his underestimation of Sadat and overestimation of Israeli military prowess.[1]

Another reason for some of the continuing uncertainty about what happened at crucial moments in the 1972–1973 period is that the written record is overwhelmingly weighted to the American and Israeli sides of the story. American archives have been open for years and have been quite carefully reviewed by many scholars.[2] Israeli archives have recently also been opened and are providing a sharper picture of what took place at crucial moments.[3] These archives, especially the documents reserved for the restricted Israeli security cabinet, include insights into how Kissinger often communicated directly with Meir through the Israeli ambassador in Washington—Yitzhak Rabin until March 1973 and thereafter Simcha Dinitz—without leaving any record of these conversations in the American files. As these Israeli archives become more accessible, we can expect to fill in a few of the holes in the narrative of what occurred before and during the war.[4]

Although several useful memoirs and firsthand accounts of the war have been written by Egyptians—including Sadat—and there are even a few from Syrian sources, the Arab documentation is not nearly as complete as that from the American and Israeli sides. The same is true to a lesser degree for Soviet/Russian sources.[5] One result of this imbalance is that significant questions remain about important dimensions of the crisis. This volume tries to highlight some of them, and I will briefly review what I consider to be the most important ones that are being addressed here. I will also indicate where I think additional attention should be paid if we want to understand more fully the many lessons that can be drawn from this crisis.

Without doubt, the October 1973 war must be seen as a major international crisis. It imposed severe human and economic costs on the immediate participants, but its repercussions were much broader. They included a marked deterioration in the détente-like relationship that was still intact between the United States and the Soviet Union; an unprecedented use of oil supplies from Arab countries as an economic and political weapon, which resulted in a rapid rise in oil prices in the months following the war; and a reordering of the interstate system of the Middle East, with Egypt beginning to shift away from its previously strong alignment with other Arab states and toward becoming a major client of the United States, allowing Cairo to move toward reconciliation with Israel in the process. The war was also accompanied by more than a hint of nuclear menace, especially in its dramatic final days, when the United States declared a DEFCON 3 military alert in response to a perceived threat of unilateral Soviet military intervention in the conflict.

The above considerations lead to the obvious question of whether a crisis of this magnitude could have been avoided, and if so, how? Counterfactuals can never be easily addressed, but they nevertheless deserve consideration. And here we have two significantly different schools of thought. One maintains that the war could not have been easily avoided because the positions of the two key parties, Egypt and Israel, were so far apart, and the chance for diplomatic initiatives to narrow those gaps so limited, that some resort to force was inevitable. Sadat himself essentially promoted this line of argument, claiming that only Egypt's heroic crossing of the Suez Canal was able to break the logjam that had blocked diplomacy.[6] Some Israelis, self-servingly, have also argued that Sadat needed "his war" to restore his dignity and legitimacy in order to reinvent himself as a statesman and peacemaker.

An alternative view is that the war could and should have been prevented. In this volume, Yigal Kipnis presents the strongest case that the Egyptians in early 1973 had conveyed to Kissinger a clear willingness to proceed with a plausible diplomatic initiative that was not intrinsically hostile to fundamental Israeli interests. In his retelling, even the main skeptic on the American side—Kissinger—concluded belatedly that the war could have been avoided if only Meir had been more of a realist and less of a politician. Kipnis views her as the main obstacle to an effort to test Sadat's intentions by means of negotiations. He cites her as saying that if war came, it would be to Israel's advantage, since Egypt would lose even more decisively than it had in 1967, a view partially shared by Kissinger. She also, correctly, said that Sadat would demand a high price—the return to Egypt of all of the Sinai Peninsula—for something that might turn out to be less than peace. Her view was that Israel needed to keep a significant portion of the Sinai as a security buffer, and she understood that no Egyptian leader could accept that. Thus, she chose to continue to rely on deterrence, believing that even if that failed, Israel could fight and win another war, which might actually strengthen the Israeli hand in future negotiations. As long as Israel could count on unqualified American support, this sounded like a plausible stance. But by early 1973, Nixon was already talking to Kissinger about the danger of an explosion in the Middle East and about the need to squeeze the "old woman."

After Kissinger's meetings with Sadat's national security adviser, Hafiz Ismail, in February and May 1973, it was clear that the Egyptians were moving in the direction of meeting several of Israel's most important concerns, especially on security. Kissinger had introduced the idea of distinguishing between sovereignty and security—in other words, Egypt might be able to reclaim sovereignty over the Sinai, but Israel would be given time to withdraw its forces, and security arrangements would go into effect that would limit Egypt's ability to use the Sinai as a staging area for future wars against Israel. In addition, Egypt had made it clear that while it would publicly espouse the need for an overall Arab-Israeli peace, Sadat would leave the Palestinian question for the Jordanians and Palestinians to sort out, and he would be prepared to reach an agreement with Israel without it being contingent upon Syria, Jordan, and the Palestinians doing so. This, in fact, is what Sadat eventually settled for at Camp David in September 1978, but only after the October 1973 war had shattered a number of unwarranted assumptions.

Based on the evidence we now have, I think it is fair to conclude that the war could have been avoided if a major diplomatic effort had been launched in mid-1973. That would have required American leadership to persuade the Israelis to take some risks, and real progress in the negotiations would not have come until after Israel's elections, then scheduled for October. But it seems quite possible that Sadat would have put his war plan on hold to see

Introduction   xi

if his opening to the United States could produce a diplomatic breakthrough. Most Egyptian accounts claim that the final decision for war was not made until after the US-Soviet summit in June, which seemed to indicate that the United States had no intention of supporting a new diplomatic effort in the Middle East.

A second important but still unanswered question is whether the war could have been brought to an end within its first week. This would have required a serious parallel effort by the United States and the Soviet Union to press for a ceasefire, backed by a United Nations (UN) Security Council resolution. This is what one might have hoped for if the principles of superpower détente had been in play. And, indeed, there was a serious move in this direction. But the precise details of why it failed are still obscure, and the archival records have not yet shed much light on how close Kissinger came to getting a ceasefire in place on October 12–13—just before the Egyptians launched their second offensive toward the Sinai passes, just before the massive US military airlift to Israel got underway, several days before the Arab oil producers announced their oil embargo and production cuts, and two weeks before the DEFCON 3 alert.

Because the ceasefire initiative of October 12–13 failed, it has not received much attention, but one key Soviet observer, Anatoly Dobrynin, the USSR ambassador in Washington, has expressed the view that this was the best moment to end the war and preserve détente, and that the Soviets were fully behind the ceasefire-in-place initiative.[7] We also know that Meir had, reluctantly, agreed to Kissinger's ceasefire proposal, but we do not know how Kissinger managed to persuade her. Neither the American nor Israeli archives are of much help on this question. At the time, Kissinger blamed the British for a clumsy diplomatic move that led Sadat to a premature rejection of the plan. But Sadat's own account makes it seem as if he had no interest at that point in a ceasefire and was determined to move his forces deeper into Sinai in order to relieve pressure on his Syrian ally. Given how little trust there was between Asad and Sadat by this time, as Raymond Hinnebusch makes clear in his contribution to this volume, one must wonder if Sadat really took such a major military risk to assuage the Syrians. The Soviets also claim that they tried to persuade Sadat to agree to the ceasefire, but that he refused. In short, there are still many unanswered questions about this moment in the war. My own sense at the time was that it came close to succeeding, and we all would have been better off if it had.

A third bundle of related uncertainties surrounds the three days after Kissinger managed to reach an agreement in Moscow on what became UN Resolution 338, which called for a halt to the fighting. The ceasefire was to go into effect on October 22, just as the Israelis were on the verge of surrounding the Egyptian Third Army in Sinai. As Galen Jackson and Marc Trachtenberg show in their chapter in this volume, Kissinger, during his stop in Israel en route home to Washington, gave the Israelis more than a wink and a nod that they might continue fighting beyond the strict deadline set by the UN resolution. Kissinger has said that he may have unintentionally given that impression, but that the Israelis went much further than he had expected. But upon his return to Washington, according to a recently declassified Israeli cable, he told Dinitz on October 23 that the United States would not press Israel to withdraw to the October 22 lines and that, in fact: "They [the Americans] will give us all the cover support for our move." The Israeli ambassador quoted Kissinger as saying that he supported extending Israel's progress "in the field"—possibly a better translation would be "on the ground." Dinitz went on to say that Kissinger wanted Israel to improve its position as much as possible, but that he had to worry about relations with the Soviets and the Arabs. But he promised to cooperate closely with Israel in devising a postwar strategy. Then, "Kissinger added that if anyone knew about the degree of intimacy between us he [Kissinger] would be fired."[8] This seems to imply that Nixon, the only person who could fire Kissinger, was not aware of what his secretary of state was telling the Israelis and would not have approved of it if he had been.

Shortly after this exchange, the crisis got worse. On October 24, several messages went back and forth between Moscow and Washington, the last of which included Brezhnev's threat to take unilateral military action if Israel did not stop its advances. As is well known, Kissinger reacted by convening a meeting of top security officials that decided, without Nixon's direct participation, to order US troops worldwide to be placed on a DEFCON 3 alert status. The next morning, there was a brief moment of alarm in the Situation Room of the White House when an intercepted Soviet diplomatic message seemed to suggest that Soviet troops were on their way to Cairo. Kissinger immediately contacted Dobrynin and was told that these were a small contingent of military observers to monitor the ceasefire that had been agreed to when Kissinger was in Moscow. Soon thereafter, tensions began to ease, the United States strongly urged Israel to allow food and water to get to the Egyptian Third Army, and the ceasefire finally took hold. A few days later, Kissinger made his famous "we are in the catbird seat" comment. But he had gotten there with what seems like a highly risky series of steps that might well have led to further escalation. And, as Jackson and Trachtenberg argue, the DEFCON 3 crisis helped put an end, at least for the remainder of the time Kissinger was in power, to any effective policy of détente.

One other angle of this crisis that has received relatively little attention is the nuclear shadow that loomed over it. Since at least mid-1967, it was generally known in US policy circles that Israel had acquired some degree of nuclear capability. Meir had told Nixon as much in September 1969, and presumably the Soviets and their Arab clients knew as well. During the 1973 war, there were a few moments other than the DEFCON 3 alert when nuclear dangers were part of the drama. From my position on the National Security Council staff, I recall on about October 8 or 9 seeing an intelligence report that the Israeli Jericho missiles had been placed on a higher alert status. Nothing was said about the kind of warheads they might have carried, the issue was not discussed in any meeting that I attended, and no one has managed to unearth the document. Still, knowledgeable Israelis have confirmed to me that Israeli defense minister Moshe Dayan, without cabinet authorization, might have given the order to make sure the Jerichos were ready for possible use. It is also now known that on about October 8, Dayan sought a meeting of the security cabinet to discuss his idea of a demonstrative nuclear blast, and he wanted Meir to allow Israel's top nuclear specialist to brief the cabinet. She refused, and the issue reportedly did not come up again.[9]

Even if the Israelis did not make any explicit nuclear threats during the October 1973 war, the mere existence of their nuclear capability almost certainly had an impact on Arab war planning. For example, Syrian tanks were given orders to stop if they reached the Israeli border, as some of them almost did in the first days of the war. Egyptian forces concentrated on crossing the Suez Canal and then consolidating their foothold on the eastern bank. Only a week after crossing the canal did they move their tanks toward the passes, some thirty miles or so farther east. At no point did Egyptian forces launch strikes into pre-1967 Israel. Sadat, years later, was reportedly asked by an Israeli general why he had not moved more swiftly and aggressively to take the passes after crossing the canal. He replied, in a joking manner: "You have nuclear arms. Haven't you heard?"[10]

The only other hints of some nuclear dimension of the crisis involve reports of Soviet ships passing through the Dardanelles and triggering a monitoring system that was looking for signs of nuclear weapons on the ships. At least one of the ships that had triggered an alarm was seen in mid to late October docking in Alexandria. Some wondered if the Soviets might be sending nuclear warheads for the Scud missiles that were known to exist in Egypt. US secretary of defense James Schlesinger later said that he was concerned, although he considered it a low probability.[11] It should also be noted that just before the October 22 ceasefire went into effect, the Egyptians, with Soviet support, fired two Scud missiles at Israeli troop concentrations in Sinai, doing a small amount of damage. They were not, of course, armed with nuclear warheads. Still, without factoring in the nuclear shadow caused by these events, one misses part of what made this a crisis that was widely considered to present the most serious risk of nuclear war since the Cuban missile crisis.

A final issue that deserves more discussion is whether or not détente could have been preserved after the October War. In one of their discussions in the middle of the war, Nixon and Kissinger had a very frank exchange:

> Nixon: As far as the Russians are concerned, they have a pretty good beef insofar as everything we have offered on the Mid-East, you know what I mean, that meeting in San Clemente [in June 1973], we were stringing them along and they know it. We've got to come up with something on the diplomatic front, because if we go with [only] the ceasefire, they'll figure that we get the ceasefire and the Israelis will dig in and we'll back them, as we always have. That's putting it quite bluntly, but it's quite true Henry, isn't it?
>
> HK: There's a lot in that.
>
> Nixon: Because we've got to squeeze the Israelis when this is over and the Russians have got to know it. We've got to squeeze them goddamn hard. . . . We told them before we'd squeeze them and we didn't. . . . We ought to tell Dobrynin . . . that Brezhnev and Nixon will settle this damn thing. That ought to be done. You know that.
>
> HK: Exactly. Exactly right.[12]

This exchange strongly suggests that Nixon, had he managed to remain in power, might well have tried to preserve the core principles of détente, unlike Kissinger, who seemed distinctly unenthusiastic, even while voicing his apparent agreement with his boss. So it is possible to argue that it was not only the DEFCON 3 alert, and Kissinger's role in triggering it by his nudging the Israelis to keep going after negotiating the ceasefire in Moscow, that undermined détente—as important was Nixon's loss of authority and eventual departure from office in August 1974. With Kissinger at the peak of his power by then, détente no longer had an advocate in the White House.

Whereas Nixon seems to have genuinely believed in some sort of US-Soviet condominium as the central element of détente, Kissinger's view was much more that the facade of diplomacy offered by détente would allow him to outmaneuver the Soviets in the Middle East. The key would be convincing Sadat to place his bets on Washington to use its influence to help him recover his territory. Once Kissinger actually met with Sadat in early November 1973, he realized that he had a real chance of sidelining the Soviets, provided that he could produce at least some initial results that responded to Sadat's desperate need to lift the Israeli siege surrounding the Egyptian Third Army in Sinai. This led to Kissinger's step-by-step diplomacy, which for the next two years left the Soviets essentially on the sidelines and produced three disengagement agreements, setting a pattern for US-led peacemaking in the region for the next two and a half decades.

Jeremy Pressman's contribution to this volume adds a slightly different twist to my analysis in the preceding paragraphs. He notes that the peace process after the war was a means for reducing the risk of another conflict, with the attendant danger of superpower confrontation, but also was a way to ease the pressure brought by the Arabs with the embargo of oil and production cutbacks. As long as these pressures continued, the United States had an incentive to pursue some form of Arab-Israeli settlement. This led Kissinger to work seriously on three disengagement agreements, but he was not prepared to spend much energy on a Jordanian-Israeli interim agreement, nor was he prepared to make any overtures to the Palestinians, as Khaled Elgindy rightly notes in his chapter in this volume. But as the risk of war and the pressure from Arab oil producers faded, as Pressman notes, the United States stepped back from treating the Arab-Israeli conflict as a central preoccupation, turning its attention, especially after the attack on the Twin Towers on September 11, 2001, to the war on terrorism.

By way of conclusion, I want to reflect briefly on several of the key analytical errors made during the crisis. First, despite ample warning by mid-1973 that Egypt and Syria were preparing for war, both the Israeli and American leadership generally adopted the view that deterrence would work, and if it did not, Israel would easily defeat the Arab armies as they had in 1967. As Risa Brooks notes in her chapter in this volume, the Egyptians had, in fact, made significant improvements in their military organization and capabilities after the 1967 debacle, and Sadat was therefore able to exert his authority over a highly professional officer corp. The Israelis and Americans badly underestimated these improvements, as well as misunderstood the nature of Egypt's limited war plan. They also failed to recognize the extent to which Sadat's frustration was increasing, after two serious attempts at dialogue with the United States earlier in the year. Ismail, at the end of his second meeting with Kissinger, had urged the latter to come to Cairo to meet directly with Sadat. One can only wonder what might have been the result if Kissinger had accepted the Egyptian invitation.

Second, Kissinger more than Nixon was very wary of coordinating too closely with the Soviets in the Middle East. He had publicly talked about his goal of "expelling" them.[13] And yet he was in regular, and often productive, contact with Ambassador Dobrynin and with Brezhnev himself. In retrospect, his willingness to urge the Israelis to ignore the ceasefire agreement that he had just negotiated in Moscow was reckless and was bound to produce a sharp Soviet response. The whole DEFCON 3 drama could have been avoided, and Kissinger would still have been in a commanding position to take the lead in the postwar diplomacy.

Third, there was a woeful misunderstanding at the top levels of the US government of the new realities surrounding energy supplies. In previous crises in the Middle East—in particular, the 1956–1957 Suez crisis and the June 1967 war—the Arab oil producers were unable to have any serious impact on the political and military events. The slogan was frequently heard that the Arabs had to sell their oil; the only alternative was to drink it.[14] In short, they could not credibly threaten an oil embargo. But they could and they did, and it had a major impact on the world economy, resulted in the transfer of huge revenues to key oil producers, and brought the crisis home to American consumers in a dramatic way. One day before the oil embargo was declared, Kissinger proudly told the members of the Washington Special Actions Group (WSAG)—an assemblage of many of the top national security officials in the US government—that the Arab foreign ministers whom he and Nixon had met with on October 16 had made no mention of oil.[15]

Like the Cuban missile crisis, the October 1973 war did not lead to a full-scale superpower confrontation. But that is no reason to conclude that management of the crisis, and especially the diplomacy in the months preceding the crisis, could not have been much better. Much of the fault, I believe, lies with the Israeli stubborn refusal to believe that Sadat was serious about wanting to move the conflict into a US-led negotiation. Kissinger was more willing to test Sadat's intentions, but felt that there was no urgency, since the balance of power was so clearly on Israel's side. And when Brezhnev did try to warn Nixon that war was coming, Kissinger saw this as a ploy to get the United States to put one-sided pressure on Israel.[16] Thus, an opportunity to prevent the October 1973 war may well have been lost. We will never know how different the Middle East might have been if the "peace process" had gotten underway in mid-1973 instead of after the October War. But having lived through the crisis at close hand—and having devoted much of my time subsequently to thinking about and working to achieve Arab-Israeli peace—I think we would have all been better off if the war had been avoided.

NOTES

1. Henry Kissinger, *Years of Upheaval* (Boston: Little, Brown, 1982), 545–613; Henry Kissinger, *Diplomacy* (New York: Simon & Schuster, 1994); Henry Kissinger, *Crisis: The Anatomy of Two Major Foreign Policy Crises* (New York: Simon & Schuster, 2003).

2. For example, see United States Department of State, *Foreign Relations of the United States* [*FRUS*], *1969–1976*, vol. 25, *Arab-Israeli Crisis and War, 1973* (Washington, DC: Government Printing Office [GPO], 2011). I should note here that I played a minor role during the crisis as the acting head of the Middle East office of

the National Security Council from October 6 to October 26, 1973. As such, I was present at most of the meetings of the Washington Special Actions Group, which met almost every day, and had access to most of the diplomatic communications and intelligence reports. In 1977, I published *Decade of Decisions: American Policy Toward the Arab-Israeli Conflict, 1967–1976* (Berkeley: University of California Press, 1977), which contains my first public account of the events surrounding the 1973 war.

3. Yigal Kipnis in his chapter in this volume makes ample use of both American and Israeli archival material, as he also does in his important book *1973: The Road to War* (Charlottesville, VA: Just World, 2013).

4. The most recent contribution based on US and Israeli archives, as well as extensive interviews with Kissinger, is Martin Indyk, *Master of the Game: Henry Kissinger and the Art of Middle East Diplomacy* (New York: Knopf, 2021).

5. Two important memoirs by key Egyptian actors in 1973 are Anwar el-Sadat, *In Search of Identity: An Autobiography* (New York: Harper & Row, 1977) and Mohamed Abdel Ghani El-Gamasy, *The October War: Memoirs of Field Marshal El-Gamasy of Egypt* (Cairo: American University in Cairo Press, 1993). See also Ahmed Aboul Gheit, *Witness to War and Peace: Egypt, the October War, and Beyond* (New York: American University in Cairo Press, 2018). For a rare Syrian insider's account, see Bouthaina Shaaban, *The Edge of the Precipice: Hafez al-Assad, Henry Kissinger, and the Remaking of the Modern Middle East* (Beirut: Bissan, 2017). The best account by a Soviet official who was present during Politburo deliberations is Victor Israelyan, *Inside the Kremlin during the Yom Kippur War* (University Park: Pennsylvania State University Press, 1995). See also Anatoly Dobrynin, *In Confidence: Moscow's Ambassador to Six Cold War Presidents* (Seattle: University of Washington Press, 1995), 287–301. For more on the superpower rivalry, see Craig Daigle, *The Limits of Détente: The United States, the Soviet Union, and the Arab-Israeli Conflict, 1969–1973* (New Haven, CT: Yale University Press, 2012). On the twenty-fifth anniversary of the war, a conference which included participants from nearly all the involved parties was held in Washington, DC. The results were published in Richard B. Parker, ed., *The October War: A Retrospective* (Gainesville: University Press of Florida, 2001).

6. Sadat, *In Search of Identity*, 244.

7. Dobrynin, *In Confidence*, 296, describes Sadat's rejection of the ceasefire-in-place proposal of October 12–13 as "a gross political and strategic blunder, because it brought military disaster some days later."

8. For some of the translated Israeli archival materials, see the appendix to "A Self-Inflicted Wound? Henry Kissinger and the Ending of the October 1973 Arab-Israeli War," by Galen Jackson and Marc Trachtenberg, http://www.sscnet.ucla.edu/polisci/faculty/trachtenberg/cv/selfinflicted(appendix).pdf. The Dinitz-Kissinger conversation quoted here may be found in this collection and is titled Document 3 (n. 81): Dinitz to Gazit, October 23, 1973, 6 p.m. reporting 3:00 p.m. meeting [frames 281–82].

9. See Elbridge Colby et al., "The Israeli 'Nuclear Alert' of 1973: Deterrence and Signaling in Crisis," Center for Naval Analyses, April 2013, https://www.cna.org/reports/2013/DRM-2013-U-004480-Final.pdf, 2. For more on Israel's nuclear

program, see, for example, Avner Cohen, *Israel and the Bomb* (New York: Columbia University Press, 1998) and Avner Cohen, *The Worst-Kept Secret: Israel's Bargain with the Bomb* (New York: Columbia University Press, 2010).

10. Dan Sagir, "How the Fear of Israeli Nukes Helped Seal the Egypt Peace Deal," *Haaretz*, November 26, 2017.

11. Schlesinger's comments on the DEFCON 3 alert can be found in Parker, *October War*, 174–76, 200.

12. Transcript of a Telephone Conversation between Nixon and Kissinger, October 14, 1973, in *FRUS, 1969–1976*, vol. 25, 496, 499.

13. Quoted in Henry Kissinger, *White House Years* (Boston: Little, Brown, 1979), 579–80.

14. Nixon himself made comments to that effect on occasion. For example, see Memorandum of Conversation, "President's Meeting with his Foreign Intelligence Advisory Board," June 5, 1970, in *FRUS, 1969–1976*, vol. 24, *Middle East Region and Arabian Peninsula, 1969–1972; Jordan, September 1970* (Washington, DC: GPO, 2008), 80.

15. Minutes of a WSAG Meeting, "Subject: Middle East," October 16, 1973, in *FRUS, 1969–1976*, vol. 25, 577.

16. Kissinger, *Years of Upheaval*, 297–300.

Chapter 1

The October 1973 War

Culmination of the Failure of Political Analysis

Yigal Kipnis

"We were not surprised," Prime Minister Golda Meir declared on a televised broadcast to the Israeli public on the evening of October 6, 1973, several hours after the war had broken out.[1]

"A coalition of Arab nations led by Egypt and Syria launched a surprise attack on October 6, the day of Yom Kippur.... The offensive surprised US policymakers as well as Israel," stated a special publication issued by the Central Intelligence Agency (CIA) thirty-nine years later.[2]

So what actually took place?

The development of historical research enables us today to look deeply at events from the distance of time. The rich documentation that has been revealed in archives in both Israel and the United States, and the integration of the information from both of those sources, provides an in-depth look into the secret channels of discussion conducted by Henry Kissinger, the US national security adviser and secretary of state, with the president of Egypt, Anwar Sadat, and with the Israeli prime minister, Golda Meir, and enables us to investigate this question. At the beginning of 1973, there was a real change in the political situation in the Middle East, as Sadat indicated his desire for peace talks with Israel, with Kissinger acting as intermediary. This new reality forced decision-makers in Israel to choose between two alternatives. The first was to respond to Kissinger's proposal and to conduct secret peace negotiations between Israel and Egypt. The second was to wait for the Egyptians and the Syrians to initiate a war during the second half of 1973. Israel's refusal to pursue the first of these options—in other words, to abstain from a political process which would have involved an American confrontation with Israel—meant, in effect, that it had instead decided to wait until after its October elections to negotiate.

The war, despite its military outcome, is perceived in Israel as a failure and a disaster, while in Egypt, it is viewed with pride. Kissinger subsequently defined the war as "the culmination of a failure of political analysis on the part of its victims."[3] Kissinger was the most influential political player involved in the Arab-Israeli peace process—almost alone, he conducted the channels of communication between the two superpowers, the United States and the Soviet Union, in addition to the secret communications with Meir and with Sadat. Nearly all the information relevant to these issues was concentrated on his desk and, in many cases, this knowledge was his exclusively.

This chapter investigates the circumstances of the war in October 1973 against the backdrop of Kissinger's characterization, an analysis that included a core insight: it was a political failure, one that had a starting point and a culmination—the war. As he commented to Meir after the war, "I don't want to accuse anyone, but during 1973, the war could have been prevented."[4] In order to answer the questions of how and why this happened, we must first clarify what actually did happen. Up-to-date research confirms Kissinger's version of these events, indicating the central role of political conduct preceding the war—and reducing the role of the failure in decision-making by Israeli military intelligence—as the Yom Kippur War did not surprise the Israeli leadership. Recent scholarship also shows that Israel's decision to neither launch a preemptive attack nor mobilize its reserves, as would have been expected following the deployment of Egyptian and Syrian troops, was not due to intelligence considerations. This was a political dictate imposed on the Israeli military a long time before the war.

Thus, current research enables us now to examine the two main questions about Israeli conduct leading up to the war: First, what was the political alternative offered to Israel? Second, what caused Israel to be more unprepared than it should have been in acting in advance of the outbreak of war? These questions are this chapter's main focus.

THE TURNING POINT

"We were not surprised," stated Meir, just after the war had broken out, as noted above. So what about the alternative of trying to prevent it?

Until the beginning of 1973, Kissinger, with the approval of President Richard Nixon, and in coordination with Israel, had attempted to thwart any peace initiatives by the State Department. This policy stemmed from the fact that the Soviets would have been involved in any proposed solution and would then be representing Egypt in achieving any peace agreement. Kissinger wanted to reach a settlement that would return sovereignty to Egypt over the territories it had lost in the June 1967 war as a means of driving the Soviets out of the region. He planned to lead negotiations only when the Soviets had been eliminated from the political process, so that the United States would be the only mediator. That was also the reason he preferred US mediation, rather than direct talks between the two sides.

When 1971, the "year of decision" between war and peace, as proclaimed by Sadat, had ended, nothing had happened.[5] In December, Meir had visited Washington for talks with Nixon and Kissinger, and reached a number of secret understandings—the "Understandings of December, 1971," as termed by then–Israeli ambassador to the United States, Yitzhak Rabin.[6] These included the abandonment of the Rogers Plan—which Secretary of State William Rogers had publicly laid out in December 1969—for peace in the Middle East, an implicit freeze on political steps toward peace, and a continuing supply of Phantom and Skyhawk jets to Israel.[7] "Now having said that, we then move to the *'appearance' of negotiations*, under the Department of State's auspices. That's why I use the term appearance," Nixon had told Meir.[8] A few days later, Nixon met with Kissinger and they agreed to hide these understandings from Rogers and to prevent the State Department from taking any further steps toward a Middle East solution.[9]

At the beginning of 1973, a turning point took place in the political situation. To be sure, Sadat's aim to replace Soviet patronage with American sponsorship of Egypt, to establish ties with the US government, and to recognize Israel was not new. However, in early 1973, these plans received practical expression.[10] Nixon and Kissinger's policy "to frustrate Egypt . . . [from thinking that] their salvation would come from Moscow" had succeeded, Rabin reported just after this shift in policy had taken place.[11] After a seven-month waiting period that had followed Sadat's decision to modify the relationship between Egypt and the Soviet Union by expelling USSR military personnel from his country, Kissinger and Sadat opened a direct and secret channel, with the latter's national security adviser, Hafez Ismail, acting as his representative. Simultaneously, Sadat was preparing his army for a limited war as a means of motivating a political process if his peace initiative was not accepted.[12] "Henry, the time has now come that we've got to squeeze the old woman," Nixon said to Kissinger a month before both Ismail and Meir were due to arrive in Washington.[13]

Kissinger knew the positions of the two sides regarding a peace agreement and could analyze them. He was able to identify the important points for each side and to understand where each of them could compromise. It was not the gaps in the Egyptian and Israeli positions that deterred him from making a major effort. His expertise was in overcoming such difficulties, and he knew that, during negotiations, the two sides would become more flexible. His position about a peace border between Israel and Egypt was well known. It was very different from the Israeli demand that it be allowed to annex about a third of the Sinai desert. Like Nixon, Rogers, and Sadat, Kissinger favored the international border, or at the very most, "tiny changes," as he put it.[14]

On February 23, just before Nixon met with Ismail, Kissinger presented the president with three possible modes of action. "We could," he wrote, "*stand back* and let the two sides reflect further on their position." The president reacted negatively to that suggestion, correctly anticipating events by writing: "*Absolutely not*. . . . I totally disagree. This thing is getting ready to blow." The second option was "to renew the efforts to achieve an *interim settlement* that lost momentum in 1971." The president opted, however, for the third alternative—to work simultaneously in two channels. One would be public and focus on an interim deal, whereas the other would be secret and aim at coming up with understandings for an overall agreement. "It would stand or fall on whether Israel can be persuaded to think in terms of restoring Egyptian sovereignty over most of the Sinai while retaining control at strategic points—rather than insisting on a permanent change in boundaries," Kissinger explained to the president. "[That is the] preferred track for action," the president replied, adding: "The time has come to quit pandering to Israel's intransigent position."[15]

After Ismail's public meeting with the president, he secretly met for two days of discussions with Kissinger, at which Ismail presented Sadat's initiative. The Egyptian leader hoped to achieve understandings with the United States on the principles of a peace agreement with Israel, and on that basis, to conduct negotiations with Israel via Kissinger's mediation. Egypt, Ismail said, would disengage from the patronage of the Soviet Union. Ismail could not completely hide his talks with the Americans from the Soviets, but he kept from them the existence of the secret track with Kissinger. Thus, he had to mislead the Soviets by misrepresenting the nature of his discussions with the Americans.

During the talks with Ismail, Kissinger did not engage in negotiations—he simply listened.[16] The lengthy protocols of the two days of discussions between Kissinger and Ismail indicate the dynamics that Kissinger was employing toward the Egyptian emissary, who, as required at this early stage of the process, did not reveal much of his willingness to make concessions. In addition to what was said in the official discussions, Kissinger also made use of unofficial talks, which were an inseparable part of the diplomatic process, as what was revealed, free from the limits of the official protocol, clarified important points.[17] He asked questions and analyzed what he was hearing rigorously, in accordance with Nixon's directions, in order to identify Egyptian positions which might make it possible to bridge the gaps between

Egypt and Israel. And he found what he was seeking. He knew that what he was hearing from Ismail were not dictates but were instead points preliminary to the initiation of negotiations. According to Kissinger, these were "points which were raised in the framework of the exchange of views and had not been considered as agreed upon."[18]

Even before his meeting with Kissinger, Nixon had advised Ismail that he did not have to volunteer his positions during the first meeting. Ismail requested that Kissinger develop the issues that were raised in the discussions, and Kissinger later reported to Meir, "He asked for us to draw up a paper with their and your views as a kind of starting point." He stressed to Meir that the Egyptians were demonstrating flexibility, "especially in the field of the time limit between the ending of the state of war and the beginning of normal peace."[19]

During the two days of discussion, in accord with Kissinger's request, Ismail exhibited flexibility on two key points. About the first, he stated that the Egyptians were ready "to change the demand for evacuation from all Egyptian territory to a demand for recognition of Egyptian sovereignty over Egyptian territory." They would be ready to accept recognition of Egyptian sovereignty over Sinai for a long period, rather than a full evacuation, to be seen "as a possible response to the security needs of Israel." After the meeting, Ismail increasingly referred to the "new formula," thinking about "the untapped possibilities in that formula." He explained that recognition of sovereignty was "solid enough for them to defend to their own people, yet flexible enough to accommodate practical arrangements that may be necessary." Kissinger updated Meir with this information in a report to Ambassador Rabin.[20] This was also true of the second point, that "the Egyptian issue, that is, Egypt's agreement to such a solution, could be separated from dealing with an agreement with Jordan and/or Syria." Later, Kissinger was even more decisive. In June, he said, "This time it is completely clear . . . that the Egyptians are concerned only with themselves and don't tie an agreement with them to the other Arab states." And in September, he similarly reported, "Egypt is already willing to make a separate peace."[21]

Sadat was well aware of the severe criticism he would receive in the Arab world if he set his sights on a separate peace with Israel. At this early stage, Ismail would only pay lip service to the prediction that "[a]s Egypt and Israel move through the above stages, Syria and Jordan would be roughly one stage behind." And "[a] Syrian settlement had to be based on the same principles as Egypt's." Regarding the Palestinians, he said that "Egypt would consider whatever [Jordan's King] Hussein worked out with the West Bank Palestinians as an internal Jordanian matter, not an Arab-Israeli matter."[22] Ultimately, Ismail's comments about the Syrians were identical to what was later written into the 1979 Israeli-Egyptian peace agreement, and Sadat's demand for Palestinian autonomy at that time was his way of minimally fulfilling his obligation to relate to the Palestinian issue.

The flexible points that Kissinger noted in the Egyptian positions caused him to hurry to Nixon immediately following the end of the discussions to tell him: "Frankly, until this weekend, I didn't know how to do it. . . . I had no concept of how to get this thing done. . . . I now see a glimmer of how we might do it."[23] Kissinger informed the president that he "thought the most important thing, that he's [Ismail] never said to anyone and won't say to anybody" was that the Egyptians were "willing to make a separate Egyptian-Israeli deal, because they know that afterwards the Jordanians and Syrians are going to follow the same procedure." He requested and received approval from the president to advance negotiations on two parallel tracks, one in public that Rogers would lead, and whose goal would ostensibly be an interim agreement for an Israeli withdrawal from the Suez Canal, and the other a secret track between him and Ismail that would discuss the details of a peace agreement. On the basis of what he had heard from Ismail, he estimated that "by September 1st . . . we have two things going, an interim settlement and direct negotiations between the Arabs and the Israelis. And it will look lovely, and it will be a tremendous boon." Nixon had actually presented this approach to Ismail when they met on February 23.[24] As a matter of fact, Nixon and Kissinger were adopting a draft for discussion that was similar to what had been proposed by Israeli deputy prime minister Yigal Allon three months earlier.[25]

"They would be flexible," Kissinger similarly emphasized to Meir when they spoke two days later. He also told her that after the United States and Egypt had reached understandings, "they will sit down with you." He tried, unsuccessfully, to counter her claim that there was nothing new in the Egyptian proposal. "There is a new Egyptian approach," Kissinger explained, but Meir reacted with stiff opposition. He added, "Again, I would only try if you and I agree." "Then we will just not go along with this," she responded.[26]

Kissinger and Hal Saunders, a National Security Council official, summarized the discussions in a memorandum that "described Ismail's position as it evolved over two days of talks and the process he envisage[d] over the coming months."[27] The document, which was immediately transmitted to Rabin, opened with the schedule that Ismail had suggested. Although it noted that "fundamental principles of an agreement would [be] agreed by this September," the timetable indicated that implementation "[c]ould take well beyond the end of 1973 to complete." Kissinger explained that Ismail was considering separating the issue of recognition of sovereignty from the issue of withdrawal and, as such, integrating the demand for Israeli security. As Ismail had put it, "If the issues of territory and sovereignty could be put aside, we could be open-minded." "This of course, could be quite significant," Kissinger emphasized to Rabin.[28]

On March 6, Kissinger transmitted a summary memorandum to Nixon as well. He was aware of the president's desire to advance negotiations, but after his final discussion with Meir, he was also aware of Meir's adamant opposition to such a move. He added a moderating sentence to the memorandum, noting that Ismail's opening positions were no different than Egypt's positions in the past. But he also stressed that this time Ismail was open to considering other approaches in order to reach an agreement.[29] Under the heading "What Ismail Proposed," Kissinger wrote that "[t]he U.S. and Egypt could work out the principles of an agreement and then present them to Israel," and that "[t]he U.S. could listen to both Egypt and Israel and try to develop a position that would meet the reasonable interests of both sides." He added that "[i]f there were a serious process, Egypt would not feel the need to set deadlines." The positions proposed by Ismail were not dictates—as long as negotiations were continuing for a permanent solution, the Egyptians were not demanding that Israel withdraw from more than what might be determined in an interim solution.

On March 9, after Kissinger had also received intelligence information about Ismail's reactions to the talks, which confirmed that the positions the latter had presented were preliminary and open to discussion and change,[30] Kissinger presented Israel with an outline and schedule for progress in negotiations during 1973.[31] He updated Ismail that same day, saying that he was making every effort to formulate an agreement in principle, according to the draft that Egypt had presented.

The Sadat initiative, which had started to take practical shape in the form of the Kissinger-Ismail track and had initiated a change in Kissinger's approach, was exactly what Meir had feared. For two years she had been receiving information from a Mossad agent, Ashraf Marwan, that Egypt was willing to recognize Israel and to sign a peace agreement, without consideration of the Palestinian issue.[32] In fact, she feared negotiations based on the Nixon-Kissinger outline even more than she feared war. Thus, she ignored this turning point and rejected Kissinger's ideas. She termed his proposal "Kissinger's cockroach," even though it represented the alternative to the war facing Israel.[33]

THE OUTLINE

As Kissinger described it, this was the outline that he proposed to Meir in March 1973: "The creation of three security areas in Sinai for the stage following the attainment of a peace agreement (creating a state of peace) until full normalization. In one area, Egyptian forces would be stationed, primarily in the canal sector, the second area in which Israeli forces would be stationed and a third area covering most of Sinai, which would be a demilitarized zone, constituting a demarcation between the sides. The stage between achieving a peace agreement up until the transition to normalization, could be long and might continue for many years." Kissinger stressed that this draft was based on Egyptian flexibility, which could be identified "at two main points." The first was the conversion of the Egyptian demand for complete withdrawal to a demand to recognize Egyptian sovereignty over Sinai. The second was the Egyptian approach to the possible implementation of the agreement in stages and over a period of time—Egyptian willingness to see two main stages in the progress to *a real peace*," as Rabin reported. Rabin added that "Shaul [Kissinger] sees the possibility to respond to Israel's security needs between the period from achieving a political agreement signed by the sides creating a state of peace, until the completion of *the normalization process in relations between two states*, by leaving Israeli military forces at critical points in Sinai, but without harming the principle of Egyptian sovereignty."[34]

Kissinger also proposed stages to achieve a comprehensive agreement. At the first stage, Egypt and the United States would conduct secret negotiations in order to reach an agreement on understandings between the two states, and in this framework, the Americans would recognize Egyptian sovereignty over Sinai. Kissinger would inform Israel of this step when he saw fit. This stage would end, by September 1, in a mutual statement "of general principles between the two superpowers," which was Kissinger's way of enabling the Soviets to maintain the appearance of partnership in this political process. During this stage of the negotiations, there would also be a parallel channel for an interim settlement, which would involve Israeli withdrawal from the Suez Canal.[35] "What we lose is the commitment of the US to the sovereignty of Egypt," reacted Rabin. And regarding the proposed schedule, the ambassador responded: "It comes with principles publicly, say July or August, which will be very unpleasant to the prime minister. That is two or three months before our election."[36]

The second stage would begin after Israel accepted the US-Egyptian understandings. It would aim at summarizing the specifications for implementing the agreement and the commitments of each of the sides. At this stage, for which Ismail did not set a time limit, the negotiations would take place directly. The third stage would be implementation of the agreement in phases.

Kissinger attached great importance to the "stages of implementation." In his view, structuring the process this way "would grant opportunities and time when passing from stage to stage," which he felt was responsive to "the security needs of Israel to maintain military forces at vital points in Sinai."[37] He was fully aware of the suspicions on both sides and thus found the idea of a lengthy implementation period appealing. He intended to act on this plan following the Israeli elections—and he did—but during the interim, war broke out.

Israel was not facing a dictate that had to be obeyed. At the beginning of 1973, it was handed a proposal by the most influential political figure in the world to initiate negotiations. The offer was aimed at preventing a war and attempting to achieve a peace agreement. Kissinger, therefore, simply wanted to know "whether we [Israel] are ready to digress from the demand for significant border changes in comparison to the international border [i.e., annexation of about a third of Sinai]."[38] He did not set any other condition for Israel in order to begin negotiations. Neither Egypt nor Kissinger was demanding immediate implementation of a complete Israeli withdrawal with the signing of a full agreement, and the latter, for his part, had only requested the elimination of Israel's demand for annexation of a large part of Sinai.

Rabin discussed this proposal with Meir for about two hours, a conversation which Rabin later termed as long and difficult. Meir responded with total rejection. "For two hours, I have tried my best to explain," the ambassador told a frustrated Kissinger, who had difficulty understanding Meir's negative reply—which prevented him from immediately beginning negotiations to implement his proposed plan.[39] In May, Kissinger again requested that Israel reconsider its position and eliminate the obstacle to the political process. He explained, "I do not share Israel's optimism about the low probability of renewing the war."[40]

HOW ISRAEL RELATED TO KISSINGER'S PLAN AS AN ALTERNATIVE TO WAR

Three decision-makers in Israel reacted to the Kissinger plan: Meir, Defense Minister Moshe Dayan, and Minister without Portfolio Yisrael Galili. For his part, Allon was only partially informed about this secret proposal. Likewise, even though Rabin knew about all of the details and developments until mid-March, he was kept in the dark following the end of his term as ambassador, and as Israel's elections approached, was involved in political activity and far removed from the focus of decision-making.

Allon and Rabin felt that Israel should enter negotiations in accord with Kissinger's plan and, as Kissinger intended, conduct two channels—the secret channel for a permanent settlement and the public channel for an interim agreement. That may be the reason both of them were denied key information and kept out of the decision-making process. Dayan, like Meir, was initially opposed to the alternative that Kissinger had laid out. But whereas Meir continued to resist the US proposal, Dayan eventually changed his opinion, and was ready by mid-June to accept an agreement which would include recognition of Egyptian sovereignty over Sinai, with security arrangements for Israel, on the condition that negotiations start after the Israeli elections. Dayan informed the Americans of his views, but did not tell his decision-making companions.[41]

It was Meir, however, who was the first to react to Kissinger's outline. As noted, as early as February she had already completely rejected his request to eliminate her demand for Israeli sovereignty over a large part of Sinai. Kissinger was thus prevented from beginning the political process.

In April, Sadat was waiting for Kissinger to set a date for an additional meeting with Ismail, while Kissinger, who was trying to postpone continuing clarifications with Egypt until after the Israeli elections, delayed appointing a time for the meeting. Meanwhile, Israel received targeted information about Sadat's intention to start a war in May. The intelligence turned out to be incorrect, but the warnings of war were nevertheless probably a reflection of Sadat's desire to pressure Kissinger into acting. That, at any rate, was how Israeli leaders interpreted this intelligence when "Golda's kitchen cabinet" met on April 18 to discuss the alert. The meeting opened with an evaluation of the probability of war and its possible scenarios. Chief of Staff David Elazar, who was known as "Dado"; the head of the Mossad, Zvi Zamir; and the head of army intelligence, Eli Zeira, all reported in detail. The ensuing discussion proceeded on the assumption that, as Dayan put it, sooner or later "they were moving towards war."[42]

In the second part of the meeting, Galili forced Meir and Dayan to discuss Kissinger's proposal. This was the only part of the conversation during which the principal decision-makers directly talked about the political alternative and, as such, merits particularly close examination. "Is there anything that we could do so that that [war] will not happen?" asked Galili. Meir tried to avoid dealing with Galili's queries and chose instead to focus on three main questions. The first was how to avoid war by deterrence: "Could we bring what we know [the information from Mossad agent Marwan about the intention to initiate war] to our friends [Kissinger] or not, with all of the danger that entails?" Her additional two questions were about preparing the home front and whether to update the government about the possibility of war. "How can we do that without arousing panic that war is on the way?" she asked. Consequently, she directed the discussion toward minimizing reporting about a coming war because of the "dangers" involved. Specifically, the prime minister worried that having a more open discussion about the risks of war might expose the fact that Israel had a high-quality source of information, and feared that Kissinger would leverage the tension to try to get negotiations started. Even when Galili again requested that they devote an "internal discussion" to the political alternative, Meir avoided the question and returned to talking about matters relating to how to prepare the home front, such as the "gasoline that we need. Maybe there are other things, Civil Defense, cleaning the shelters and of course, many of them have been filled with old furniture, etc."[43]

But Galili did not give up. There were very few who dared to face up to Golda's stubbornness, but Galili was one of them. Indeed, although he worded his comments carefully, he kept pressing the prime minister in an almost nagging fashion. "It seems to me," he said, "that internally, we are not in a good place, that is, all of these developments stem from the fact that we do not agree to return to the previous line." Galili did not allow Meir and Dayan to evade "the elephant in the room" and not even to avoid recognizing that the "elephant" was actually "Kissinger's cockroach." "If you take *what Hafez (Ismail) said to Shaul (Kissinger) and the paper he left with him*," said Galili, "then their starting point is that *they are ready for peace* and for a system of agreements and international assurances and so forth, and all of that on condition that we completely withdraw to the previous line."[44]

Galili persisted. "I think that basically, we have to bring this up to the government. Because I think *this requires a new mandate, that is, a new exclusive mandate* from our side that we do not agree to withdraw to the previous line, nor will we begin negotiations on the basis of the demand to withdraw to the previous border." Galili also challenged the basic idea that the plan proposed to Israel "was Kissinger's 'vision' and not what he had heard from Ismail."[45] As for Dayan's belief that in the absence of a political solution there would be a war, Galili said: "But relating to that, *there is also a possibility of avoiding all of this 'tribulation' if we are ready to enter a series of discussions on the basis of a return to the previous border*." Galili, therefore, wanted to discuss the political alternative with the Americans and to consider the point of view of Allon, who felt that Israel should begin negotiations:

> I would really be "thirsty" for such a discussion, in this framework [of the "kitchen cabinet"] with Yigal [Allon], to try to work out what Kissinger is hinting at *time after time, when he talks about strategic strongholds as an alternative to a change in borders*. We are always trying to educate him that when we talk about a change in borders with Egypt, *we are talking about* [Israeli] *sovereignty* and not about all of Sinai [but a third of it]. In contrast, they [the Egyptians] have come out with the formula of [Egyptian] sovereignty on Egyptian ground, but which will take the security needs of Israel into account, sovereignty in exchange for security.[46]

Galili, in other words, was expressing opposition to Meir and Dayan's preference for war over negotiation. "I see another state of war as a threat that will deepen hostility, hatred," he said, adding: "It will involve great destruction and many lives lost. And so (we are talking about) a very long-term postponement of any possibility of a return to quiet." He proposed considering the alternative of negotiations in order to reduce the likelihood of war and to begin moving toward reconciliation. His proposal stemmed from the fact that, unlike the others, he understood that "our potential to deter them is limited, but I would like to be able to tell ourselves that everything possible [to achieve progress] has been done." Galili also felt that giving a positive reply to Kissinger would earn points for Israel when it began moving into a political process, which would obviously occur sooner or later.[47]

In short, the key Israeli decision-makers could no longer ignore the fact that they were facing two alternatives: to agree to conduct negotiations or to wait for a war initiated by the Egyptians and the Syrians. They also had to decide whether to share this information with the rest of the government. Ultimately, Meir left no doubt as to her refusal to accept Kissinger's plan: "[Kissinger] should be told again, that he must know, what he has heard from us many times, that this is not our conception, and he cannot propose such a plan in our name."[48]

In the end, Meir, Dayan, and Galili agreed that the government should be told about the war alerts, but that they would not provide the details of the political alternative. "Yisrael, I wouldn't suggest that this should be placed before the government in this context, that is, are we willing to go to war only on condition that we don't return to the Green Line?" Dayan responded to Galili. Thus, Meir agreed to inform the rest of the government of the possibility that war might break out, but not of the possibility of preventing it by negotiating.[49]

About six days later, the full government met. The ministers heard a summary of the warnings of war. Nothing was said of Kissinger's proposed political alternative.[50] In the discussion that followed, Dayan estimated that the Egyptians would not initiate a war because they had demanded a political process. Moreover, "if Egypt initiates a war in the middle of the discussions, if Egypt begins to fire, it won't end well for the Egyptians." "[W]hat they are doing," he concluded, "is to threaten, to say that the situation is on the eve of a blow up, and if there is no political progress, there will be a military action." Thus, he assumed that "Egypt was on the path back to war." This was echoed by Foreign Minister Abba Eban, who stated, "The fact is that Egypt is in a state of very deep frustration. The common strategy of Israel and the United States is aimed at deepening this frustration and there is another possibility, that frustration will actually lead to an act of despair, an act of war."[51]

Neither was the Israeli military command focused on a political alternative. Deputy Chief of Staff Yisrael Tal was an exception. "A total war," he said, "no matter who delivers the first blow, who wins and what the scope of the victory will be, its chances of promoting our national objectives are minimal, if not nonexistent. And in contrast, there are many dangers, great human and material losses; negative effects on Israeli society itself; undermining the status of the existing lines; and a worsening of our international situation." Consequently, Tal wanted Israel to explore the possibility of a political solution: "As things stand, our goals should be both an effort to prevent war by political activity, which is not in the realm of responsibility of the Israeli army, in addition to military deterrence of the enemy to prevent them from going to war."[52]

Kissinger was aware of the fact that Sadat might go to war. He especially feared that this would take place before the summit meeting between Nixon and the Soviet leader, Leonid Brezhnev, that was scheduled for June. His second meeting with Ismail had been set for May 20. A week earlier, he met with Israeli ambassador Simcha Dinitz, who had taken Rabin's place, and again asked if Israel was ready to accept his proposed course of action. "Why couldn't you take it in the form of security zones instead of annexation? Sovereignty will be Egyptian but in actuality, you will be present there," Kissinger emphasized. Kissinger also wanted to make sure that he understood Israel's demand that it be allowed to annex a significant portion of the Sinai, which he felt was preventing him from initiating negotiations. "My estimate of what you want," he said, "is a straight line west of El-Arish." Dinitz confirmed that Kissinger was indeed correct: "It might not be a straight line . . . but in general terms you are right. In strategic terms we need sufficient depth to make it secure. But three-quarters of Sinai would go back. . . . I really think it is reasonable!"[53]

The result, as Kissinger had understood it might be, was that Sadat determined that the only alternative left to him was the military one. Neither the second meeting between Kissinger and Ismail in May nor the summit meetings between Nixon and Brezhnev in June set a political process in motion, which left the Egyptian president no viable course other than war. As a consequence, the Egyptians accelerated their joint military planning and coordination with Syria's president Hafiz al-Asad. On September 12, Sadat and Asad determined that the war would commence on October 6, and from mid-September onward military preparations began to appear in the field.

On September 22, Kissinger was appointed secretary of state. "Israel and the Arabs must be ready to make difficult decisions based on an agreement," Kissinger had said during his Senate confirmation hearings, at which he called for negotiations in the Middle East.[54] Leading up to his appointment, he had repeatedly prodded Israel to cooperate to advance negotiations. To the Israelis, he clarified that he would not try to start a political process until January, after the Israeli elections and immediately following the formation of a new government.[55] To that end, it was also determined that on December

8, Dayan would travel to the White House for talks in Washington.[56] This was also reported in the press.[57]

Dinitz left the United States for consultations in Israel about the expected political attack on Israel.[58] By the time he returned to Washington, the threat of war was concrete. Six days before the outbreak of war, Dinitz transmitted Meir's response to Kissinger's demand that she advance negotiations: "As he (Kissinger) knows, I do not think that the present situation (military tension) is ideal, but a time of elections is not convenient for serious discussion."[59] "That horse is finished," said Kissinger when he heard Meir's response. The secretary of state emphasized that the December 1971 understandings had now expired, and that, come January, a new political era would begin in the Middle East.[60] Apparently, it was no coincidence that, at the beginning of October, an editorial appeared in the *London Times*, saying: "Israel will be behaving with foolishness if it rejects the Kissinger plan. . . . Israel will be very foolish if it tries to prevent an agreement by procedural objections or territorial claims."[61]

The failure of political analysis, which had begun at the end of February, reached its peak at the beginning of October. No one involved knew that within less than a week, a war would break out, one that would mark the collapse of the Israeli approach of preventing war by deterrence. Thus, the Egyptian-Syrian military attack preceded—indeed, postponed—the political offensive by Kissinger. And it came at a heavy price.

On the basis of his earlier outline, which Meir had not accepted, Kissinger led the political process immediately following the war. This was a war that Meir and Dayan had not wanted, but which they had preferred over the implementation of the Kissinger plan. When they had made this decision, moreover, they well knew that the Israeli army would be limited in the steps it could take in advance of the fighting. Indeed, they believed that Israel would win the war, but they also knew that its costs would be heavy.

THE COMMITMENT

"We were not surprised," Meir told the Israeli public a few hours after the war had broken out on October 6. What, then, actually had taken place?

On the morning of the day that the war would begin, Meir reacted with anger toward one minister, who objected to the decision not to approve a preemptive attack. "We are fighting for our lives," she said. "But that does not mean just fighting at the borders; it also means fighting to stand with our friends, that is, one friend." Dinitz, who was standing nearby, intervened, saying: "He also said this to Rabin." "Do you think I have forgotten?" Meir replied.[62] Meir remembered the nature of an important pledge she had made to Washington very well. "Kissinger always told me that what would be, was not important; don't be the first ones to attack." Furthermore, "It will help," she had noted after her consultations with the Americans in December 1971, "if we wait 'for more than two hours' for a military retaliation."[63]

Indeed, Meir had promised Nixon and Kissinger to wait for longer than two hours to respond in the event that war broke out, and that had become a political directive to the army—the opening moves of the war would be made by the other side. This commitment meant that Meir and Dayan could approve neither a preemptive attack nor a comprehensive military mobilization. In other words, it was Meir—not a failure of intelligence—who bore the responsibility for preventing the military from preempting the combined Arab attack on October 6. As recently as December 1972, Kissinger had again warned Israel not to carry out a preemptive strike if Egypt attacked.[64] Minutes before the outbreak of war, he repeated that message, saying: "We demand that you not take any preventive action."[65]

And Meir fulfilled her promise, which created difficult conditions for the Israel Defense Forces (IDF) at the start of the war. Although Meir and Dayan did not want war, they feared the political moves that Kissinger was attempting to set in motion even more. Thus, the army's preparations were forced to conform to their wish that military tension that would motivate Kissinger to initiate a political process along the lines that Sadat desired be avoided. "We do not," Elazar had therefore stated in May, "want to inflate preparations *that will serve the (Egyptian) political aims without going to war*."[66]

While the military commanders did not know of the commitment that Meir had made to Nixon and Kissinger, they understood that the IDF had to prepare for a war that would be initiated by the enemy, probably during the second half of 1973. The commitment was not a last-minute consideration or demand. "We are preparing plans on the assumption that we will not be the ones to initiate the war but rather, we must 'welcome' them," Elazar had told Meir and Dayan when he presented them with the war plans.[67] Although he preferred to strike preemptively, "I understand that we cannot initiate a preventive strike." "Gentlemen, prepare for war!" Dayan had ordered the General Staff in May. But he had made clear that he was talking about an attack by Egypt and Syria.[68]

Thus, on the morning of October 6, when the outbreak of war was already a certainty, the political leadership refused to allow the IDF to strike the first blow. "The answer is no," Dayan told Elazar when he requested that the military be allowed "to carry out a preventive strike on airports in Egypt and Syria," or alternatively, to attack airports in Syria and missiles in Egypt.[69] Dayan explained, "In my estimation, it is important, even if the Americans are 100% certain, they will not let us attack first." "Regarding a preventive strike, fundamentally, we cannot let ourselves do that this time," he similarly told Meir, adding, "We cannot carry out a preventive strike. Even five minutes."[70] "He was schizophrenic," recalled Dinitz about Dayan's misgivings during the hours leading up to the war. "As a general he felt that they must but as a member of the Cabinet, he knew that they couldn't."[71] That was true of Meir as well. "A preventive strike—really attractive. But this is not 1967," she said. Meir and Dayan's considerations were political—they likely would have chosen not to preempt even if Zeira had not been mistaken in his evaluation and had correctly thought that war would break out.

The second aspect of the Israeli commitment was not to call up the reserves on a large scale. "We do not want, nor do we propose to mobilize the reserves on a large scale, or do anything else that might deteriorate into war," Elazar told Meir and Dayan when he presented them with his war plan.[72] Thus, in October, the army was operating according to this political directive. "Don't move troops unless war has actually started," Dayan ordered Elazar the day before the outbreak of the war. "Don't concentrate your forces or send out alerts."[73] "Mobilizing the reserves is an act of war," Dayan said on the morning that the conflict began in explaining his opposition to Elazar's request to call up about 200,000 reservists. Instead, the defense minister agreed to a limited call-up, only for defensive needs.[74] "If things get more serious, and firing has begun," he told Meir and Elazar several hours later, "we will call up the full formation. Otherwise it will seem as though we are making war."[75]

The failure of the intelligence appraisal during the days that preceded the war is not in doubt. So it has been convenient to present this as an explanation for Israeli conduct in the days and hours leading up to the war. But that interpretation lacks a strong factual basis, for Meir and Dayan's considerations were political. Indeed, their concerns would still have been operative even if Zeira had not erred in his assessment. And the political leadership's directives guided the military commanders' preparations, such that they had planned for war on the basis that Israel would not preempt for many months, an approach that nevertheless created great difficulties when the conflict actually did break out.

Golda Meir did not forget about the pledge she had made to Nixon and Kissinger in December 1971. She had given her word and made sure to uphold her commitment. This created difficult opening conditions for the Israeli military. The IDF command knew that this time, unlike 1967, Israel would not initiate the battle. However, they had not internalized the significance of this constraint and had not prepared for it as they should have.

CHAOS

The failure of the Israeli leadership's political analysis—starting from the decision to prefer war over negotiation—had culminated in the Egyptian-Syrian combined attack, and only then did Meir and Dayan understand that they had made a mistake by trying to rely on deterrence to prevent war. Israeli deterrence, meant to dissuade Sadat from initiating a comprehensive war, was not effective in preventing a limited war that would serve his political objectives. To the contrary, depending on deterrence turned out to be an approach that was fatally flawed. In order to deter, Israel would have had to transmit messages to Egypt that it had credible information that Egypt was about to initiate fighting, and to warn Egypt that Israel would react with great intensity. However, such a message would have not only revealed the sources of Israel's information, but also allowed Kissinger to leverage the danger of war to advance his political plan, which Israel did not want. "At this stage, we won't ask them to be concerned about [war] breaking out because you know about your friends there. They will act in their own interests at your expense," in Dayan's words.[76]

The IDF ultimately paid a high price for the political directive it received to not initiate the fighting. Waiting for more than two hours forced the Israeli military to deviate from its combat culture, which was based on initiative, surprise, and the transfer of the fighting to enemy territory. It also became clear that the Israeli plan to contain the Egyptian-Syrian assault was not practical, as it rested on an internal contradiction. It relied on the air force as a central factor in the holding defense, but also assumed the need to grant it two days to destroy the missile batteries and attack the airfields in Egypt and Syria.[77]

The top decision-makers' political conception of the situation was also mistaken. Although the Egyptian and Syrian concentration of forces was known, Meir and Dayan still assumed that Sadat's political goals created "a low probability that he would initiate a war"; that he would instead wait for Kissinger to put his plan into action after the Israeli elections; and that the Syrians would not go to war without Egypt. "I accept that conception about the difference between Egypt and Syria one hundred percent," Golda had said, responding to the approach offered by Dayan. Dayan considered that the "Egyptians would now prefer an additional political round to a military round"[78] and that "on the way to peace, or at least the non-renewal of war, I expect that there will be a decline of hostility, or no fanning of the flames into an active state."[79] He added, "I don't expect a renewal of war in the battlefields, but I do expect a difficult political struggle"[80] and that "the Egyptians will now prefer to 'gather the fruits' of the political campaign that they have begun."[81] "What is the logic in beginning a war?" Zamir similarly wondered during a conversation with Marwan a few hours before the war broke out. "Starting a war now will do harm to recent Egyptian political gains and the chances of reaching understandings with Kissinger."[82] These assessments, it turned out, ultimately amounted to wishful thinking.

These failures of analysis became clear on the morning of October 6. The IDF also realized that day that it would have to pay a heavy price for the political demand that it hold on to the water line along the Suez Canal. And still another weak point in the Israeli position became palpably apparent, namely the inferiority of American-supplied weaponry in the ensuing confrontations between the Arabs' SAM and antitank missiles on the one hand and, respectively, Israeli planes and armor on the other.

TECHNOLOGICAL-MILITARY INFERIORITY

In August 1970, Israel had lacked the weapons to gain a victory in the War of Attrition, which Egypt had initiated the year before. The technological inability of the West to deal with the air defense missile system provided to Egypt by the Soviet Union compelled Israel to end the exhausting war. Having no choice, Israel accepted a ceasefire resolution that Rogers had mediated, a political solution which it had adamantly opposed. The plan was accompanied by a very significant development—Egypt's movement of its missile batteries to the canal zone, which violated the terms of the ceasefire; turned the surrounding area, in effect, into a missile defense zone; and left the IDF in a weakened military position. The situation had not changed by 1973, and its implications were well known.

On May 9, Elazar presented the IDF battle plan to Meir and Dayan. Israel's inferiority in the canal zone would ultimately cause the plan to fail. "We are building the Egyptian and Syrian fronts on complete containment," Elazar said. He outlined the basic premise of the plan, saying, "We view the air force as the primary factor both in defense and in attack." He further explained that "the fact that we are venturing not to call up the preliminary reserves" stemmed from the assumption that the air force could stop attacks on both fronts. Responding to Dayan, who objected that the air force could not participate in containment, Elazar stated that the air force would begin by attacking either the missile batteries or the airfields, a decision that would depend on the hour of the Egyptian crossing of the canal. About the northern border, he said, "Exactly the same principle that I have described with Egypt."[83]

Elazar did not recognize—or at least did not discuss openly—the internal contradiction in his plan. Employing the air force as the primary factor in defense would leave Israel without a containment plan for the first two days of the war. Consequently, Dayan found it necessary to give additional clarification:

> What may happen is that they begin with an attempt to cross the canal in the evening. Basically, it won't be the air force which deals with them. And in a battle to prevent the incursion, most of the burden may be on the armored forces or the forces of the Southern Command. The one who will have to deal with the invader will be Arik [Ariel Sharon, the head of Southern Command] with tanks. On the following day, the air force will be busy, destroying the missiles and planes.[84]

In short, Elazar's war plan—which put the air force at the center of the initial defense—was hamstrung by the fact that the air force could not effectively participate in the containment effort.[85]

As a result, Elazar conceded that the containment effort would have to be made without the air force's involvement. But the chief of staff did not present an alternative plan. Instead, he hoped that a suitable rationale would be found to enable a preemptive attack on Egypt, which would shorten the time that the ground forces would have to stop the Egyptians without the help of the air force.[86]

Elazar's thinking in this respect was not wholly without foundation. At the end of April, Dayan had said that even if the air force did not carry out a preemptive attack, as it had in 1967, there was a possibility that it could carry out some kind of preliminary step.[87] Elazar, in other words, was relying on Dayan's judgment when he said, "It is not impossible, as I am relying on the Arabs to make even the tiniest mistake, and we don't need more than one mistake." Elazar even cited some specific examples: "Firing rockets at a photo sortie or 'a fiery speech' and an Egyptian statement that 'we are going to war.' Or the possibility that we (Israel) will also choose some kind of story on that morning. There is hope, but it isn't a certainty as in 1967."[88] At that same discussion, Dayan requested preparation of a plan "for that eventuality," and Elazar was evidently hoping for such a scenario when he devised his containment plan.[89] But Elazar's wishes ultimately did not square with reality on the afternoon of October 6, 1973.

Starting in September, and even more so in October, the Egyptian and Syrian deployments for war were evident. The top Israeli decision-makers knew that they would not approve a preemptive strike, and therefore appraised the situation at the front with growing concern and misgivings. Zeira, however, continued to estimate that the chances of war were low, an assessment with which Zamir agreed. "If we are dealing with an appraisal for a year, they (Egypt) are tending not to go to war," the head of the Mossad said after receiving at update from Marwan at the beginning of September.[90] For his part, Elazar also felt that the potential for war was low because Marwan had not transmitted any alert. "What we knew about previous dates sometimes was more practical than what we know now," he said three days before the war broke out.[91] And less than a day before it erupted, he declared, "We will have indications and additional information (about Egyptian plans)."[92] As long as this additional information had not arrived, the estimation remained that there would be an alert from Marwan at least forty-eight hours before war broke out, an assumption that proved mistaken when Zamir reported at four o'clock the next morning that fighting would commence later in the day.

Even after this information arrived, there was another setback. Zamir had reported that the war would begin "towards evening," Dayan "a bit after darkness falls."[93] The IDF was told that this meant 6:00 p.m., which became the time that was used as a basis for preparations during the coming hours.[94] However, the war actually began at 1:55 p.m. The incorrect information about when the war would break out played a central role in the chaos of the following hours, both practically and psychologically.

The air force, in accord with instructions from its commander, General Benny Peled, was already making preparations for the outbreak of war on October 4, and thus provided cover for the absence of the forty-eight hours necessary to prepare electronic warfare for attack. On the morning that the war began, the air force was ready for the order from the chief of staff to attack the Syrian missile batteries and, later, because of weather limitations, the Syrian airfields. This situation continued until 1:00 p.m., such that Peled was only belatedly informed of Meir's decision not to approve a preemptive attack. And so, for a precious amount of time, the air force was busy with preparing a step which was not to be taken.[95]

The report received at 1:55 p.m. that the radar screens had picked up signs of hundreds of planes from Egypt and Syria moving toward Israel left the top decision-makers off-balance. All of their assumptions had been upended. Elazar and Dayan hurried to the narrow command room of the air force commander. There they discovered that they could not operate according to plan; half an hour before, after a preemptive strike had not been approved, Peled had ordered the air force to return to its primary function—safeguarding the country's skies. Peled was not satisfied with the interceptors which were ready for that task and had therefore ordered that their configuration be changed from attack mode to interception mode. It quickly became clear that the air force was disorganized, with attack planes being launched without having been provided targets.[96] The planes, moreover, were operating at a height that exposed them to Egypt's ground-to-air missiles. Within minutes, Israel's technical inferiority also became clear, as the air force was even unable to assist in the missile-free area of the front.

The unexpected advance in timing caught the command chiefs far from their command positions and far from the storm of events at the front, where the chaos was tangible and tragic. The rapid pace of events provided fertile ground for mistakes in decision-making, which, in turn, paved the way for additional mistakes. There was no one to provide details to the air force that would enable it to immediately assist in the containment effort. The location of forces, information almost indispensable for planes to perform effectively at the front, was not transmitted. Additionally, communication channels for coordination, guidance, and identification of attack targets were nonexistent.

Dayan soon realized that there was a great gap between how he had envisioned the war would unfold and what actually happened, which soon instilled enormous fear in him. He viewed fighting on the canal and the cease-fire lines of the Golan as tantamount to the destruction of "the Third Temple," even though neither the Egyptians nor the Syrians had the intention or the ability to move beyond the 1967 lines and into Israel directly. To the contrary, the aim of the Egyptian army had been the command systems of supervision and control in the west and south of Sinai. As for Elazar, he was soon exposed to the contradiction between his intention to rely on the air force for containment and the knowledge that, to assist the ground forces fighting to retain their defensive positions in the battle zone, what was needed was two days to attack the Arabs' missile batteries and the airfields.

The next morning, the air force began its operation, codenamed Tagar, to attack the air defense missiles in Egypt. But Elazar ordered Peled to stop the operation and to instead attack the missiles in Syria—the mission was code-named Doogman—to aid in the containment in the Golan. It became clear that, under conditions of extreme pressure, even the IDF's well-oiled and efficient system could be thrown off-balance, and that its talented and experienced commanders could go wrong.

SADAT'S INTENTIONS, MOTIVATIONS, AND ACTIONS

Sadat—along with Asad—initiated the war, even though he and the heads of the Egyptian military knew that a war could not return Sinai to Egyptian sovereignty. He intended to achieve that goal in a political agreement. So the obvious question is why he chose to go to war in October instead of waiting until after elections in Israel. At that point, Kissinger would have been able to advance peace negotiations between Israel and Egypt, having been freed from the difficulty of applying pressure on Israel during an election period.

From the standpoint of the Israelis and Americans, these are reasonable questions. To answer them, they must be examined from the Egyptian point of view. The goal, in other words, must be to understand Sadat's objectives, the difficulties he faced in trying to achieve them, and how he chose to deal with those difficulties.

Fundamentally, Sadat had to find a way to return the territory that Israel had conquered in 1967—the Sinai Peninsula—to Egyptian sovereignty. His solution to this problem was to exchange Soviet patronage for American patronage so that Egypt would receive economic and political support from both the United States and the oil countries that were tied to Washington, first and foremost Saudi Arabia. Sadat understood that in order to do this, he would have to cut Egypt off from the other tracks of the dispute between the Arab world and Israel. He knew that the Israeli-Syrian and the Israeli-Palestinian conflicts might take a much longer time to resolve. Consequently, in July 1972 he had sought to create the necessary conditions to bring about this shift in patronage by significantly downgrading his relationship with the Soviets and, via the CIA, establishing a secret back channel with Kissinger. His aim was to reach agreement on understandings with the United States in 1973, and on that basis, to achieve the framework of a peace agreement between Egypt and Israel before the Israeli elections. As Ismail had told Kissinger, the Israelis "could present their nation with the question of peace or war and we will see what the nation has to say about that."[97]

Thus, Sadat operated simultaneously on two tracks. The first was direct communications with Kissinger, conducted through Ismail both via messages and at the secret meetings between the two men that were held in February and May 1973. The second was preparations for a war, the goal of which was to motivate the political process if the diplomatic track did not yield results. The war plan had limited objectives—it called for Sadat's forces to cross the Suez Canal under the umbrella of a SAM missile battery and to then hold on to the eastern bank—and was thus consistent with Egypt's military capabilities. The instructions to the heads of the army to prepare a limited war plan had already been given in October 1972. The commanders began their preparations, set a schedule to complete them, and acted with no knowledge of the political track.[98]

In May, after the second meeting between Kissinger and Ismail, Sadat understood that the diplomatic track with Kissinger was not achieving results and announced that he was suspending it.[99] He also requested that the Soviet Union be involved in the political process and try to advance the negotiations at the US-Soviet summit in June.[100] However, at the meeting Nixon and Kissinger pushed the Middle East to the margins, and no progress was made.

By July, Sadat had realized that only the military option remained. He accelerated Egyptian military coordination with the Syrians, as well as political coordination with the Saudis. The aim of the latter was to get Riyadh to activate the oil weapon when the war broke out. On August 23, Sadat and

Asad were given the dates on which the military leadership preferred to initiate the fighting.[101]

Based on a reconstruction of events, it is now possible to pinpoint the following key factors relating to the question of why Sadat chose war, instead of waiting until after Israel's elections in October, to try to jumpstart the political track again:

1. Even during the meetings at the end of February, Ismail emphasized to Kissinger that Sadat's schedule to reach an agreement was timed so that he would be able to meet the test and trial of the Israeli public during elections. This point came up several times.[102]
2. In 1971 and 1972, Sadat had experienced the failure of his attempts to reach an agreement during his negotiations with Rogers and Undersecretary of State Joseph Sisco, as well as with the United Nations envoy, Gunnar Jarring. Likewise, the ideas that Sadat expressed via the back channel with Kissinger had been met with rejection. Initially, Sadat was told that serious negotiations would have to wait until after the 1972 US elections. Subsequently, the Egyptians encountered problems scheduling talks with Kissinger, who was very busy. The second meeting between Kissinger and Ismail was also postponed a number of times—it did not take place until May 20—and without the preparations necessary to achieve an agreement on understandings. Sadat assumed that the delay had been coordinated between Kissinger and Meir. Then, the superpower summit yielded no progress. Thus, Sadat had reason to suspect that this conduct would continue after the elections in Israel.
3. Sadat did not know the details of the exchanges that were taking place between Kissinger and Meir. Nor did he know that already at the beginning of March, Kissinger had presented the outline for an agreement, and a schedule to conduct negotiations, to Israel. And he knew nothing about Dayan's intention to try to move toward an agreement after the Israeli elections, one that, in principle, was similar to his own initiative.[103]
4. The preparations for war were based on their own schedule, independent of the political moves that were taking place at the same time. The heads of the Egyptian army planned to complete their preparations by the autumn of 1973 and were unaware of the political track. As such, they determined that the possible dates to initiate the fighting would be in September or October. Sadat would have faced great criticism if he had allowed these dates to pass without starting the war.
5. In 1971, his first full year as president, Sadat had announced that it was a "year of decision" for either war or peace. By October 1973, he would

have been in power for three years, and he would have had difficulty explaining an additional postponement of decision-making.

6. On September 4, the "Galili document," which laid out the Labor Party's policy for developing settlements in the occupied territories, had been made public in Israel.[104] This document included the establishment of a bloc of settlements and the city of Yamit, which would include a large port, in northwestern Sinai. Discussions about formalizing the plan were publicized in the media. Sadat viewed this document as the Israeli reaction to his peace initiative.

Sadat would have preferred that his political efforts succeed, instead of having to choose the military alternative. When Marwan had alerted Israel of the likely dates that war would break out the previous year, he had simultaneously emphasized that political moves initiated by the United States, the Soviet Union, or Israel would prevent Sadat from giving the final order to attack. This message was also transmitted by King Hussein of Jordan, who had arrived in Israel several days after discussions with Sadat and Asad in Cairo for a meeting with Meir, at which he tried to warn her of the coming war.[105]

After the war, many officials and analysts claimed that a key objective for Sadat had been to restore the honor and pride, which had been lost in the June 1967 Six-Day War, to Egypt and its army, as well as to regain Egyptian sovereignty over Sinai. That assertion, however, gained prominence mainly due to the impression that Egypt had won a great military victory and had its pride restored—it had not been the objective of the war. To the contrary, this argument does not take into account the possibility that the war might have ended with an additional defeat for Egypt and an expansion of the Israeli occupation on the west side of the canal.

Ex post explanations usually arise because key participants have an interest in cultivating them. In this case, Israel had an interest in promoting this narrative to prove that the war was unavoidable and would have broken out even without Israel's refusal to negotiate. Similarly, Sadat supported this version of events to foster the idea that Egypt had recovered its honor so that he could justify the heavy price that came with the military losses from the war, and to rebut criticism that he should have waited for a political solution to present itself. And this narrative also served Kissinger's purposes by creating a justification for the fact that he had not used US influence to advance a political agreement before the war.

The argument that the political initiative was fraudulent and meant to camouflage the Arabs' military planning should also be rejected. Egyptian and Syrian preparations for war were open and public, and Sadat did not hide his intention to go to war if there was no progress in the political track. These messages were transmitted openly in the media, as well as through quieter diplomatic channels. It is not reasonable to think that Sadat would have risked initiating a war if Kissinger had succeeded in advancing a political process, as going to war with negotiations ongoing would have created a serious crisis of confidence between him and the United States, whose patronage he sought.

THE OUTLINE RETURNS

From the moment that the fighting broke out, Kissinger's goal was to put the United States in a position that would allow it to facilitate the postwar negotiations. Sadat had a similar objective. But, in contrast to Sadat, Kissinger also had a great effect on the war's ending. Kissinger had not wanted this war. But when it broke out, he knew how to use it to his advantage so that he could establish the undisputed status of the United States as the key outside player in the peace process, as well as strengthen his personal position for the purpose of being able to guide political developments during and after the war.

What Kissinger had avoided before the war, he undertook decisively and with great talent afterward. And he did so according to the outline he had presented to Israel in March, which was based on the principles of Sadat's initiative: preliminary understandings between the United States and Egypt; recognition of Egyptian sovereignty over Sinai as a substitute, at least temporarily, for full withdrawal; a withdrawal which would take place gradually and would respond to Israel's security needs; and separation between the Egyptian track and the other elements of the dispute—that is, basing an Israeli-Syrian agreement on the one between Israel and Egypt and treating the Palestinian problem as an internal Jordanian matter, rather than as a central factor in the Arab-Israeli conflict.

From the end of the war, the Egyptians became full partners with Kissinger in the political process. Already at the end of October, Ismail Fahmi, the new Egyptian foreign minister, arrived in Washington and assisted Kissinger in conducting talks with Meir and General Aharon Yariv. About a week later, Kissinger traveled to Egypt and, in a lengthy private discussion with Sadat, began implementing the outline that he had presented to Israel in March. This time he went ahead with his initiative without requesting that Israel withdraw its demand to annex a part of Sinai. To put pressure on the Israelis, Kissinger hinted that he alone was capable of shielding them from Nixon, who, he claimed, wanted to take a harder line. "Edward (Nixon) wanted to issue an announcement supporting Israeli withdrawal to the 4 June 1967 lines," the secretary of state reportedly said, adding that he had prevented the president from doing so.[106]

At Kissinger's meeting with Sadat, the two men agreed upon the understandings that Ismail had wanted to advance after his first meeting with the Americans at the end of February. Statesmen like Kissinger and Sadat needed only one discussion to take that step. "He is the best hope for peace in the area," said Kissinger about Sadat. In contrast to the Israelis, the secretary of state added: "He is a person who can make decisions."[107]

On November 11, Egypt and Israel signed the so-called Six Point Agreement to stabilize the ceasefire.[108] On December 21, Kissinger opened the Geneva conference, a meeting with only symbolic significance, the main objective of which was to give the appearance of the inclusion of the Soviet Union in the peace process. Egypt, Israel, and Kissinger finalized what they had agreed upon previously, beginning with a discussion about a separation of forces, followed by the beginning of the Israeli withdrawal from Sinai.[109]

On January 18, 1974, Egypt and Israel signed a disengagement agreement, often referred to as the Sinai I agreement, which "would represent the first step towards a final, just and lasting peace."[110] This was the beginning of what was termed "a state of peace" in Sadat's initiative, and in Kissinger's outline, implementation of the partial agreement and continuing discussion on a full agreement. Israel withdrew from the Suez Canal to a line that, at this stage, secured its security needs. To that end, Sadat agreed that the Israeli withdrawal would be to the western, rather than the eastern, side of the Sinai passes. Sadat explained to his army chief of staff that it would be a pity to postpone the signing of the agreement over an argument about withdrawal from an area from which Israel would withdraw in the future.

On May 31, "one step" after Egypt, Syria also signed a separation of forces agreement with Israel. In coordination with Sadat, Kissinger pressured Israel to accept a withdrawal in the Golan that would symbolically be from an area it had conquered in June 1967.

On September 4, 1975, Egypt and Israel signed another interim agreement—Sinai II—agreeing that "[t]he conflict between them and in the Middle East shall not be resolved by military force but by peaceful means" and that "[t]hey are determined to reach a final and just peace settlement by means of negotiations."[111] Israel continued to withdraw eastward. There was also an agreement between Kissinger and Rabin—the latter had replaced Meir as prime minister in June 1974—that, on the Syrian track, they would skip the interim agreement stage, as the geographical conditions in the Golan would make a partial withdrawal difficult.

The final stage of implementation of the outline, a peace agreement, was led by a new American government. The Sadat formula to separate Egypt from the other Arab actors involved in the conflict was included in the agreement. It stipulated that a solution to the Palestinian problem would be achieved by granting the Palestinians autonomy, and that agreements between Israel and the other Arab states would be based on the Israeli-Egyptian settlement. Syria declined to join the process, despite an invitation from Israel's new prime minister, Menachem Begin, but was later forced to negotiate after the collapse of the Soviet Union.[112] Since 1992, the prime ministers of six Israeli governments have conducted negotiations with Syria in an effort to reach a peace agreement, with the Egyptian agreement serving as a model, including the territorial aspect of full Israeli withdrawal from the Golan. During this period, a peace agreement was signed with Jordan, and like the agreement with Egypt, the "international border" was determined as the boundary.

The peace process during the 1970s ultimately culminated in the implementation of the Sadat initiative, which was reflected in Kissinger's outline. The opportunity to conduct serious negotiations on that basis had existed before the outbreak of the October 1973 war. In other words, the war could have been prevented, as Kissinger had warned Meir.

NOTES

1. Golda Meir, in an address to the nation, October 6, 1973, Channel 1—Israel Broadcasting Authority.

2. Central Intelligence Agency, "President Nixon and the Role of Intelligence in the 1973 Arab-Israeli War," 2013, https://www.cia.gov/resources/publications/president-nixon-and-the-role-of-intelligence-in-the-1973-arab-israeli-war.

3. Henry Kissinger, *Years of Upheaval* (Boston: Little, Brown, 1982), 459.

4. Matti Golan, *Ha-Sichot Ha-Sodiot Shel Henry Kissinger* [The Secret Conversations of Henry Kissinger: Step-by-Step Diplomacy in the Middle East] (Tel Aviv: Shocken, 1976), 142.

5. Address by President Anwar Sadat to the nation on Revolution Day, July 23, 1971, *Davar*, July 25, 1971.

6. See Yigal Kipnis, *1973: The Road to War* (Charlottesville, VA: Just World, 2013), 78–79; Yitzhak Rabin, "First Thoughts," February 18, 1973, Israel State Archives (ISA), 7061/6-Aleph.

7. The Rogers Plan proposed a withdrawal from the areas conquered by Israel in June 1967 and related to all dimensions of the Arab-Israeli dispute.

8. White House Tapes, Conversation 628–016, December 2, 1971, Richard M. Nixon Presidential Library, Yorba Linda, California (RMNL), https://www.nixonlibrary.gov/white-house-tapes/628/conversation-628-016.

9. National Security Council (NSC) Files, Box 1166, Hal Saunders Middle East Negotiations Files, RMNL.

10. Yitzhak Rabin, *Pinkas Sherut* [The Rabin Memoirs] (Tel Aviv: Sifriat Ma'ariv, 1979), 345–46. See also Henry Kissinger, *White House Years* (New York: Little, Brown, 1979), 1,329; Kipnis, *1973*, 38; CIA Document Summarizing the Creation of the President's Track, Box 131, NSC Files, Kissinger Office Files (HAKOFF), RMNL; Kissinger-Rabin Meeting, December 6, 1972, ISA, 7061/5-Aleph.

11. Rabin to Meir, "First Thoughts about the Expected Visit of Ismail to Washington," February 18, 1973, ISA, 7061/6-Aleph.

12. Kipnis, *1973*, 38.

13. Conversation between Nixon and Army Vice Chief of Staff Alexander Haig, January 23, 1973, in United States Department of State, *Foreign Relations of the United States* [*FRUS*], *1969–1976*, vol. 25, *Arab-Israeli Crisis and War, 1973* (Washington, DC: Government Printing Office, 2011), 8.

14. Rabin, "Report—Conversation with Shaul," March 9, 1973, ISA, 7062/8-Aleph.

15. Memorandum (Memo) from Kissinger to Nixon, "Subject: Background for Your Meeting with Egyptian Emissary Hafiz Ismail," February 23, 1973, in *FRUS, 1969–1976*, vol. 25, 70–71; Kissinger, *Years of Upheaval*, 212.

16. Kipnis, *1973*, 64–72.

17. Summary Memo by Kissinger and NSC Staffer Hal Saunders, February 27, 1973, ISA, 7062/8-Aleph.

18. Meeting between Kissinger and Rabin, March 9, 1973, ISA, 7062/8-Aleph.

19. Meeting between Meir, Rabin, and Kissinger, February 28, 1973, ISA, 4239/3-Aleph.

20. Meeting between Kissinger and Rabin, March 9, 1973, Box 135, NSC Files, HAKOFF, RMNL; About the Private Discussion, ISA, 7062/8-Aleph. Kissinger showed Rabin important information that had been transmitted by Eugene Trone, the CIA station chief in Cairo, who had accompanied Ismail on his visit and conversed with him on February 26–27.

21. Kipnis, *1973*, 156, 203. Kissinger to Dinitz, June 2, 1973, Box 135, NSC Files, HAKOFF, RMNL; Dinitz Report about His Meeting with Kissinger, September 10, 1973, ISA, 4996/2-Aleph.

22. Memo from Kissinger to Nixon, "Subject: My Talks with Hafiz Ismail—Summary," February 25–26, 1973, March 6, 1973, Box 131, NSC Files, HAKOFF, RMNL.

23. Editorial Note, in *FRUS, 1969–1976*, vol. 25, 85. See also Kipnis, *1973*, 71.

24. Editorial Note, 85–86. The meeting took place without the presence of Secretary of State Rogers.

25. Kipnis, *1973*, 51, 158. Allon tried to return to this proposal in June 1973 but was thwarted by Meir.

26. Kipnis, *1973,* 80–83; Meeting between Kissinger and Meir, February 28, 1973, ISA, 4239-Aleph. There is no American protocol for this meeting. The following day Meir was forced to agree that Kissinger could continue the secret track with Ismail, on the condition that "he does not do anything behind our backs." Telephone Conversation, Kissinger-Rabin, 28/2/1973, 23:15, NARN, Hak Telcon Files, Box 18. Also, Telephone Conversation, Kissinger and the President, 28/2/1973, 23:30, NARN, Hak Telcon Files, Box 18; website of the archives of the President Gerald Ford Library, www.fordlibrarymuseum.gov/default.asp; ISA, 7038/12-Aleph; quote from Meir's Report to the Limited Forum of Ministers, March 13, 1973, ISA, 7062/8-Aleph; Kipnis, *1973*, 87.

27. Summary Memo by Kissinger and NSC Staffer Hal Saunders, February 27, 1973.

28. The president had reacted to an additional earlier memorandum from Kissinger prior to his meeting with Meir by writing: "This is the time to get moving—[and] they must be told that *firmly*." See Memo from Kissinger to Nixon, February 23, 1973, 71n7. See also Kipnis, *1973*, 58; Kissinger, *Years of Upheaval*, 212.

29. Memo from Kissinger to Nixon, March 6, 1973.

30. NA RN, Box 135; ISA, 7062/8-Aleph. Ismail had said that unfortunately, it had not been possible for him to be very specific this time. Kissinger showed Rabin the intelligence information about what Ismail had said.

31. Kipnis, *1973*, 93. Researchers of the period who did not combine American and Israeli documentary sources erred in reconstructing these events. For example, Craig Daigle, editor of the *Foreign Relations of the United States* volume on the October 1973 war, did not make use of Israeli documentation. He thus overlooked important pieces of information when trying to understand these events. One of them was the outline presented by Kissinger to Israel, which is documented only in the Israeli archives. Consequently, Daigle ignored the public part of the discussion in which Kissinger detailed the schedule for the implementation of his plan. This is also true of the Israeli editor, who did not integrate American documentation into his research.

32. Kipnis, *1973*, 313. Meir avoided transmitting this information to the Americans because she thought it would lead to pressure on Israel to enter negotiations on the basis of the Rogers Plan, which she opposed. See Rabin, *Pinkas Sherut*, 345–46.

33. Meeting of the "Cabinet 2," April 18, 1973, Israel Defense Forces (IDF) Archives 175/383/1975.

34. Kipnis, *1973*, 91–96. See also Meeting between Rabin and Kissinger, "Report of a Discussion with Shaul," March 9, 1973, ISA, 7062/8-Aleph.

35. Memo from Kissinger to Nixon, March 6, 1973.

36. Meeting between Kissinger and Rabin, March 9, 1973. This document is not included in the *Foreign Relations of the United States* volume.

37. Meeting between Rabin and Kissinger, March 9, 1973, ISA, 7062/8-Aleph.

38. Ibid.

39. Kipnis, *1973*, 96.

40. Ibid., 140–41.

41. Ibid., 200–203.

42. "Cabinet 2," April 18, 1973, ISA, Yom Kippur War Documents, ISA online, www.archives.gov.il. For further details, see Kipnis, *1973*, 97–100.

43. Ibid.

44. Ibid.

45. Interpretation proposed by Yoav Gelber; Y. Gelber, *Rahav* [Arrogance] (Kinneret Zmora-Bitan Dvir, 2021), 273.

46. "Cabinet 2," April 18, 1973.

47. Ibid.

48. Ibid.

49. As Meir put it, "We won't be doing the right thing if we tell the government that there were signs in the past, and we thought that here it is (war), it's coming, and the information was false. . . . The government must know that it is possible. And we are talking about weeks. That is to say, Sadat is talking about only a few weeks."

50. Cabinet Meeting, April 24, 1973, ISA, Yom Kippur War Documents, ISA online, www.archives.gov.il.

51. Ibid.

52. Kipnis, *1973*, 153–54. Quoted in Hanoch Bartov, *Dado, 48 Shanim V'od 20 Yom* [Dado, 48 Years and 20 Days] (Or Yehuda, Israel: Dvir, 2002), 283–84.

53. Kipnis, *1973*, 141; Memorandum of Conversation (Memcon), May 13, 1973, Box 135, NSC Files, HAKOFF, RMNL.

54. Nahum Barnea, "Kissinger Calls for Negotiations in the Middle East," *Yedioth Ahronoth*, September 12, 1973. See also Kipnis, *1973*, 203–5.

55. Memcon, September 10, 1973, *FRUS, 1969–1976*, vol. 25, 265; Dinitz to Mordechai Gazit, September 10, 1973, ISA, 887/Lamed Vav.

56. Dinitz to Gazit, September 30, 1973, ISA, 934/Lamed Vav, 4996/2-Aleph.

57. For example, see Philip Ben, "Kissinger Will Demand an Initiative by Israel to Break the Stagnation in the Dispute," *Haaretz*, September 23, 1973; Moshe Carmel, "Expectations and Fears Approaching 1974," *Davar*, September 26, 1973; also the headline in the *Haaretz* daily newspaper, "Dinitz: The Americans Are Talking a Lot about Movement and Are Expecting an Initiative by Israel," September 17, 1973.

58. See Kipnis, *1973*, 203.

59. Dinitz to Meir, September 30, 1973, ISA, 934/Lamed Vav, 4996/2-Aleph.

60. Dinitz to Gazit, September 30, 1973.

61. *Haaretz*, October 2, 1973. Quote from an editorial of the *London Times*.

62. Meeting between Kissinger and Dinitz, October 7, 1973, RG 59, Box 25, RMNL; National Security Archive, *The October War and U.S. Policy*, ed. William Burr, 5.

63. Meeting between Kissinger and Rabin, December 24, 1971, ISA, 7052/20-Aleph; Kipnis, *1973*, 79–80.

64. Dispatch from Rabin, December 1, 1972, ISA, 7043/16-Aleph.

65. Memcon, October 6, 1973, Box 136, NSC Files, HAKOFF, RMNL; Henry Kissinger, *Crisis: The Anatomy of Two Major Foreign Policy Crises* (New York: Simon & Schuster, 2003), 11; Message from Meir to Kissinger, undated, in *FRUS, 1969–1976*, vol. 25, 284–85. After the war, Kissinger claimed that he had never made that demand to Israel, but real-time documentation negates this claim.

66. Presentation of War Plans to Meir and Dayan, May 9, 1973, Israeli Defense Forces Archives (IDF Archives), 2016/264/41.

67. Ibid.

68. Kipnis, *1973*, 147.

69. https://archive.kippur-center.org/discussions/d-md-06101973-0545.pdf.

70. Consultation with Meir, October 6, 1973, 8:05 a.m., 7049.19-Aleph. Dayan even made sure to tell the prime minister, "I told Dado not to do air patrols over the border today. It must be clear that we didn't start this."

71. Meeting between Kissinger and Dinitz, October 7, 1973, RG 59, Box 25 RMNL; National Security Archive, *The October War and U.S. Policy*, ed. William Burr.

72. Presentation of War Plans to Meir and Dayan, May 9, 1973.

73. Bartov, *Dado, 48 Years*, 316; Eli Zeira, *Mitos mul Metziut* [Myth versus Reality: The Yom Kippur War] (Tel Aviv: Yedioth Aharonoth, 2004), 183.

74. Consultation with Dayan, October 6, 1973, 5:45 a.m., Yom Kippur War Center, https://kippur-center.org.

75. Consultation with Meir, October 6, 1973.

76. "Cabinet 2," April 18, 1973.

77. Presentation of War Plans to Meir and Dayan, May 9, 1973.

78. Cabinet Consultation, October 3, 1973, website of the State Archives; IDF Archives 1975 175.383; Kipnis, *1973*, 247.

79. Bartov, *Dado, 48 Years*, 317. See also Kipnis, *1973*, 247–48.

80. "Dayan Views Positively the Possibility of Kissinger Taking the Initiative," *Yedioth Ahronoth*, September 11, 1973.

81. "Dayan Views a Possible Kissinger Initiative Positively," *Davar*, September 11, 1973.

82. Notes of Meeting by Zamir and Dubi Asherov, Marwan's Contact Person, with Marwan in London, October 6, 1973, ISA online, www.archives.gov.il.

83. Presentation of War Plans to Meir and Dayan, May 9, 1973.

84. Ibid.

85. The Agranat Commission defined the military agenda of the air force as: (1) defense of the country's skies; (2) attacking the airfields; (3) destroying the missile batteries; and (4) aid to the ground forces. See Agranat Commission Partial Report, vol. 2, 214.

86. "I am making the assumption that we cannot initiate a preventive war out of the blue on two fronts," Elazar said during the discussion. "Nevertheless, we are preparing ourselves for the possibility of a partial blow. If that is possible before the start or at the same time." See Presentation of War Plans to Meir and Dayan, May 9, 1973.

87. Dayan even illustrated with an example. If there was a large offensive concentration of forces in the Golan, the Americans might accept a preemptive strike understandingly, and then: "If we need a provocation that they fired first, we will get that." Dayan gave another example in May, saying, "If it becomes clear that tomorrow, they may fire on Tel Aviv—we don't have to wait for them to do that." See Golan, *Ha-Sichot*, 67.

88. Golan, *Ha-Sichot*, 67.

89. Yigal Kipnis, *The Golan Heights: Political History, Settlement and Geography since 1949* (New York: Routledge, 2013), 37. The skirmishes that had broken out on the Syrian-Israeli border in the years before the June 1967 Six-Day War were such an example. They were the result of IDF provocations that aimed to take advantage of the superiority of the Israeli air force to strike at the Syrians. Dayan admitted, "I did it, Laskov and Chara (Tzvi Tzur) did it. Yitzhak Rabin did it when he was there. But it seems to me that the one who most enjoyed those games was Elazar." All of those mentioned were Israeli generals at Northern Command.

90. General Staff Discussion, September 24, 1973, Agranat Commission Report, Additional Partial Report, Explanations and Additions, vol. 1, 167. The commission determined, "Basically, there were no differences of opinion among them, and during the days before war broke out, he was relying on the military intelligence appraisal.

91. Consultation with Meir, October 3, 1973, IDF Archives, 175/383/1975.

92. Meeting of the Government, October 5, 1973, IDF Archives, 175/383/1975.

93. Meeting of the Government, October 6, 1973, IDF Archives, 173/383/1975.

94. Consultation with Meir, October 6, 1973, ISA, 7049.19-Aleph.

95. Shmuel Gordon, *Thirty Hours in October* (Tel Aviv: Maariv, 2008), 251.

96. In addition, it was impossible to attack strategic targets in Syria. "What should we do until more tanks are brought in?" Dayan asked three days before the war broke out. Israel, he anticipated, would attack deep in Syria, "even including putting Damascus under fire." See Cabinet Consultation, October 3, 1973, IDF Archives, 175/283/1975.

97. Kipnis, *1973*, 64–72.

98. Saad el-Shazly, *The Crossing of the Suez* (San Francisco: American Mideast Research, 1980); Muhammad Abd-al-Ghani el-Gamasy, *The October War: Memoirs of Field Marshal El-Gamasy of Egypt* (Cairo: American University in Cairo Press, 1993); Dani Asher, *Breaking the Conception* (Tel Aviv: Maarachot, 2003).

99. Message from Ismail to Kissinger, June 2, 1973, Box 132, NSC Files, HAKOFF, RMNL.

100. "There is no doubt therefore that the Soviet Union will find in the Summit Meeting an opportunity to resume its discussions with the U.S. which were started in May 1972 and, knowing the Egyptian position." Message from Ismail to Kissinger, June 2, 1973.

101. Mohammad Hassanein Heikal, *The Road to Ramadan* (New York: Quadrangle, 1975), 1–4; Shazly, *Crossing of Suez*, 146–47.

102. Kissinger was told the following in his conversation with Ismail on February 25–26: "I assume that in the coming days Mrs. Meir will tell you that in Israel there will be elections this year. But the elections in Israel do not enter into our considerations. It's enough that we waited until after the election in the United States. They [the Israelis] have to raise questions of war and peace and let's see what the Israeli nation has to say about that." NARN, NSC Files, Box 131.

103. Kipnis, *1973*, 154–55.

104. Ibid., 191–92. For his part, Nixon, when he learned of the plan, wrote: "This is an enormous mistake—tell the Israelis in unmistakable terms that I believe they hurt their cause and jeopardize our (my) support by such brutal tactics." See Memo from Kissinger to Nixon, September 1, 1973, in *FRUS, 1969–1976*, vol. 25, 260.

105. Kipnis, *1973*, 213–14; Shlaim, 2009, 315–18; Shalev, 2007, 108–18.

106. Report from Eban, December 22, 1973, ISA, 7035/12-Aleph.

107. Memcon, January 16, 1974, Box 133, NSC Files, RMNL. "You don't have anyone who can make decisions on foreign policy," Kissinger said to Dinitz at one point. See Kissinger, *Crisis*, 316.

108. The agreement stabilized the ceasefire, provided for an exchange of prisoners, and arranged for the removal of the blockade around the Third Army. The agreement was signed at Kilometer 101 by General Gamasy and General Aharon Yariv.

109. This decision had been accepted by Egypt, Israel, and Kissinger previously. The idea to call for the conference came from Sadat. See Farhi-Kissinger Meeting, October 31, 1973, Box 132, NSC Files, RMNL. For Sadat, the aim of the conference

was to give the impression of cooperation between the various tracks of the dispute. The Syrians declined to participate and stated that Egypt would represent them.

110. The separation of forces agreement between Israel and Egypt was signed by the heads of the Egyptian and Israeli armies. Knesset, www.knesset.gov.il.

111. The Interim Agreement between Israel and Egypt. Knesset, www.knesset.gov.il.

112. Yigal Kipnis, *1982, Lebanon: The Road to War* (Modi'in, Israel: Dvir, 2022), 174.

Chapter 2

Egypt's Military Effectiveness in the October War

Risa Brooks

In the annals of military history, Egypt's performance in the 1973 war has become a near iconic example of a state that was able to dramatically improve its military capabilities in a short period of time. The Egyptian experience accordingly has been mined for larger lessons on operational and tactical adaptation, organizational learning, and military effectiveness.

Yet, while there has been significant study of the war itself, less attention has been devoted to understanding the underlying factors that laid the foundation for the dramatic enhancement of Egypt's military capabilities just six years following its disastrous performance and ignominious defeat in the 1967 Arab-Israeli War. In Israel, the focus has mainly been on the conflict's causes and, more specifically, on the character of the intelligence and political failures that obscured Egyptian president Anwar Sadat's intention to go to war in 1973. Another large body of scholarship has examined the war for what it reveals about the nature of strategic surprise, broadly understood.[1]

Moreover, even when Egypt's performance in the war is the central focus, existing scholarship has a hard time accounting for the changes observed. Scholars, for example, have made essentialist claims about how supposed deficiencies in Arab culture account for ongoing deficits in military competence. That approach nonetheless predicts constancy in military activity and has a hard time accounting for the change in military effectiveness that occurred between 1967 and 1973.[2] Studies that point to the autocratic character of Egypt's regime also falter, as there was no transformation in the country's political system during this time.[3] And scholars who claim that different coup-proofing tactics shape military effectiveness do not emphasize the factors that enabled both Sadat and, in his final years, his predecessor, Gamal

Abdel Nasser, to regain control of the military and manage it differently than Nasser had in the 1960s.[4]

To understand what happened, I contend, one has to dig deeper into the domestic political bases of civil-military relations in the regime.[5] Specifically, I argue that understanding the Egyptian performance in the war requires, paradoxically, examining factors that seemingly have little to do with the war itself. What happened in 1973 was the product of more fundamental changes in the country's domestic politics and developments within the armed forces—changes that altered the country's civil-military relations and laid the foundation for reform within the military. These developments were rooted in the fractious character of Egypt's civil-military relations in the 1960s—which culminated in Egypt's defeat in the 1967 war and, ultimately, in domestic political shifts—that allowed Nasser to reestablish control over the military in the final three years of his presidency.

When he assumed office following Nasser's death in September 1970, Sadat then benefited from and capitalized upon these prior transformations in civil-military relations. Sadat also used his powers of appointment to put in leadership positions officers who identified themselves as professionals and saw the military's engagement in politics as contrary to the military's principal role and mission. It was this combination of underlying shifts in the civil-military balance of power in the regime, Sadat's skill as a tactician in managing his generals, and his ability to play upon fundamental ideational shifts in the officer corps that explain the improvements in Egypt's war-making capacity in 1973.

In this chapter, I detail these changes, showing how they influenced three key attributes of military effectiveness—the integration, responsiveness, and skill exhibited in Egypt's military activity in 1973. As a result of these changes, Egypt proved to be a significantly more effective fighting force than it had been in 1967, even while it continued to suffer from intractable deficits related to the character of its human capital and other training and organizational limitations. As a result of those enduring shortcomings, in both tactical and operational terms, Egypt lost the war, or at least was on the precipice of doing so, to the more capable Israeli military. Nonetheless, when the role and purpose of the military campaign is analyzed within the context of Sadat's larger strategic and political goals, Egypt's successes are more apparent.

This chapter begins with a brief overview of the major developments in the 1973 conflict, and then discusses changes in Egypt's civil-military relations following the 1967 war and under Sadat. It also defines the concept of military effectiveness. It then analyzes Egypt's military effectiveness, focusing on several important examples of its armed forces' integration, responsiveness, and improved skill.

BACKGROUND TO THE WAR

Following the 1967 war, Nasser sought to rebuild the Egyptian military and use it to maintain pressure on Israel through what came to be known as the War of Attrition. Thousands of Egyptian troops were deployed to the Suez Canal, where they engaged in artillery barrages and occasional raids against Israeli forces stationed on its east bank. The Israelis in turn established defensive fortifications that spanned one hundred miles along the canal and comprised over thirty positions, which were defended by soldiers armed with small arms and mortars. The string of fortifications, dubbed the Bar-Lev Line, was named for Israel's chief of staff, General Chaim Bar-Lev. By 1970, the War of Attrition and Israeli counterattacks had failed to produce any change in the military situation, and a ceasefire was brokered in August.

Sadat thus inherited a military stalemate when he assumed office, and faced the reality that Israel still controlled the territories it acquired from Egypt in the 1967 war, namely the Sinai Peninsula and Gaza Strip. Sadat initially sought to win back Egypt's territories diplomatically.[6] Yet, it soon became clear that Israel's political leaders, in great part because of their country's military superiority, had little inclination to negotiate.

The concept for the 1973 war emerged in this context. During the summer of 1972, Sadat increasingly became convinced that Egypt needed to demonstrate that the costs to Israel of holding Egyptian territory were significant and unsustainable, and thereby spur the Israelis to negotiate. The war aimed to demonstrate those costs, while also highlighting the dangers that the unresolved conflict posed to the stability of relations between the United States and the Soviet Union. Sadat, George Gawrych writes, hoped that the war "would shake the superpowers, in particular the United States, out of their diplomatic lethargy with respect to the Arab-Israeli conflict and force a positive attitude and policy toward Egypt."[7] As Sadat himself described it, the goal of the war was "to challenge the Israeli Security Theory by carrying out a military action according to the capabilities of the armed forces aimed at inflicting the heaviest losses on the enemy and convincing him that continued occupation of our land exacts a price that is too high for [Israel] to pay."[8] Operation Spark, as it was called, therefore never sought victory through exclusively military means—seizing and maintaining physical control of the Sinai—but relied on a coercive logic, aimed at shaking up the bargaining situation with Israel.

On the afternoon of October 6—during Ramadan and on Yom Kippur—Egypt took Israel by surprise with its offensive across the Suez Canal. The crossing operation included thousands of men and their supporting equipment. It employed innovative anti-armor tactics and was protected by a dense zone of anti-aircraft missile defenses in the canal zone.[9] Overall, the Egyptian crossing and assault against the Bar-Lev Line employed over 100,000 men and 1,700 tanks. By contrast, at the time of the initial attack the Israelis had just 91 tanks stationed in the canal zone. Israel was caught off-guard and ill-prepared to repel the assault, suffering as a consequence more than 700 casualties in the war's first two days, "a toll magnitudes higher than in any other Israeli war in such a short time period."[10] By October 8, Egypt succeeded in overtaking the Bar-Lev Line and establishing several bridgeheads on the canal's east bank.

Subsequently, on the night of October 15–16, Israel breached Egyptian lines and crossed behind Egypt's forces in the canal zone on the west bank. When the war ended with a United Nations–sponsored ceasefire on October 25, the section in the south, held by 20,000 soldiers of Egypt's Third Army, was isolated and surrounded, and Israeli forces were just sixty miles from Cairo.[11]

Even so, Egypt still retained its bridgeheads on the east bank of the canal. More importantly, from Sadat's perspective, the war had succeeded in surprising Israel and the world with its military effort, and Egypt had inflicted heavy casualties on the Israelis. As one Israeli general observed, "It's not the Egyptian Army of 1967."[12] Similarly, General Ariel Sharon said: "I have been fighting [Arab forces] for 25 years, and all the rest were just battles. This was a real war."[13] Sadat had succeeded in improving Egypt's capabilities and demonstrating that it would be costly for Israel to maintain control of Egypt's territory, which served his larger political goals. The leverage he gained from the war would later enable him to reach two disengagement agreements in 1974 and 1975 with Israel, as well as a peace treaty in 1979, which laid the groundwork for Israel's phased withdrawal from Sinai.[14]

CIVIL-MILITARY RELATIONS IN THE 1960S

To understand how Sadat accomplished these goals, one has to first understand the evolution of Egyptian civil-military relations. During the 1960s, Nasser faced a fierce challenge to his authority from the head of the Egyptian armed forces, Abdel Hakim Amer, a close friend and fellow Free Officer from the July 1952 coup that brought Nasser to power. Amer had been appointed head of the military by Nasser in the late 1950s, and steadily built a faction within the armed forces that was loyal to him, in part by enlarging the officer corps and providing them many privileges and perquisites.[15] By the mid-1960s, the rivalry between Nasser and Amer had devolved into a quiet competition for control of the military. That contest, in turn, had devastating consequences for strategic assessment and preparation in the crisis that preceded the June 1967 war with Israel, and for Egypt's military performance during it.[16]

The fallout from the war led to major changes in civil-military relations that subsequently laid the groundwork for Sadat's war planning in 1973. Following Egypt's disastrous performance in 1967—and even before the war had ended—Nasser offered to resign. Egyptians, however, poured into the streets in support for him. Indeed, "[t]he demonstrators constituted a massive plebiscite compelling Nasser to remain in power."[17] Sixteen hours later, Nasser reinstated himself as the country's president. Critically, "[a]t this moment [Nasser] discovered that he was more powerful than the army."[18]

A tense few months followed, filled with intrigue on both sides, which ended in Amer's arrest by Nasser's allies and his reported suicide on September 16. Three days later, the Egyptian paper *Al-Ahram* reported that 181 officers and civilians had been arrested. More than 1,000 officers were forced to retire.[19] This was an important turning point because the purge effectively eliminated the competing power center within the military and paved the way for Nasser to establish control over it.

In addition, Nasser benefited from two other postwar dynamics. First, blame for the defeat in 1967 was placed squarely on the military, not on any of the decisions Nasser had made. The military was publicly shamed for its incompetence. For example, on June 22, the respected Egyptian newspaper *Al-Goumhouria* published an article criticizing the military, something that would have been unheard of prior to the war.[20]

Second, a narrative emerged within the officer corps linking the military's politicization to its poor preparation for war in 1967. Nasser, and later Sadat, would benefit from the emergence of a class of military officers who identified as professional soldiers. These commanders were committed to staying out of politics, a normative conception that was bolstered by evidence of the military's poor discipline, inattention to duty, and organizational failures under Amer.[21] Consequently, there emerged at the time a belief that the armed forces' involvement in political activities had been detrimental to the officer corps' preparation for war.[22] These material and ideational factors combined, in turn, to produce a dramatic change in Egypt's civil-military relations in the final years of Nasser's rule.

CIVIL-MILITARY RELATIONS UNDER SADAT

Ironically, when he first assumed the presidency following Nasser's death, Sadat was seen as a relatively weak leader whom different political factions had elevated as a compromise candidate.[23] He lacked an independent power base within the regime. Still, Sadat benefited from several dynamics that enabled him eventually to oversee dramatic improvements in Egypt's military effectiveness. First, the balance of power between the political and military leadership had shifted considerably in the former's favor by the time Sadat took office, which he capitalized on. He also built upon changes in the social bases of the regime that Nasser had initiated. In his final three years in office, Nasser had begun to shift away from a socialist model toward policies that favored middle-class interests. Likewise, Sadat continued to liberalize Egypt's economy and political sphere—initiatives that presaged his subsequent open-door policy (*al infitah*) of economic liberalization following the 1973 war. Under Sadat, there would be notable policy adjustments with respect to the sequestration of capital, taxation, and landholding. Sadat, in other words, was shifting and expanding his political coalition. As such, Sadat's authority within the regime was underpinned by "the solid base given to his rule by his alliance with the bourgeoisie, both its state and private wings."[24]

In addition, Sadat consolidated power within the regime's civilian elite. As president, Sadat faced opposition from powerful leftists, which culminated in a confrontation in May 1971 that ended in him effectively sidelining his opponents. Notably, his ability to do so in part reflected the absence of powerful factions within the military. For example, Egypt's minister of war, General Mohammed Fawzi, had sided with the leftist camp, but Sadat was able to appeal to the chief of staff of the army, General Mohamed Sadiq, and win his support in outmaneuvering his opponents.

The consequences of these domestic political developments may seem to have little to do with war planning in 1972 and 1973, but, in fact, they enabled Sadat to establish and maintain political control of the military, bolstering his domestic political power and giving him firm control over decisions about political and strategic issues.[25] As Raymond Hinnebusch writes, "The army's claims for a decisive role or veto in its field of responsibility had been repeatedly defeated. . . . The military still had some input . . . into defense policy, but its role had been reduced to that of simply giving professional advice."[26]

Sadat also controlled appointments and promotions, the practical authority over which Nasser had lost during his competition with Amer in the 1960s.[27] After the 1967 war, there was a "conscious effort to promote the most competent officers regardless of political sentiments [which] resulted in very capable leadership at the senior levels of the Egyptian military."[28] Consequently, as one analyst puts it, "considerations of merit now weighed in promotions alongside considerations of loyalty."[29]

In November 1971, Sadat changed the process for deciding military promotions, issuing a presidential decree that first increased the authority of the service branches' Armed Forces Officers' Committees, and then expanded the president's control over the membership of the committees and the rules under which they operated. These changes "helped Sadat make sure that the major posts in the armed forces were staffed by loyal officers; and that there was a high risk involved in not remaining loyal."[30] Sadat adeptly manipulated appointments to ensure that the commanders remained subordinate to him, from early in war planning through the war's execution. Sadat would counterbalance the influence of particular individuals by appointing rivals to key posts and then sidelining certain individuals when he anticipated they might oppose his initiatives or authority.[31]

Sadat also followed in Nasser's footsteps by appointing officers who were critical of the state of the officer corps in the 1960s and wary of the corruption and lack of discipline that was pervasive under Amer's leadership.[32] Indeed, the president's appointees favored the overall "professionalization" of the Egyptian military.[33] Among the most pivotal of Sadat's appointments was Mohammed Abdel al-Ghani al-Gamasy, chief of operations in the October War and later minister of war. Gamasy represented "the very model of the respected non-political professional" military officer.[34] The general, for example, recounts in his memoirs that he disagreed with many of Sadat's decisions during and after the 1973 war, but that his view of himself as a professional required that he obey them nonetheless.[35] War Minister Ahmed Ismail also saw himself as a professional officer.[36] In turn, these values "were diffused throughout the officer corps" by the top military leadership.[37]

In addition, like Nasser, Sadat benefited from the existence of an external challenge to Egyptian national security interests in the form of Israeli control of the Sinai Peninsula and its extensive fortifications on the east bank of the Suez Canal, a visible and visceral reminder of the security challenges facing Egypt in reclaiming its territory. From the vantage point of the Egyptian armed forces, the country faced a military challenge of paramount importance, which helped focus its attention on the task at hand.[38]

THE CONCEPT OF MILITARY EFFECTIVENESS

Broadly defined, military effectiveness is the ability of a military to translate basic material and human resources into power in war in service of a state's larger political and strategic aims.[39] A military, in turn, is effective—that is, best able to maximize its own potential—when it exhibits three properties. First, military activity is integrated, such that it is internally consistent and self-reinforcing. Integration occurs when political aims and strategy are aligned with operational plans for war, as well as with the tactics employed in military engagements on the battlefield. Military activity along all of these dimensions then must be aligned with the force development practices essential to building armed forces, such as those involving the recruitment and training of personnel and the procurement and employment of weapons and equipment.

Second, military activity must be responsive in that it is tailored to the state's own strengths and weakness, as well as those of its adversaries, while bearing in mind external constraints. While many militaries may recognize and capitalize on their strengths, it is much harder to explicitly plan around weaknesses. The recognition of those deficits, and the corresponding modification of military activity, is thus an especially important indicator of responsiveness.

Finally, the skill and quality of personnel and equipment are important determinants of military effectiveness. There may be hard constraints facing a military in developing its capabilities that originate in the broader features of its state and society. A military may have to draw from a population with limited literacy levels or from a poorly developed technological base, or be forced to operate in a state with a small population and limited economic wealth. The nature of the political system may also matter—such as in cases when it is especially responsive to casualties, as in many democracies—since it can constrain the strategy and tactics that the military employs. By contrast, military leaders in an autocratic political system may prioritize regime security, which requires stifling military training and discouraging the cultivation of initiative among officers, but might be more tolerant of casualties.[40] These factors can constrain the types of strategies, operational approaches, and tactics on which a military can rely, although one that is responsive will plan around these constraints.

These factors impinge on military effectiveness, especially if opponents have comparative advantages in them or face fewer constraints. For this reason, effectiveness, while related to success in war, is not the sole determinant of a war's outcome. A military with more resources can afford to waste more of those resources; it can be relatively less effective (i.e., less integrated, responsive, and skilled) but still prevail simply through attrition and costly sacrifices of personnel and equipment. Effectiveness thus captures the capacity to make the most of basic resources and to modify doctrine and training to capitalize on what is available. By these metrics, Egypt exhibited significant military effectiveness in 1973, as I explain below.

EGYPT'S MILITARY EFFECTIVENESS IN THE 1973 WAR

Below I discuss how civil-military relations affected the integration, responsiveness, and skill of Egypt's military activity in the war.

Political-Military Integration and the Limited War Strategy

To start, civil-military relations proved important in ensuring that Sadat's political goals for the war remained integrated with military strategy and operations. Sadat's latitude to overrule opponents, in particular, enabled him to develop and implement a limited war strategy consistent with his political goals.

The adoption of such a strategy was not a foregone conclusion. To be sure, the loss of Egyptian territory in June 1967, and the generals' interest in reclaiming it, helped harmonize civil-military preferences in favor of improving the military's capabilities.[41] Beyond that, however, preferences diverged between Sadat and many of his military leaders over the best strategy to achieve that goal. For example, Sadiq, who was Sadat's minister of war at the time, disliked the uncertainty and risk entailed by using a limited military victory to leverage a bargaining advantage for negotiations.[42] Rather, he and others preferred to prepare a conventional offensive that would aim to retake the territories by force.[43]

Sadat's control of decision-making and appointment prerogatives was critical to assuring the military fell in line behind his preferred goals and operational concept. Sadiq, for example, opposed the limited war plan, voicing his reservations in a contentious three-hour meeting of the Supreme Council of the Armed Forces (SCAF) in January 1972. Sadat, however, ordered the high command to prepare for a limited war nonetheless, and his control over appointments proved essential to the military actually doing so.[44] In October 1972, at another SCAF meeting, some in the military command—including Sadiq, the chief of the navy, and the heads of Egypt's First, Second, and Third Armies—contended that Egypt was not ready for war, while some expressly opposed the limited war concept.[45] Sadat then told Deputy Minister of War Hasan Abdel al-Qadir, "You don't have to tell me what to do and what not to do. . . . Keep to your limits. You are a soldier, not a politician."[46] Fed up, Sadat then fired Qadir, Sadiq, and the chiefs of the navy and the Central Military District in Cairo.[47] Ultimately, Sadat removed over one hundred senior officers in his effort to forge a compliant command.[48]

Sadat also appointed more professionally minded officers to implement his plans. This included appointing the disciplined and charismatic Lieutenant General Saad al-Din al-Shazly chief of staff and al-Gamasy director of operations.[49] Arguably Sadat's most significant appointment, however, was his designation of General Ahmed Ismail Ali as Sadiq's replacement as minister of war on October 26, 1972.[50] As Sadat characterized that decision, "The first actual decision on the October 6 war was taken when I removed former War Minister Sadiq and appointed Marshall Ahmed Ismail in his place."[51] Ismail was a skilled military leader.[52] He also was well positioned to execute Sadat's political-military goals for the war, given that he exhibited a "keen understanding of the subtle relationship between war and politics."[53] The general understood both the limitations of Egypt's capabilities and the political necessity driving Sadat's decision to go to war nonetheless.[54]

Planning for the war began in earnest in November 1972, and by January 1973 Ismail had formulated Plan Badr, which defined the overall approach that the Egyptian military would take during the war. Sadat continued to participate in war planning, helping to refine the plan in the spring of 1973. At the same time, the military command started building Egypt's capabilities and identifying tactical level objectives in support of the plan.[55]

Sadat's control of the military, moreover, helped ensure that the chain of command remained robust not just before but also during the war, and that command decisions reflected his political goals. When, for example, the military leadership pressed Sadat to expand the offensive to the mountain passes in the days following the initial success of the crossing operation, Sadat refused, viewing it as too risky to his strategic aim of retaining Egypt's positions along the canal zone.[56] It was only when Syrian pressure mounted to resume the offensive in order to divert Israeli forces from their operations on the Golan front that Sadat relented, approving an advance to the strategically important Giddi and Mitla passes in Sinai. Despite ending in a disastrous tactical defeat, the operation was guided by the clear political goal of placating the Syrians and keeping them in the war.[57] Sadat's military leaders subsequently criticized him for not making the decision immediately following the crossing, when Egypt presumably had greater momentum, but Egypt's poor performance and costly retreat belied the claim that doing so would have succeeded and confirmed the wisdom of Sadat's initial stance.[58]

In addition, on the night of October 15–16, Israel took advantage of a gap between the positions of the Second and Third Armies and circled behind Egypt's forces. In response, many of Egypt's commanders wanted to make use of forces from the strategic reserve and redeploy troops stationed on the east bank of the Suez to support a counteroffensive to relieve the pressure. Ismail, echoing Sadat, believed those moves would jeopardize Egypt's capacity to hold its positions at the canal, but some commanders persisted in their opposition, with Shazly pressuring him on October 20 to send four armored brigades to aid the encircled Third Army.

Sadat was then called to the command center, where he consulted with Ismail and Gamasy, as well as the heads of the air force, air defense forces, artillery, and military intelligence.[59] Sadat chose to keep the forces in position because retaining the bridgehead was essential to his political goals in the war.[60] As Sadat later described it, the dispute in the high command "ended only when I personally went to the operations room and made the decision that the armies would stay where they were."[61] Sadat's dominance within the chain of command ensured his political goals remained integrated with Egypt's military means. As it was, despite the breakthrough, Egypt still maintained two bridgeheads in the canal zone at the close of the war totaling 1,000 square kilometers—land Israel had held just three weeks earlier.

Responsiveness, Integration, and Strategic Surprise

Civil-military relations also had important implications for the ability to execute a key component of the war plan, which would prove essential to its success: ensuring the assault would not be anticipated by Israel. The Egyptian military command estimated that a successful effort to cross the Suez, overtake the Bar-Lev Line, and entrench positions on the east bank would depend on achieving strategic surprise.[62] This would lessen the chance that Israel could carry out a preemptive strike, and provide a window for Egyptian forces to cross the canal and entrench themselves before Israel mobilized its reserves for a counterattack.[63]

Achieving surprise would be difficult, however, and the integrity of the chain of command and Sadat's control at its apex would prove crucial to accomplishing this goal. Part of that effort required adhering to protocols over who would have access to key information. Consequently, only the top military leadership knew the actual day and hour of the attack.[64] Egypt, meanwhile, developed a detailed timetable outlining when each commander and unit would be told about the timing of the operation.[65] This capacity to understand not just its own military strengths but also its opponent's strategic concept was a key indicator of its responsiveness. As a result, "[m]ost Egyptian officers and troops had no idea war was imminent until the very last moment."[66] The Israelis later interviewed Egyptian prisoners of war, finding that nearly all of them only became aware that the attack was going to happen hours in advance.[67]

In addition to maintaining control of information flows internally, Egypt also formulated a detailed deception plan to create alternative explanations for its wartime preparations and to play upon Israeli assumptions that an attack by Egypt was unlikely. At the time, Israeli intelligence assessments of the likelihood of war were heavily influenced by the belief that Egypt would not go to war until it was able to achieve a significant improvement in its capabilities. Egypt played upon this. For example, the military planted false press reports that detailed challenges Egypt was supposedly facing in operating technologically sophisticated equipment after Soviet military advisers were withdrawn in 1972. Egypt deliberately fed Israel's prevailing narrative that inadequate capabilities would keep the country from going to war,[68] and that all the exhortations in Egypt were merely meant for a domestic audience.[69] As one analyst notes of the deception plan and its components, these "efforts were part of an imaginative, intensive and well orchestrated strategy of deception which brought rich rewards."[70]

Learning and Responsiveness in Operational Planning

Egypt also demonstrated significant responsiveness in developing the operational concept for the war and in designing key aspects of the plan. In particular, greater emphasis on merit—versus solely on political fealty—in appointments enabled greater learning and more critical reflection among military leaders. For example, a report detailing Egypt's failings in the 1956 Suez conflict was finally released and scrutinized, after being ignored by Amer. A similarly self-critical mindset was applied to studying the lessons from Egypt's failures in the 1967 war, including a study of its defeat undertaken by the army's historian, Major General Hasan El-Badri.[71] The generals also "analyzed the mistakes made by the Egyptians in the air force and air defense since the 1956 war."[72] The lessons from these efforts provided the foundation for the preparation for the 1973 war. In short, "[w]hat the Arabs did after 1967 was a much more serious and practical examination of their record. Actually, the Arab strategy in 1973 can be described as a system of remedies for the problems which had caused the Arab defeat in 1967; a set of lessons derived from their 1967 experience."[73] Learning was therefore key to war planning in 1973. But a necessary precondition was the appointment of a military command both capable of and ready to scrutinize the past—something afforded by the prior change in appointment criteria and the civil-military relations that supported it.

Perhaps most importantly, the Egyptians expressly planned around their weaknesses, choosing an operational plan that served to compensate for them, even though doing so meant forgoing the use of its air force and eschewing sophisticated doctrine. Indeed, military leaders developed the plan in light of the clear inferiority of the Egyptian air force to Israel's. They ordered only a limited number of strikes and avoided air-to-air engagements, such that, for the most part, Egypt's aircraft stayed in hardened hangars during the war.[74]

Egypt also decided to forgo reliance on offensive maneuver, the fast-paced operations that are considered by military theorists to be highly effective, but that require substantial training to execute. Instead, Plan Badr capitalized on Egypt's superiority in numbers, relying on mass in a full frontal assault during the crossing operation and then static defense, aided by the dense anti-aircraft battery it assembled in the canal zone.[75] As one analyst writes, "From the outset, Egyptian planners recognized that overall military strategy and tactics would have to be tailored to the character of the manpower available, i.e., small cadres of highly trained individuals (senior officers with extensive backgrounds, academy graduates and some pilots), but also large numbers of Egyptian peasants."[76] The plan also drew on the innovative approaches of its engineers, who themselves were highly skilled, which helped enable Egypt to transport over 800 tanks and 90,000 men across the canal in less than three days.[77] These tactics offset deficiencies in speed and mobility, while complicating Israel's ability to counterattack using its relative strength in mobile operations and penetration in depth.[78] Overall, the approach reflected the responsiveness of Egyptian military activity.

Increasing the Skill of Military Personnel

Finally, the military sought to improve its human capital. Prior to 1967, many of Egypt's conscripts lacked much education, and literacy levels were low in the ranks. Subsequent changes in personnel policy included increasing efforts to recruit from urban areas, such that in 1973 approximately one in four soldiers were from cities, where they would be more familiar with modern transportation and communication than the rural recruits on which Egypt had previously relied.[79] Military leaders also more than doubled the number of high school graduates in the ranks from 25 to 51 percent, while also increasing the number of soldiers that had attended university. Sixty percent of officers held college degrees, compared to less than 2 percent in the 1967 war.[80] Nasser again set the stage for changes in educational proficiency by requiring that officers serving in roles that required technical know-how have engineering or technical degrees. Under Sadat, the military maintained and expanded its emphasis on educational standards.

The fate of the Soviet military advisers, who were deployed to Egypt from 1970 to 1972, also offers an interesting wrinkle on the responsiveness of Sadat and the military command to the operational needs and morale of its personnel. Following the 1967 war, Nasser had relied heavily on what some analysts approximate to have been upwards of 20,000 Soviet trainers. So intensive was the effort that artillery and armor units in the army were reported to have at least ten Soviet advisers in each battalion.[81] Yet, this was not an unalloyed good. One problem was that Soviet doctrine, based on combined-arms fire and maneuver, was poorly suited to the skill and needs of Egyptian soldiers, and USSR trainers were known to be disrespectful of Egyptians, creating friction in the ranks. Following tense disputes between Sadat and the Soviets over weapons systems deliveries to Egypt, Sadat expelled the bulk of the trainers in July 1972, while retaining those in charge of technically sophisticated equipment. As James Powell describes the implications of Sadat's decisions:

The abrupt removal of a large portion of this foreign contingent reveals much about the institutional awareness of Sadat and his senior commanders. In dismissing the advisors seeded throughout various echelons of the armed forces, while allowing Soviet technical experts to stay, the Egyptians acknowledged certain strengths and weaknesses. Aligning war aims with the military means readily available, Sadat astutely shed superfluous Soviet assistance but retained what he considered essential.[82]

In other words, Sadat and the military were responsive to the advantages and disadvantages of relying on Soviet trainers in improving the skill level of their personnel.

In sum, Egypt exhibited significant strengths in its military effectiveness, originating in its responsiveness to resource constraints, capacity to integrate military activity and align it with Sadat's political goals, and improvements in the skills of its personnel. Yet, it was still constrained by the nature of the resources it possessed, both materially and in terms of its human capital. It was also not able to overcome other limitations on the tactical abilities of both its ground and air forces, especially relative to Israel's strengths in these areas.

Thus, while Egypt made the most of carefully scripted operations, the mass and attrition approach on which Plan Badr relied was inferior to a doctrine based on offensive maneuver, at which the Israelis excelled. This became abundantly clear with the successful breach of Egypt's defensive line and Israel's encirclement of its forces ten days into the war. It was also apparent in Egypt's failed advance to the mountain passes in Sinai.[83] Egypt also exhibited other persistent weaknesses, such as the quality and maintenance of equipment.[84] Hence, while Egypt's military effectiveness improved in 1973, in an absolute sense its war effort still exhibited serious shortcomings—deficits that Israel was able to exploit once it recovered from Egypt's initial assault across the canal. Still, the changes in Egypt's military effectiveness were dramatic and politically consequential in catalyzing negotiations with Israel, as Sadat had intended.

CONCLUSION

This chapter explores the reasons for Egypt's military effectiveness in the 1973 war, contending that its improvements depended on prior and fundamental shifts in the domestic politics of its autocratic regime and how they in turn influenced civil-military relations. The balance of power in civil-military relations shifted, first under Nasser with the loss of popular support for the armed forces and the purging of Amer's faction, as well as the former's efforts to expand his coalition and bolster his regime's bases of support. Subsequently, Sadat proved an adept tactician at sidelining opponents to his rule and appealing to middle-class interests, and he benefited from the changes in the military initiated by Nasser. He then used his control over the military, and his powers of appointment, to create a compliant command that would translate his political concept for the war into a military plan tailored to Egypt's resources. In the process, he also benefited from a narrative in the officer corps that linked its poor performance in 1967 to the corrosive impact of the military's engagement in politics. Combined, these factors ensured that Egypt's military activity exhibited higher levels of skill and remained relatively integrated and responsive, especially in comparison to the country's performance just six years earlier in the 1967 war.

Egypt's experiences in the 1973 war are important on their own terms, especially given the momentous impact of the conflict, particularly the role it played in laying the groundwork for eventual peace accords with Israel. Egypt's experiences, however, also offer several lessons for the broader study of authoritarian regimes and military effectiveness.

First, they illustrate the complexity of the impact of the threat environment on civil-military relations. Scholars have argued that where external threats are present, military and civilian preferences are much more harmonious, which facilitates the establishment of civilian control.[85] The Egyptian case, though, suggests that the relationship between these variables is more complicated. While Sadat ultimately prevailed in seeing his vision through, Egyptian civil-military relations were plagued by tensions during the planning for the war. Recall that Sadat clashed with military leaders, both before and during the war, over the operational plan and key decisions related to its execution. Sadat's ability to draw on a reservoir of officers who saw it as their professional responsibility to defer to civilian authority as well as his adept shuffling of military commanders and astute appointments are as, if not more, important in understanding how civilian control was maintained. The mere existence of a threat in the form of a loss of territory may have been a necessary condition for Egypt's success, but it was not sufficient. The internal politics of civil-military relations were crucial.

The case also speaks to larger scholarship on the importance of purges in authoritarian regimes.[86] Recent years have seen a surge of interest in understanding the timing and implications of purges of civilian and military elites, especially for a leader's capacity to secure himself in office and for the qualifications and capacity of the regime's elite. Most of this scholarship emphasizes the role of purges in consolidating autocratic authority and in generating a tradeoff between expertise and loyalty. The Egypt case, however, suggests that purges, and the broader phenomenon of political dominance of appointments and promotions, may play a more nuanced, and even potentially positive, role in autocracies. They influence the dominant views held by the military leadership and create commands that may be more committed to a professional ethic of nonintervention in politics. Purges may be an important contributor—not just detractor, through a loss of expertise and ensuing politicization—to military effectiveness by shaping ideational trends and incentives to adhere to professional standards.

Finally, the analysis highlights lessons for the vibrant scholarship on autocracy that has emerged in the last decade in the discipline of political science. Much of this scholarship has focused on parts of the state unrelated to the coercive apparatus, such as the politics of patronage and role of legislatures, or autocratic regime type, and do not treat the military and security apparatus as either distinct entities or distinctive in their roles and influence in the regime.[87] On the other hand, scholars of security forces often treat them as operating apart from other regime institutions, and may at times neglect to embed the coercive sector in broader domestic or regime politics.[88] The case of Egypt after 1967 shows how these elements interact: understanding Egyptian civil-military relations requires looking more deeply into aspects of domestic politics well beyond the military. At the same time, it reveals that any full appreciation of the character of the autocratic regime demands attention to variation in the military's power in the regime, institutional character, and relation to other coercive bodies and to the rest of the state. The military is part and parcel of domestic politics in autocratic regimes, as Egypt's military effectiveness in the 1973 war demonstrates.

NOTES

1. See Carly Beckerman-Boys, "Assessing the Historiography of the October War," in *The Yom Kippur War: Politics, Diplomacy, Legacy*, ed. Asaf Siniver (New York: Oxford University Press, 2013), 11–28.

2. Kenneth M. Pollack, *Arabs at War: Military Effectiveness, 1948–1991* (Lincoln: University of Nebraska Press, 2002).

3. Dan Reiter and Allan C. Stam, *Democracies at War* (Princeton, NJ: Princeton University Press, 2002).

4. James T. Quinlivan, "Coup-proofing: Its Practice and Consequences in the Middle East," *International Security* 24, no. 2 (Fall 1999): 131–65; Risa Brooks, *Political-Military Relations and the Stability of Arab Regimes* (New York: Oxford University Press, 1998).

5. For further discussion of Egypt's civil-military relations and the 1973 war, see Risa Brooks, "An Autocracy at War: Explaining Egypt's Military Effectiveness, 1967 and 1973," *Security Studies* 15, no. 3 (July/September 2006): 396–430; Risa A. Brooks, "Civil-Military Relations and Military Effectiveness: Egypt in the 1967 and 1973 Wars," in *Creating Military Power: The Sources of Military Effectiveness*, eds.

Risa A. Brooks and Elizabeth A. Stanley (Stanford, CA: Stanford University Press, 2007), 106–35; Risa Brooks, *Shaping Strategy: The Civil-Military Politics of Strategic Assessment* (Princeton, NJ: Princeton University Press, 2008).

6. William B. Quandt, *Peace Process: American Diplomacy and the Arab-Israeli Conflict since 1967* (Berkeley: University of California Press, 2005).

7. George W. Gawrych, *The Albatross of Decisive Victory: War and Policy between Egypt and Israel in the 1967 and 1973 Arab-Israeli Wars* (Westport, CT: Greenwood, 2000), 148; Raymond A. Hinnebusch, *Egyptian Politics under Sadat: The Post-Populist Development of an Authoritarian-Modernizing State* (Cambridge: Cambridge University Press, 1985), 46.

8. Anwar El-Sadat, *In Search of Identity: An Autobiography* (New York: Harper & Row, 1978), 326–28.

9. John W. Amos III, *Arab-Israeli Military/Political Relations: Arab Perceptions and the Politics of Escalation* (Oxford: Pergamon Press, 1979), 176; Anthony H. Cordesman and Abraham R. Wagner, *The Lessons of Modern War*, vol. 4, *The Gulf War* (Boulder, CO: Westview, 1996), 74, 94; Gawrych, *Albatross of Decisive Victory*, 83; Saad El-Shazly, *The Crossing of the Suez* (San Francisco: American Mideast Research, 1980), 19; Pollack, *Arabs at War*, 104.

10. Rami Rom, Amir Gilat, and Rose Mary Sheldon, "The Yom Kippur War, Dr. Kissinger, and the Smoking Gun," *International Journal of Intelligence and Counterintelligence* 31, no. 2 (2018): 358.

11. The United Nations Security Council first passed Resolution 338, which called for a ceasefire, on October 22. The Israelis, however, continued their operations against Egypt's Third Army and also refused to abide by a second resolution that passed on October 23. On October 24, the Soviets threatened to intervene unilaterally in the conflict if Israel failed to comply with the ceasefire resolutions. Ultimately, Resolution 340, which required Israel to return to its position as of October 22, also passed the Security Council, and the ceasefire was finally implemented on October 25. See Yaacov Bar-Siman-Tov, *Israel, the Superpowers and the War in the Middle East* (New York: Praeger, 1987).

12. Quoted in Gawrych, *Albatross of Decisive Victory,* 190.

13. Quoted in John Keegan, *World Armies* (New York: Facts on File, 1979), 167.

14. While the war itself is celebrated in Egypt, how Sadat employed the political opportunities it generated was at the time—and remains—much more controversial among Egyptians. Critics portray Sadat as squandering the hard-won bargaining leverage generated by the war and claim that he failed to use it to advance Egypt's true strategic interests. Sadat's grand strategic shift toward the United States and ensuing peace initiatives, which culminated in the 1979 treaty with Israel, were especially controversial. See Yoram Meital, "The October War and Egypt's Multiple Crossings," in *Yom Kippur War*, ed. Asaf Siniver, 65. Indeed, opposition to the peace treaty with Israel was probably the main reason for Sadat's assassination in 1981 by religious militants within the military, which, ironically, took place during a parade commemorating Egypt's success in the 1973 war.

15. Richard B. Parker, *The Politics of Miscalculation in the Middle East* (Bloomington: Indiana University Press, 1993), 84; Kirk J. Beattie, *Egypt during the Nasser Years: Ideology, Politics, and Civil Society* (Boulder, CO: Westview, 1994), 125.

16. For details, see Brooks, *Shaping Strategy*.

17. While the Arab Socialist Union may have helped orchestrate the protests, many observers contend that they were largely organic and reflected Egyptians' sentiments. Beattie, *Egypt during the Nasser Years*, 211, 230.

18. Comments by Dr. Rifaat Said, interview, Cairo, June 1996.

19. Beattie, *Egypt during the Nasser Years*, 212; Gawrych, *Albatross of Decisive Victory*, 73; A. I. Dawisha, *Egypt in the Arab World: The Elements of Foreign Policy* (New York: Halsted, 1976), 117.

20. "Leftist Cairo Paper Scores Army Chiefs," *New York Times*, June 22, 1967.

21. On global norms of military professionalism, see Theo Farrell, "World Culture and Military Power," *Security Studies* 14, no. 3 (July/September 2005): 448–88. To be sure, these ideas do not forestall political engagement among militaries that emulate global norms of professionalism, but they do create a foundation for arguing about why such interventions are problematic and for maintaining normative arguments against such engagement.

22. Mohamed Abdel Ghani El-Gamasy, *The October War: Memoirs of Field Marshal El-Gamasy of Egypt* (Cairo: American University in Cairo Press, 1993); Hinnebusch, *Egyptian Politics under Sadat*, 109.

23. Raymond William Baker, *Egypt's Uncertain Revolution under Nasser and Sadat* (Cambridge, MA: Harvard University Press, 1978), 123–24; Mohamed Hassanein Heikal, *The Road to Ramadan* (New York: Quadrangle, 1975); Mohamed Hassanein Heikal, *Autumn of Fury: The Assassination of Sadat* (New York: Random House, 1983); Anthony McDermott, *Egypt from Nasser to Mubarak: A Flawed Revolution* (London: Croon Helm, 1988), 41.

24. Hinnebusch, *Egyptian Politics under Sadat*, 89.

25. On the importance of political leaders' coalitions and support base in shaping the political-military balance of power, see Brooks, *Shaping Strategy*.

26. Hinnebusch, *Egyptian Politics under Sadat*, 131; Ibrahim Karawan, "Egypt's Defense Policy," in *Defense Planning in Less-Industrialized States*, ed. Stephanie Neuman (Lexington, MA: Lexington, 1984), 152.

27. Ahmed Abou-Zeid El-Sherif, "The Pattern of Relations between Sadat's Regime and the Military Elite," MA Thesis, American University in Cairo, 1995, 229–32.

28. Pollack, *Arabs at War*, 127.

29. Gawrych, *Albatross of Decisive Victory*, 77. See also Hinnebusch, *Egyptian Politics under Sadat*, 38.

30. El-Sherif, "Pattern of Relations," 230.

31. Brooks, *Shaping Strategy*, 132–37.

32. George W. Gawrych, "The Egyptian High Command in the 1973 War," *Armed Forces and Society* 13, no. 4 (Summer 1987): 545.

33. Kirk J. Beattie, "Egypt: Thirty-Five Years of Praetorian Politics," in *Military Disengagement from Politics*, ed. Constantine Danopoulos (London: Routledge, 1988), 214.

34. Quoted in Hinnebusch, *Egyptian Politics under Sadat*, 129. See also "Sadat's Power Base," *Journal of Palestine Studies* 7, no. 2 (Winter 1978): 159–61.

35. See El-Gamasy, *October War*.

36. El-Gamasy, *October War*, 155; Heikal, *Road to Ramadan*, 182. Many of these were officers who had been marginalized by Amer in the 1960s. See Ehud Ya'ari, "Sadat's Pyramid of Power," *Jerusalem Quarterly*, no. 14 (Winter 1980): 115.

37. Ya'ari argues that access to sophisticated weaponry and recruitment of officers from a broader stratum of society reinforced these trends. See Ya'ari, "Sadat's Pyramid of Power," 113–14. Despite professed adherence to these professional norms, these generals were not truly apolitical. For example, Mohammed Fawzi, who was appointed by Nasser following the 1967 war, was ostensibly an "apolitical" general given the task of reforming the military. He later supported the leftist faction in May 1971 that was challenging Sadat's authority and was fired as a result. General Sadiq, who replaced him as minister of war, was also purportedly an apolitical leader, but he too often sought to bolster his position in the officer corps. See Heikal, *Autumn of Fury*, 40. See also El-Gamasy, *October War*, 157; Ya'ari, "Sadat's Pyramid of Power," 113, 115.

38. On the influence of international threats on civil-military relations, see Michael C. Desch, *Civilian Control of the Military: The Changing Security Environment* (Baltimore, MD: Johns Hopkins University Press, 1999); Barry Posen, *The Sources of Military Doctrine: France, Britain, and Germany between the World Wars* (Ithaca, NY: Cornell University Press, 1984).

39. For this definition, see Risa A. Brooks, "Introduction: The Impact of Culture, Society, Institutions, and International Forces on Military Effectiveness," in *Creating Military Power*, 1–26.

40. On these issues, see Brooks, *Political-Military Relations*.

41. Gawrych, *Albatross of Decisive Victory*, 75.

42. These differences were acute and without Sadat's control of the military would have been difficult to overcome. In November 1972, rumors surfaced of a conspiracy within the officer corps called "Save Egypt." Its members opposed any effort to go to war prior to Egypt receiving more offensive weapons. The conspirators were subsequently arrested. Among their ranks was the chief of military intelligence, commander of the central district (Cairo), commander of a ranger group, and two division commanders. See El-Shazly, *Crossing of the Suez*, 192; El-Sherif, "Pattern of Relations"; David Hirst and Irene Beeson, *Sadat* (London: Faber and Faber, 1981), 144; Jon Kimche, "The Riddle of Sadat," *Midstream* 20, no. 4 (April 1974): 27. In fact, the dominant view within the officer corps was that Egypt should not attempt a war until it could reclaim its territory through force. Indeed, this was the basis for opposition to the limited war concept. See El-Shazly, *Crossing of the Suez*, 189–90. At the same time, many in the officer corps also opposed negotiations with Israel. Mohamed Heikal observes, for example, that Fawzi told Sadat that the army found proposals by US secretary of state William Rogers for a settlement with Israel unacceptable. The

dominant view was that Sadat would be compromising Egypt's interests for the sake of improving its relations with the United States. See Heikal, *Autumn of Fury*, 41.

43. Mahmoud Riad, *The Struggle for Peace in the Middle East* (London: Quartet, 1981), 211.

44. Gawrych, *Albatross of Decisive Victory*, 11; Donald Neff, *Warriors against Israel: How Israel Won the Battle to Become America's Ally* (Brattleboro, VT: Amana, 1988), 100–101.

45. Gawrych, *Albatross of Decisive Victory*, 133; Michael I. Handel, *The Diplomacy of Surprise: Hitler, Nixon, Sadat* (Cambridge, MA: Harvard University Center for International Affairs, 1981), 248; Amos, *Arab-Israeli Political/Military Relations*, 104; Abraham Rabinovich, *The Yom Kippur War: The Epic Encounter That Transformed the Middle East* (New York: Schocken, 2004), 25; Gawrych, *The 1973 Arab-Israeli War*, 133; Uri Bar-Joseph, *The Watchman Fell Asleep: The Surprise of the Yom Kippur War and Its Sources* (Albany: State University of New York Press, 2005), 2.

46. Quoted in Meital, "Egypt's Multiple Crossings," 52.

47. Gawrych, *1973 Arab-Israeli War*, 11; Gawrych, *Albatross of Decisive Victory*, 128; Heikal, *Road to Ramadan*, 181.

48. Amos, *Arab-Israeli Political/Military Relations*, 106.

49. On these and other key appointments, see Gawrych, *Albatross of Decisive Victory*, 136–37; Gawrych, *1973 Arab-Israeli War*, 10.

50. Amos, *Arab-Israeli Political/Military Relations*, 139–40.

51. Quoted in Amos, *Arab-Israeli Political/Military Relations*, 118.

52. Gawrych, *Albatross of Decisive Victory*, 136; Amos, *Arab-Israeli Political/Military Relations*, 141; Insight Team of the London Sunday Times, *The Yom Kippur War* (Garden City, NY: Doubleday, 1974), 221–22; Karawan, "Egypt's Defense Policy," 153.

53. Neff, *Warriors against Israel*, 101–2.

54. On Ismail's role in refining the limited war plan, see Amos, *Arab-Israeli Political/Military Relations*, 139–40; Rabinovich, *Yom Kippur War*, 27.

55. Amos, *Arab-Israeli Political/Military Relations*, 313; El-Shazly, *Crossing of the Suez*, 31–39; Heikal, *Road to Ramadan*, 220.

56. Gawrych, *Albatross of Decisive Victory*, 54. Note that while Shazly later vigorously denied in his memoirs that he ever supported continuation of the offensive, in the days immediately following Egypt's successful crossing operation, a large contingent in the military high command initially supported an advance to the passes.

57. Sadat had deceived the Syrians prior to the war. He told them that Egypt's plan was to continue the offensive in Sinai and not just limit itself to claiming ten kilometers of land in the canal zone, as Sadat intended all along. See Meital, "Egypt's Multiple Crossings," 54.

58. El-Shazly, *Crossing of the Suez*, 164, 166.

59. Gawrych, *Albatross of Decisive Victory*, 224.

60. Gawrych, *1973 Arab-Israeli War*, 69; Trevor N. Dupuy, *Elusive Victory: The Arab-Israeli Wars, 1947–1974* (New York: Harper & Row, 1978), 519.

61. Quoted in Amos, *Arab-Israeli Political/Military Relations*, 184. Shazly was fired by Sadat after the war over the disagreements about the conduct of the war. See Hinnebusch, *Egypt under Sadat*, 60–61; Frank Aker, *October 1973: The Arab-Israeli War* (Hamden, CT: Archon, 1985), 116–17; McDermott, *Egypt from Nasser to Mubarak*, 49.

62. Hassan El-Badri, Taha El-Magdoub, and Mohammad Dia El-Din Zohdy, *The Ramadan War, 1973* (New York: Hippocrene, 1978), 45; Insight Team, *Yom Kippur War*, 64.

63. Amos, *Arab-Israeli Political/Military Relations*, 167.

64. Ibid., 171.

65. El-Gamasy, *October War*, 196.

66. Anthony Cordesman and Abraham R. Wagner, *The Lessons of Modern War*, vol. 1, *The Arab-Israeli Conflicts, 1973–1989* (Boulder, CO: Westview, 1990), 22–23.

67. Amos, *Arab-Israeli Political/Military Relations*, 330.

68. Ibid., 172.

69. On the components of the deception plan, see El-Badri, El-Magdoub, and Zohdy, *Ramadan War*, 46–47; Amos, *Arab-Israeli Political/Military Relations*, 171–72; Bar-Joseph, *Watchman Fell Asleep*, 25–32; Avi Shlaim, "Failures in National Intelligence Estimates: The Case of the Yom Kippur War," *World Politics* 28, no. 3 (April 1976): 348–80. See also the interview with Ismail in Heikal, *Road to Ramadan*. There remains a persistent debate about the importance of the deception plan relative to other factors in contributing to Israel's intelligence failure. Unlike Shlaim, Bar-Joseph contends that the deception plan was not especially well-developed, and places more weight on organizational factors in Israel for the intelligence failure. See Bar-Joseph, *Watchman Fell Asleep*, 31. Still, many observers note that Egypt successfully obscured a large amount of information about its war plans from Israel. In short, it seems likely that the intelligence failure would not have occurred without both the deception plan and Israel's intelligence problems.

70. Shlaim, "Failures in National Intelligence," 355–56.

71. El-Gamasy's memoirs provide many specific examples of these lessons. See El-Gamasy, *October War*.

72. Gawrych, *Albatross of Decisive Victory*, 90.

73. Quoted in Louis Williams, ed., *Military Aspects of the Israeli-Arab Conflict* (Tel Aviv: University Publishing Service, 1975), 173.

74. El-Shazly, *Crossing of the Suez*, 19–20; Pollack, *Arabs at War*, 104; Amos, *Arab-Israeli Political/Military Relations*, 176; Aker, *October 1973*, 54; Cordesman and Wagner, *Lessons of Modern War*, vol. 1, 94; Lawrence L. Whetten, *The Canal War: Four-Power Conflict in the Middle East* (Cambridge, MA: MIT Press, 1974), 275.

75. Allan C. Stam III, *Win, Lose, or Draw: Domestic Politics and the Crucible of War* (Ann Arbor: University of Michigan Press, 1996).

76. Amos, *Arab-Israeli Political/Military Relations*, 195.

77. James S. Powell, "Taking a Look under the Hood: The October War and What Maintenance Approaches Reveal about Military Operations," Land Warfare Paper No. 128, Institute of Land Warfare at the Association of the United States Army,

August 2019, https://www.ausa.org/sites/default/files/publications/LWP-128-Taking-a-Look-under-the-Hood-The-October-War-and-What-Maintenance-Approaches-Reveal-about-Military-Operations.pdf, 4.

78. Amos, *Arab-Israeli Political/Military Relations*, 143, 212.

79. Edgar O'Ballance, *No Victor, No Vanquished: The Yom Kippur War* (San Rafael, CA: Presidio, 1978), 16; Powell, "Taking a Look," 7.

80. Pollack, *Arabs at War*, 104; Powell, "Taking a Look," 7.

81. Powell, "Taking a Look," 9.

82. Ibid., 10.

83. Lorris Beverelli, "The Importance of the Tactical Level: The Arab-Israeli War of 1973," *Strategy Bridge*, November 19, 2019, https://thestrategybridge.org/the-bridge/2019/11/19/the-importance-of-the-tactical-level-the-arab-israeli-war-of-1973.

84. The reliance on less technically sophisticated Soviet tanks partially offset some of these weaknesses. See Powell, "Taking a Look," 9.

85. Desch, *Civilian Control of the Military*.

86. For a discussion of this scholarship, see Edward Goldring and Austin S. Matthews, "To Purge or Not to Purge? An Individual-Level Quantitative Analysis of Elite Purges in Dictatorships," *British Journal of Political Science* no. 53 (December 16, 2021): 575–93.

87. See Risa A. Brooks, "Integrating the Civil-Military Relations Subfield," *Annual Review of Political Science* 22, no. 1 (2019): 379–98.

88. On the importance of doing so, see Brooks, *Shaping Strategy*.

Chapter 3

A Self-Inflicted Wound?

Henry Kissinger and the Ending of the October 1973 Arab-Israeli War

Galen Jackson and Marc Trachtenberg

The United States and the Soviet Union seemed determined in 1972 to put the Cold War behind them. The US president, Richard Nixon, flew to Moscow that year and signed a number of important agreements with his Soviet counterpart Leonid Brezhnev—important above all for what they symbolized. In Moscow, Nixon declared that a foundation had "been laid for a new relationship between the two most powerful nations of the world"; a process had started which could lead to a lasting peace.[1] But the great hopes of 1972 faded rapidly, and by the end of 1973 many Americans had begun to turn against the Nixon administration's détente policy. By 1976, Nixon's successor, Gerald Ford, was so embarrassed by the word *détente* that he announced he would stop using it.[2] And by 1980, as John Lewis Gaddis later noted, détente "was almost universally regarded as having failed."[3]

But why exactly had it failed? The many critics of the détente policy would not have found that question hard to answer. It had failed, in their view, because détente had been based on an illusion—on the view that the Soviet Union was now willing to coexist peacefully with the United States.[4] But Moscow's fundamental goals, the argument ran, had not changed. The Soviets still sought to bring about a "decisive shift in the world balance of power" in their favor. And détente had merely served to blind the Western countries to that core reality: "The Soviet Union saw it as an opportunity to lull Western public opinion into a lack of vigilance towards the perils it was facing."[5] So from that point of view, the collapse of détente was easy to explain: the policy was abandoned when the American people came to see

Soviet policy for what it was and realized that a very different kind of policy was called for.

The champions of détente—especially Nixon's national security adviser, Henry Kissinger, who, with Nixon, was the main architect of the policy—naturally took a very different view. As they saw it, the policy failed not because it was politically or morally defective but rather because it had been overwhelmed by anti-détente forces at home. As Kissinger put it when he was about to leave office in late 1976, "our difficulties have been almost entirely domestic" in nature.[6] The Nixon administration, he often argued, had tried to pursue a policy attuned to the nuances and ambiguities of international political life, but that kind of policy just did not sit well with the American public.[7] And many scholars take much the same view. "The Nixon-Kissinger variant of détente," one of them writes, "failed for primarily domestic political reasons."[8] Or as another scholar put it: "The foreign policy of détente drowned in the turbulent waters of domestic politics in the 1970s."[9]

Gaddis made much the same point. Whereas Nixon and Kissinger had a "sophisticated and far-sighted strategy," and despite their generally honest efforts to explain what it was, "they never really succeeded in putting it across, whether to their own bureaucracies, the Congress, or the public as a whole."[10] But there is one basic problem with that line of argument: the country had no trouble supporting détente in 1972; it was only later that opinion turned against it; and you cannot explain a change by a constant. The shift must have been caused by something. Specific events must have played a major role in this process.

And the evidence strongly suggests that the events surrounding the October 1973 Arab-Israeli War were of fundamental importance in that regard. Attitudes toward détente, as reflected in the press, shifted quite sharply at that point. Indeed, by the end of 1973 some observers were already talking about how détente had failed.[11] And the critics pointed above all to Soviet behavior in the Middle East. The Soviet Union, it was said, had played a key role in bringing on the October War. One early attack on détente referred, for example, to the "incendiary Soviet role" before the war, and that charge remained a staple of the anti-détente literature well into the 1980s.[12] The Soviet leadership was also blamed for threatening to intervene unilaterally at the end of that war. Brezhnev made that threat in a famous letter he sent Nixon on October 24, 1973—the same day the ceasefire decreed by the United Nations (UN) Security Council finally took hold.[13] That threat, as is well known, led the United States to put its military forces around the world on alert. But if the US government, the argument ran, had been forced to make that kind of move, the provocation must have been quite extraordinary. The Soviet Union, it seemed, was as aggressive as ever and could only be restrained by a tough American policy.[14]

What are we to make of arguments of that sort? Kissinger at the time characterized the claim that the Soviets had instigated the war as "absolutely preposterous."[15] And the evidence now available makes it abundantly clear that the Soviets had tried hard to work with the Americans in reaching a settlement that would have made the war unnecessary, had very much wanted to avoid a new Middle East war, and had warned US leaders repeatedly that if nothing were done an armed conflict was unavoidable.[16] The implication is that if the Americans had been more forthcoming and more willing to work with the Soviets in dealing with the problem—that is, if they had pursued a policy more in line with what détente was supposed to be—the war would never have broken out in the first place.

As for the narrower issue of the Brezhnev threat, the real question here has to do with the degree to which the US government was directly responsible for creating the situation that led the Soviet leader to send Nixon the October 24 letter. Kissinger, after all, had worked out a ceasefire agreement with Brezhnev during a visit to Moscow on October 21. The ceasefire was supposed to go into effect on October 22, and Kissinger flew directly from Moscow to Israel for talks with the Israeli leaders that day. But the ceasefire did not take hold, mainly because the Israelis very much wanted to continue military operations. Indeed, on October 23, as Kissinger put it the next day, the Israelis "grabbed a hunk of territory and cut the last supply line" for Egypt's Third Army.[17] And Brezhnev threatened to intervene unilaterally only after that Israeli policy had become clear. If Kissinger had encouraged Israel to ignore the ceasefire, as many people—including the Soviets themselves—suspected, then the Brezhnev threat can scarcely be viewed as an act of aggression pure and simple. And that in turn would imply that Kissinger himself should be held responsible for triggering the chain of events that led to the Brezhnev threat and the US alert, with all of their consequences, especially in terms of how people at home came to view détente.

So it is important to understand what actually happened at the end of the October 1973 Arab-Israeli War. Had Kissinger in fact given the Israelis a green light to continue their advance? For many years, in dealing with that issue, scholars have tended to accept Kissinger's claim that he had not deliberately encouraged the Israelis to violate the ceasefire, at least not in any major way. The account of the crisis that Richard Ned Lebow and Janice Gross Stein gave in 1994 is a good case in point. In a passage dealing with Kissinger's meetings with the Israeli leaders on October 22, they note that some officials who had taken part in those talks claimed that "Kissinger quietly encouraged Israel to violate the ceasefire and continue its offensive, at least for several hours," while other participants "insist that Kissinger was tough and emphasized the importance of the cease-fire." They then point out that Kissinger himself "adamantly denies that he encouraged Israel to violate the cease-fire" and quote from an interview they conducted with him in 1991:

> I did not encourage the Israelis. I did not want to see the Third [Egyptian] Army destroyed. I thought that they [the Israelis] were emotionally exhausted and did not need a big sales pitch for a cease-fire. After all, they had gotten the direct negotiations they had always wanted. I didn't press them hard because I didn't think that they needed to be pressed. I did not encourage the Israelis with more than minor adjustments. It is quite possible that the commanders in the field ran away with [Israeli Prime Minister] Golda [Meir].[18]

And it was largely on the basis on that testimony that Lebow and Stein concluded that Kissinger had not intentionally encouraged the Israelis to continue their advance. They state, for example, that Kissinger had "*inadvertently* created false expectations among Israel's leaders" about how much extra time they had for military operations. And they later say that "Brezhnev suspected, *wrongly*, that Kissinger had deliberately deceived him and encouraged Israel to violate the cease-fire."[19]

But important evidence at odds with Kissinger's account came out a few years after the book by Lebow and Stein was published. Indeed, a number of writers concluded on the basis of that evidence that Kissinger had done more to sanction the Israeli violations than he had suggested in that interview with Lebow and Stein, in his memoirs, and elsewhere.[20] But even then there was a certain tendency to minimize the importance of that evidence and essentially accept Kissinger's story. One document, for example, recorded a meeting Kissinger had with Meir just after he had worked out the ceasefire agreement with Brezhnev in Moscow. Meir said that if the Egyptians didn't stop military operations, Israel wouldn't either. Kissinger replied, "most tellingly," as one scholar put it, "even if they do. . . . "[21] But that comment is generally not taken too seriously. As one of Kissinger's biographers put it in 2004, it was an "almost off-handed" remark. Even his assurance that the Israelis would not get "violent protests" if the fighting continued during the night is not seen as very important. It had been "designed reflexively to sweeten the ever-suspicious Israeli leader," another historian wrote, and Kissinger would soon regret what he had said.[22]

Even scholars who do say that Kissinger deliberately gave the Israelis a green light to violate the ceasefire are often quick to qualify that conclusion in some way—by suggesting, for example, that the message he was giving was not explicit; or that he was sanctioning only minor, short-term, violations of the agreement; or that he quickly changed his mind and demanded that the Israelis put a stop to their offensive.[23]

How, then, are we to get to the bottom of this issue? Our plan here is to attack the problem on two levels. Given the importance of Kissinger's own testimony in supporting many historical accounts of the episode we are concerned with here, our first goal is to assess Kissinger's reliability as a source by examining a number of claims he has made over the years in the light of the massive body of evidence we now have access to. We will then take a close look at his specific claim that he "did not encourage the Israelis" to violate the ceasefire in 1973—not deliberately, at any rate, or in a way that really mattered—also in the light of the important body of declassified material now available.

A RELIABLE SOURCE?

What in general can be said about Kissinger's reliability as a historical source? To get at that issue, we will look in this section at four claims he made on matters not directly related to the issue at hand. The first relates to his position on the Vietnam War. In an August 1968 *New York Review of Books* article, Hans Morgenthau had identified Kissinger as one of a number of supporters of the war who were now trying to "cover their tracks" and make it seem that their real position had been very different. That charge led to a private exchange of correspondence between the two men. In one letter, written just before Nixon asked him to serve as his national security adviser, Kissinger stated flatly that he had "never supported the war in public."[24] What was extraordinary here is that he had in fact defended America's Vietnam policy in a televised debate in December 1965, and that same month he, along with a large number of other academics, had signed a petition supporting the Johnson administration's conduct of the war.[25] Not just that, but in 1966 he had published a short opinion piece in *Look* magazine arguing that the United States had to prevent a Communist victory in Vietnam.[26] And that same year, he told a group in North Carolina: "We have no choice now but to maintain our commitment to prevent a Communist takeover in the south."[27] Given all this, it is hard to understand why Kissinger would simply deny that he had ever supported the war in public. But the fact that he did so certainly tells us something about his commitment to the truth as an end in itself.

The remaining three cases relate directly to the Middle East. Kissinger claimed, first of all, that on the eve of the October War he had not urged Israel not to attack preemptively. Rumors to the effect that he had insisted that the Israelis not strike first began to circulate very early on, but Kissinger from the start strongly denied that he had done any such thing. Meeting with a group of Jewish leaders a few weeks after the war, for example, he referred to "the great myth" that the US government had "pressured them not to preempt."[28]

But the "myth" did not disappear. It instead resurfaced in two apparently well-researched books by respected journalists that came out in the next few years. Kissinger, their authors argued, had made it clear to the Israelis, just as the war was about to break out, that they were not to strike first.[29]

Kissinger, however, did not give an inch, and over the years has repeatedly denied that the United States was in any way responsible for Israel's decision not to attack preemptively. In the second volume of his memoirs, for example, he quoted from a message Meir sent him on October 7, the second day of the war. Meir had strongly implied that it was because of American pressure that the Israelis had not taken "preemptive action," and that their failure to do so was "the reason for our situation now." Kissinger was clearly irritated by that claim. Yes, it was true, he wrote, that "in years past" he had expressed his "personal view" to the Israelis that "America's ability to help Israel in any war would be impaired if Israel struck first." But in the run-up to the October War, "the subject of preemption had not been discussed." Meir, he said, had merely "volunteered" to the US ambassador that "Israel would not preempt. The decision had been her own, without benefit of recent American advice."[30]

Even in 2013, Kissinger was still taking the same line. Israel's decision not to preempt, he told an interviewer that year, had been "taken on its own volition and not at our request."[31] And that claim was not just for public consumption. In meetings with his staff at the time, he denied having warned the Israelis not to strike first. "Since there will be all sorts of legends when this is over," he said on October 10, "one legend that has absolutely no foundation in fact is that we prevented an Israeli pre-emptive attack. We were authorized by the Israelis to inform the Arabs and the Soviets that they were not planning a pre-emptive attack, in order to comply with their wish that we prevent the war. But we made no recommendation to the Israelis about any course of action."[32] He made the same point in another high-level meeting in January 1975: "We didn't keep them from preempting. That's a myth."[33]

What is to be made of that line of argument? On the one hand, the Israelis certainly did tell the Americans that they did not intend to strike first as soon as they learned that an Arab attack was imminent. And they did ask Kissinger to let the Soviets and the Arabs know about their intentions, since they thought Arab military preparations might have been rooted in an honest but mistaken fear that Israel planned to take military action against them.[34] These assurances had not been prompted by any direct American pressure related to this specific situation, since they were given well before the US government believed war was imminent or even likely. So that part of the story is certainly in line with Kissinger's account.

What Kissinger failed to note is that he had not believed the Israeli report about an imminent Arab attack when he received it at around 6:00 a.m. on October 6. That report, he thought, might have been concocted as a cover for an Israeli attack—even though that attack would be launched on Yom Kippur. As he told White House Chief of Staff Alexander Haig that morning, when he received the report he thought at first that "it was an Israeli trick for them to be able to launch an attack although this is the holiest day." He had therefore "called the Israelis and warned them to restrain" and soon "got a return call from the Israelis giving us assurances that no pre-emptive Israeli [action] would be taken."[35] Kissinger had, in fact, urged the Israelis just before 7:00 a.m. that morning "not to take any pre-emptive action."[36] As he reported to Nixon a couple of hours later, he had emphasized "the essentiality of restraint on the Israeli part, and said there must be no preemptive action."[37] Likewise, he told a high-level meeting that evening that he had made it clear that morning to the Soviets, the Egyptians, and the Israelis (including the Israeli foreign minister, then in New York) that "if Israel took preemptive action, we would oppose them."[38] All of this, of course, is very much at odds with his claim that the US government "made no recommendation to the Israelis about any course of action."

Those warnings, although issued after the key Israeli decision had been made, reflected a basic American attitude—an attitude which played a much more important role in shaping Israeli policy on this issue than Kissinger seemed willing to admit. As one well-informed writer has pointed out, the Americans had, after all, "consistently warned Israel that it must not be responsible for initiating a Middle East war."[39] And it is quite clear from Israeli sources that in considering whether to attack preemptively, concerns about how the Americans would react played a fundamental role.[40] Kissinger himself, moreover, clearly knew that this was the case. The Israeli ambassador, Simcha Dinitz, who had just flown back from Israel, briefed him on the evening of October 7 about the Israeli leadership's discussion of the preemption issue on the eve of the Arab attack. Dinitz reported one particularly striking remark Meir had made. He had reminded her that Kissinger had always told him that "whatever happens, don't be the one that strikes first." And she had answered: "You think I forgot?"[41]

All this has a direct bearing on how Meir's October 7 letter to Kissinger is to be interpreted. When she told him that he knew the reasons "why we took no preemptive action," she was almost certainly alluding to the general American attitude and not to the specific warnings issued on the eve of the war. But if that was the case, Meir's point that the Israelis had held back in large part because the Americans had made their opposition clear was absolutely correct. In dismissing that point, it was Kissinger, not Meir, who was giving a very misleading impression.

The next case has to do with an offer Soviet foreign minister Andrei Gromyko made to Nixon and Kissinger in two important meetings in September 1971. According to Kissinger's later account, Gromyko had made what was "on the surface" an attractive proposal. "In the event of a comprehensive settlement," Gromyko had said, the Soviets "were prepared to withdraw their forces from the Middle East, join in an arms embargo to the area, and participate in guarantees of a settlement." But in reality, Kissinger argued, "there was less to these proposals than met the eye." The basic problem was that the Soviets insisted that a comprehensive settlement would have to "involve total Israeli withdrawal from the occupied territories of all Arab states." Since they were "still backing the maximum Arab position" and there was "no sign" that they were willing to press their "clients toward flexibility," the United States "had no incentive to proceed jointly with Moscow." The procedure Gromyko had in mind was also unacceptable: "the promised withdrawal of Soviet forces would come at the *end* of the entire process; in other words, we would have to execute our entire contribution to this arrangement before the Soviets had to do anything." "And even then," Kissinger said, "the Soviets made their withdrawal from Egypt conditional on the withdrawal of American advisers from Iran."[42]

What is to be made of those claims? The first point to note is that whereas in his memoirs Kissinger minimized the importance of the Soviet offer, at the time both he and Nixon thought it was very significant. Kissinger's first reaction, when Nixon briefed him on what Gromyko had said, was that this was a "tremendous step" on the Soviets' part. And after meeting with Gromyko to confirm the terms of the offer, he told the president that the Soviets had made "a major concession" and that these proposals were "the biggest steps forward in the [Middle East] that have been made in your administration."[43] Even after he had had time to reflect on the Gromyko offer, Nixon still thought it was very attractive. Getting the Soviets to withdraw their forces in exchange for an Israeli withdrawal to the 1967 borders, he said a few months later, was "a damn good deal for just a few hunks of desert."[44] And the documentation that is now available fully supports that very positive appraisal.

That material shows, in fact, that contrary to what Kissinger suggested in his memoirs, with regard to the terms of the final settlement, the two big powers saw things in much the same way.[45] The evidence on this point is quite overwhelming. Gromyko, in his one-on-one meeting with Nixon on September 29, said that "if some kind of framework" was reached that would provide for the "withdrawal of Israeli troops from all occupied territories," Moscow, for its part, "would agree on the limitation, or, if you wish, even on stoppage" of arms deliveries to the area, and would be willing to withdraw its military units from the Middle East, leaving only a small number of advisers there, "like you have in Iran." The Soviets, he added, were also prepared, together with the United States and other powers, and in the context of a general agreement, to work out security arrangements for Israel.[46]

And this, it is important to note, was very much in line with the course of action Kissinger had himself laid out a year earlier: "We would require Israel's assurance that it would return essentially to her prewar borders, in exchange for Arab commitments and an enforceable peace. We would tell both the Soviets and [Gamal Abdel] Nasser [the Egyptian president at the time] that Soviet combat personnel would have to be withdrawn after an agreement."[47] Indeed, both he and other top US leaders said many times, both before and after September 1971, that as part of a settlement, Israel would have to pull back to its 1967 borders, with only minor modifications.[48] That latter provision, incidentally, was no problem for their Soviet counterparts: the Soviet government agreed that minor territorial changes, at least on the border with Jordan, were not out of the question.[49]

In the Soviet view, moreover, once the border issue was resolved, everything else, as Brezhnev later put it, would "fall into place."[50] His government, in fact, was now taking an accommodating position on all the other issues involved in a settlement: refugees, the Golan Heights, direct Arab-Israeli talks, and Israeli passage through the Straits of Tiran (through a permanent international presence at Sharm el-Sheikh).[51] So now, in agreeing to remove their military forces from the area as part of a settlement, the Soviets felt they had taken a very important step forward. Their ambassador in Washington, Anatoly Dobrynin, called it "the most generous offer the Soviet Union would ever make." They were offering to withdraw their forces, limit arms shipments to the region, and guarantee the settlement: "What more could Israel possibly want?" The Soviets, he said, "would agree to almost anything" the Americans proposed by way of guarantees. And Moscow would be "extremely flexible" in negotiating the settlement; only on the border issue did it have a fixed position—and even on that point, as we just noted, its position was not fundamentally different from what the Americans had in mind.[52]

The Politburo, Dobrynin told Kissinger, had, in effect, accepted the conditions for a peace agreement Nixon and Kissinger had laid down in July 1970. They were willing to withdraw Soviet forces from the area and would "accept almost any settlement in terms of guarantees and other requirements in return for a solution."[53] It was thus scarcely the case, as Kissinger had claimed in his memoirs, that Moscow "was still backing the maximum Arab position," or that Gromyko had given "no sign of the Soviet Union's willingness to press its clients toward flexibility," or that he had given America "no incentive to proceed jointly with Moscow."[54]

Indeed, with regard to Kissinger's comment in his memoirs that "there was no possibility of agreeing now on the shape of the final settlement," it is important to note that he told Gromyko explicitly at the time that the two powers could move ahead on the basis of the proposal the Soviet foreign minister had laid out.[55] Nixon and Brezhnev, he suggested, might be able to "agree on the nature of the ultimate settlement" at their meeting in Moscow in May 1972. But this agreement would have to be kept very secret, since Nixon could not run the risk of a leak that year, before the presidential election in November. There certainly was "no possibility of implementing a final agreement before the American election."[56] That implied that implementation would take place in 1973, and Kissinger confirmed this point in a meeting with Dobrynin a month later. His understanding, he said, "was that we would not begin implementing the agreement on our side until after the elections; I had made this point clear to Gromyko that we could come to an understanding which of course on our side would have to be very binding, but that the actual implementation would be left until 1973."[57] And in April 1972, he told Gromyko that implementation would take place "within the first six months" of 1973. He went on to specify that implementation could not "begin until January," clearly implying that it *would* begin at the start of the year.[58] All this is very much at odds with the impression a reader would have gotten from the passage in his memoirs dealing with the September 1971 meetings with Gromyko, which clearly suggested that, given Soviet policy, joint action of this sort was impossible.

There are, moreover, two other points where Kissinger's account of this episode is contradicted by the documents. He claimed in his memoirs that the "promised withdrawal of Soviet forces would come at the *end* of the entire process"—that is, after the full Israeli withdrawal had been completed. But in the record of his meeting with Gromyko, the Soviet foreign minister agreed that all the measures he had proposed, including the withdrawal of Soviet forces, "would go into effect as part of an interim settlement"—that is, it would *not* have to wait until the entire process had been completed.[59] Kissinger had also said that the Soviets had made the withdrawal from Egypt "conditional on the withdrawal of American advisors from Iran." But in reality the point about Iran was rather different. The advisers from Iran would *not* have to be pulled out—all Gromyko had said was that the Soviets could, after the agreement took effect, keep about the same number of advisors in Egypt as America had in Iran. So Kissinger's account of this episode turns out not to be very accurate.

The final but perhaps most interesting example has to do with Kissinger's account of his meetings with his Egyptian counterpart, Egyptian president Anwar Sadat's national security adviser, Hafiz Ismail. The two men met in February 1973 for two days of intense discussion. According to the account Kissinger gave in his memoirs, the Egyptians were uncompromising. Ismail, he said, had come "less to discuss mediation—and therefore compromise—than to put forward a polite ultimatum for terms beyond our capacity to fulfill." "Above all," he wrote, "Israel had to agree, before anything else happened, that it would return to its 1967 borders with *all* neighbors, with some margin for adjustment, perhaps, on the West Bank. Only on that basis would Egypt join the negotiating process, and then only to discuss security arrangements." And if an Israeli-Egyptian agreement were reached, his country would only agree to end the state of war. Full peace "would have to await a comprehensive settlement with *all* the other parties, including Syria and the Palestinians," thus giving "the most intractable parties a veto, in effect, over the whole process." The Egyptian proposal, he wrote, thus "left us with little reason for optimism." The policy Ismail had laid out was "not essentially different" from the policy that had produced the present deadlock, and he had little hope that it could lead to a negotiated settlement.[60]

But it is clear from the documentary evidence now available that the account Kissinger gave in his memoirs was again deeply misleading. As he told Nixon at the time, Ismail had in fact laid out a very new policy. "I thought the most important thing," he noted—and this was something Sadat "had never said to anyone and won't say to anybody"—was that the Egyptians were "willing to make a separate Egyptian-Israeli deal, because they know that afterwards the Jordanians and Syrians are going to follow the same procedure." This was the "first time" that the Egyptians had said anything of the sort. "Up to now" they had taken the view "that the whole package must be done as one: Syria, Jordan and Egypt."[61] To be sure, a comprehensive peace was still Egypt's long-term goal, but the connection with the Egyptian part of the settlement was, at least at first, to be fairly minimal. As one of the Egyptians taking part in the talks with Kissinger pointed out, there just had to be some indication in the Egyptian settlement "that we are going forward to a whole settlement"—just "some paragraphs" laying out basic principles of the sort contained "in the 242 document," that is, in UN Security Council Resolution 242, which had laid out in very general language the terms of settlement (and which Kissinger himself did not take very seriously).[62]

And as the lengthy transcripts of his meetings with Kissinger make clear, Ismail *was* interested in serious negotiations under mainly American auspices. He certainly never said that Israel would first have to agree to return to its pre-1967 borders, with perhaps some modifications in its border with Jordan, before there could be any negotiations at all. One could begin, in Ismail's view, by working out what he called "heads of agreement"—basic principles that would govern the *Egyptian* part of the settlement, negotiated in talks with the Americans, with the Israelis being brought in in some way at some point.[63] The "heads of agreement" would then be fleshed out in a more detailed written agreement; the Israelis would be more deeply involved in this stage.

All this would be followed by talks about implementation. Once the "heads of agreement" with Egypt were worked out, an effort would be made to "start the motors" running with Jordan and Syria. The same basic process would unfold on those fronts, but "a step behind."[64] But what if Syria refused to come along? Well, that problem could be left for later. Ismail certainly did not suggest that Egypt would be held back forever by a Syrian veto, and he probably felt that after both Egypt and Jordan had made their own agreements with Israel, it would be hard for Syria to refuse to settle on similar terms. As for the Palestinians, he at one point told Kissinger that once Israel and Jordan reached an agreement, that would "bring down the curtain" on the whole Palestinian issue, at least as an international problem; it would then be a matter for King Hussein of Jordan and the Palestinians to settle internally.[65] But Kissinger could scarcely believe that Egypt could really wash its hands of the Palestinians in that way, and when he pressed Ismail on that issue, the Egyptian agreed to give more thought to the problem. The one point that comes across from this exchange, however, is that the Palestinians would not be allowed to prevent Egypt from moving forward toward at least a partial peace agreement with Israel.

The basic plan Ismail laid out, moreover, was not too different from the kind of strategy the Americans had favored for some time. From September 1971 on, the policy, at least in theory, had been to move quickly after the November 1972 elections toward a settlement, at least with Egypt and Jordan, based on the principles the United States and the Soviet Union already shared—principles, in fact, that had more or less been agreed upon in the Moscow talks in 1972. That settlement would be worked out in further talks involving the regional actors, with the big powers helping to move matters forward behind the scenes. The Egyptian plan was very much in line with that basic approach, although it emphasized the American role in pressing Israel and played down what the Soviets were expected to do. And in substantive terms (as noted above), the Americans had for some time accepted the principle that Israel would have to return to its 1967 borders, with only minor modifications; here too they saw eye-to-eye with the Egyptians. The Americans had proposed, however, that while Egyptian sovereignty over the whole Sinai Peninsula could be recognized, Israel's security needs in that area could not be ignored, and maybe a temporary Israeli presence in the Sinai could be part of the agreement. And the Egyptians seemed willing to work out some sort of compromise on that basis.[66]

One thus comes away from the lengthy transcripts of the February 1973 Kissinger-Ismail meetings with the sense that the Egyptians were serious about moving toward peace, that Kissinger had no fundamental objection to the course of action they had proposed, and that Ismail and Kissinger had, in fact, reached a near-understanding about how matters were to proceed. That point is particularly clear from the way Kissinger summed up where matters stood at the end of the talks:

Dr. Kissinger: Now let me sum up where I understand we are, and see where we agree. And then we have to discuss who tells what to whom.

You have defined a process by which, during the course of the spring, you and we—we after discussing in general with the Israelis—would agree on some general principles, heads of agreement, whose practical concurrence would be to give some concrete meaning to 242, at least with respect to Egypt. Then when these heads of agreement have been achieved between you and us, then we should achieve Israeli acquiescence. We will have to reserve what the margin is. It may be impossible to ask us to get total acquiescence. More realistic would be to try to get the thrust of it maintained. But the spirit would be that the major thrust of it would be acceptable. After the heads of agreement are achieved, a process would start, with the Israelis engaged more, which would lead to the detailed provisions. After the heads of the agreement, then it might be possible to consider what we call an interim agreement—the initial phase. The heads of the agreement, and beginning the process of redeployment, and the opening of the Suez Canal might be agreed to by September 1.

Mr. Ismail: Or before that. June or July.

Dr. Kissinger: Or before. Yes. I am just trying to envision. And, of course, outside parties, with good will, would try to help keep the process going. As you move towards the completion of the Egyptian-Israeli negotiation, you would think that the Syrian and Jordan negotiations should have at least reached the point of agreement on the heads of agreement. Hopefully.

Mr. Ismail: Hopefully. Before we come to the final stage of agreement.

Dr. Kissinger: Yes. If those principles are well chosen, that might not be all that difficult. Because the concerns about sovereignty and security with respect to the Sinai might be the same as those for the Golan Heights. That is why a far-sighted view on your part might unlock the whole thing. With Syria it is only a security problem. The Jordan problem is more.

The completion of the Egyptian settlement might produce an end to the state of war. Its elements you have listed: free passage, an end to the boycott, a commitment against guerilla activities from Egyptian soil, an end of the reservation in international agreements, non-interference (which would include by radio). And incidentally, I might say that the more attractive that part can be made the better for us and the easier it will be. It is in that area that you can be of the greatest help to us if we are to play a role. The Jordanian settlement would be considered conclusive for the Palestine situation. Although Hussein will have to deal with the Palestinians, the question between the Palestinians and Jordan will not become a precondition for recognition.

Dr. Ghanim: It will still be an internal problem for Hussein in Jordan.

Dr. Kissinger: What we are concerned with is that the internal problem in Jordan not become an obstacle to a settlement between Israel and the other Arab countries. It is not part of this negotiation. This is what I am saying.

Mr. Ismail: Yes.

Dr. Kissinger: And at the end of that process, plus some acceptable solution of the refugee problem through the U.N., a state of peace would develop. But if I understand you correctly you said that once the Syrian and Jordanian issues were settled, then the recognition of Israel could follow that. Is that correct? Or does that also follow the refugee solution? I am a little confused.

Mr. Ismail: I will try to fix that point, that inter-relationship between recognition and the refugees at the end of the Syrian and Jordan settlements with Israel.

Dr. Kissinger: You will think about that?
Mr. Ismail: Yes. And try to make it more precise.

Dr. Kissinger: All right. So that is my present understanding of the general process as you envision it.

Mr. Ismail: Yes.

Dr. Kissinger: Now, you will do some thinking, and so will we, about some practical issues, such as who will talk to the Syrians. Don't volunteer me!

Mr. Ismail: No.

Dr. Kissinger: And at what stage. And when Israel should be brought in. But we will make a judgment of that. We will make a recommendation. We are probably the better judge. Then on the three issues I mentioned to you—the phasing of recognition, the various forms of security measures, and the precise definition of the end of the state of war. And then we should meet again around April 10.

So it really seems that Kissinger had no problem with Ismail's general approach, and appeared mainly concerned with how it could be fleshed out in practice.[67] One certainly does not get the impression that Ismail had merely "put forward a polite ultimatum for terms beyond our capacity to fulfill."[68] And in various specific ways, Kissinger's account in his memoirs of Ismail's proposal is simply not supported by those documents. Ismail, for example, had not insisted that Israel agree basically to withdraw from all the occupied territories "before anything else happened." The process, in fact, was to begin before Israel was even brought in. Nor had he insisted that "full peace" with Israel would have to "await a comprehensive settlement with *all* the other parties, including Syria and the Palestinians." With regard to the Palestinians, at least, he had simply agreed that the Egyptians needed to think more about the issue, and a lot of what he said had in fact suggested that if the other issues were resolved, the Palestinian question would not be a stumbling block to "full peace" with Egypt. So again, Kissinger's later account did not give a good sense of what had happened in his meetings with Ismail.

What general conclusions, then, are to be drawn from the whole analysis in this section? The first and most obvious point is that the accounts Kissinger later gave of what had happened during his time in office have to be taken with a grain of salt. This is not to say, of course, that his three enormous volumes of memoirs, along with his other writings and utterances dealing with these matters, are devoid of historical value. Those three volumes are, in fact, perhaps the most extraordinary political memoir ever written, and no historian interested in the period would ever dream of ignoring them. The point is simply that what he says there should not just be accepted on faith and that it is important to assess his claims in the light of the other evidence we now have access to.

A second point is perhaps a bit less obvious, and this is that the distortions were by no means random. In all three Middle East cases, the effect was to minimize America's responsibility—and especially Kissinger's personal responsibility—for what happened. The message in his passage dealing with the Gromyko offer was that the Soviets were still impossible—that they continued to "back the maximum Arab position"—so there was no point in trying to cooperate with them in working out a settlement. The message in the passage dealing with the meetings with Ismail was that the Egyptians were still impossible—that all Ismail had done was to "put forward a polite ultimatum for terms beyond our capacity to fulfill." And his account of the preemption issue on the eve of the 1973 war also suggested that America's ability to influence what happened was severely limited. Israel, the argument ran, had made the decision not to preempt entirely on her own. The subtext was that the US government had little control over what Israel did.

There is a clear pattern here, and that pattern tells us something about Kissinger's purposes in presenting things the way he did. He wanted to give the impression that America's room for maneuver was quite limited and that he personally should therefore not be blamed for the way events unfolded. But having identified the bias, we are in a position to control for it when we analyze Kissinger's account of the main issue we are concerned with here: US policy at the end of the October 1973 war.

A GREEN LIGHT FOR ISRAEL?

The tide of battle in October 1973 eventually turned against the Arabs. The Soviets then pressed hard for a ceasefire, and Kissinger agreed to go to Moscow to see what could be worked out. But, contrary to what is often claimed, he was no longer particularly interested in holding the Israelis back.[69] As he himself later pointed out, "what we wanted was the most massive Arab defeat possible so that it would be clear to the Arabs that they would get nowhere with dependence on the Soviets."[70] It was for that reason that he now sought to give the Israelis more time to complete their military operations, and in fact one of the main reasons he had agreed to go to Moscow was that the trip would give Israel another couple of days.[71] But on October 21, he did negotiate a ceasefire agreement with Brezhnev and Gromyko. That led to a UN Security Council resolution, adopted just before 1:00 a.m. on October 22. The resolution was supposed to go into effect twelve hours later—that is, just before 1:00 p.m. New York time that day, equivalent to just before 7:00 p.m. Israeli time.[72]

According to Kissinger's later account, the Israelis were not informed of the decision as promptly as the Americans had intended because of a communications problem in Moscow; he therefore indicated to the Israelis when he met with them on October 22 that he "would understand if there was a few hours' 'slippage' in the cease-fire deadline" while he was flying home, "to compensate for the four hours lost through the communications breakdown in Moscow."[73] But when the ceasefire began to unravel the next day, Kissinger wrote, he had the "sinking feeling" that those remarks might have "emboldened" the Israelis.[74]

What are we to make of Kissinger's claims in this area? Given what was shown in the previous section, neither Kissinger's own accounts nor the historical works based on his testimony should be accepted uncritically. They all have to be evaluated in the light of the massive and quite extraordinary body of evidence now available, and when one examines the sources it becomes clear that there are real problems with the way this episode is commonly interpreted. Kissinger, first of all, did *not* tell the Israelis in his meetings with them on October 22 that they had to stop their offensive, allowing only a four-hour delay. Everything he said, in fact, pointed in the opposite direction. "You won't get violent protests from Washington," he told Meir, "if something happens during the night, while I'm flying. Nothing can happen in Washington until noon tomorrow."[75] And "noon tomorrow" implied at least a sixteen-hour delay beyond the ceasefire deadline (if the reference was to Israeli time), or perhaps a twenty-two-hour delay (if, as is more likely, he meant Washington time), not the mere four-hour delay that Kissinger had admitted he had been willing to give the Israelis to compensate for the communications breakdown.[76]

In another conversation, moreover, this time with Israeli military leaders, he might have gone even further. According to Matti Golan (relying on Israeli sources), Kissinger spoke in terms not of hours but of days. When he was asked during that meeting how long it would take "to complete the encirclement of the two Egyptian armies on the east bank of the Suez Canal," the air force chief, according to Golan, answered that they could be destroyed "in two or three days." "Two or three days?" Kissinger supposedly replied. "That's all? Well, in Vietnam the cease-fire didn't go into effect at the exact time that was agreed on." To the Israelis, Golan writes, it sounded like Kissinger was giving them a green light to continue operations for two or three days more.[77] But Golan's book is not a totally reliable historical source, and this particular story should not carry much evidentiary weight.[78]

One does not need, however, to rely on sources of that kind to reach the conclusion that the green-lighting of Israel was part of a deliberate strategy. Kissinger's basic idea, as a number of documents show, was that the Israelis could take advantage of the fact that no one would really know how far they had actually advanced at the time the ceasefire was supposed to go into effect. That meant that no matter where they were at the time the shooting actually stopped, they would not have to withdraw to any particular line. As he told Dinitz in a telephone conversation at noon on October 23, since "nobody will be able to tell where" the forces were, the ceasefire resolution could not "be given practical effect," and thus the exact standstill line was "indeterminable."[79] In line with that idea, Kissinger had encouraged the Israeli leaders the previous day to "just say" they would stop where they were at the time the ceasefire was supposed to take effect provided the other side also did so, taking care to note that whether offensive operations actually continued lay within their "domestic jurisdiction" and that "reality"—meaning, presumably, "and not U.N. resolutions"—would determine where the ceasefire lines actually were.[80]

He was more explicit when he met with Dinitz in person on the afternoon of October 23. He told the ambassador that he wanted Israel to improve its position in the field as much as possible. Indeed, he said, he had made that clear to Meir when he saw her in Israel. But for diplomatic reasons it would be helpful if the Israelis accepted a UN resolution calling for a return to the original ceasefire line. That resolution, he thought, would have no substantive effect, since the Israelis would not be expected "to return to the positions from which" they had started. He asked only that they find "200–300 unimportant and insignificant yards from which" to withdraw, so that they could claim they were complying with the UN resolution. There were no threats, no demands, no criticism even of the Israeli offensive—an attitude very much at odds with the much harder line Nixon was taking with the Israelis at the time.[81]

Kissinger reiterated the point, and indeed went a bit further, in two phone conversations with Dinitz that evening. "When the pressure starts," he told the ambassador, the Israelis could withdraw a bit—just a "few hundred yards" from where they would be at that point, which was of course well beyond the original ceasefire line—but "not right now." "The time to make moves," he said, "is just a little bit before you are forced to." Israel, he thought, should continue military operations for another day: the fighting should only stop "tomorrow," that is, two days after the ceasefire was supposed to go into effect. Then someone should announce that Israel was returning to the original ceasefire line. The assumption was that since no one knew where that line was, there would be no way to prove that the Israelis, in withdrawing a few hundred yards, were not pulling back to the original line. In terms of tactics, the idea was that the Israelis should say one thing and do another, but the Israeli government was unwilling to go along with what it viewed as an unnecessarily dishonest policy, and refused to accept what Kissinger called his "strong tactical advice." In its view, the fact that some Egyptian commanders had continued to fight past the deadline, and were supposedly the first ones to violate the ceasefire, gave it all the justification it needed to do what it wanted to do anyway—namely, to cut off the Egyptian Third Army in the Sinai.

Kissinger was irritated by the Israeli response—not by the Israelis' refusal to stop fighting, but by their unwillingness to defend their actions by making false claims about where their forces were at the time the October 22 ceasefire was supposed to take effect. "The trouble with your people," he told Dinitz on the evening of October 23, "is they have too much integrity." He had clearly not given up on his plan. "In my personal opinion," he said, according to the Israeli account of these conversations, "if you could buy some time by discussing the 200–300 yards, why not give up some of your integrity? After all, within a short while it will become clear that 25,000 Egyptians do not have water or supplies and then you have the upper hand anyway." And the next day he complained to the ambassador that because of Israeli boasting—he was particularly annoyed with some remarks Israeli defense minister Moshe Dayan had just made—"the strategy which I had proposed is no longer possible." "The Israelis are not only obnoxious," he complained to other US officials a little later that morning, "they're also boastful. If they had kept their mouths shut, no one would have known where the ceasefire line was."[82]

The real problem, however, was not that the Israelis were too honest. The real problem had to do instead with the Arabs and their Soviet friends. The Egyptians especially were becoming increasingly desperate as the Israelis threatened to cut off their Third Army in the Sinai. And the Soviets were enraged by the Israelis' refusal to comply with the ceasefire—and by what they viewed as Washington's unwillingness to make them do so. The Soviet leadership had by no means been eager to intervene in the conflict. Kissinger himself understood how reluctant the Soviets were to confront the United States in this crisis. Brezhnev, he pointed out, had told him in Moscow that "détente was the most important thing and he wouldn't give it up for the Middle East," and he apparently took that statement at face value.[83] But what that meant was that the United States could go rather far before triggering Soviet military action of any sort.

The question was how far, and by October 23 Soviet patience was clearly wearing thin. There were even certain indications that the Soviets were preparing to send troops to Egypt.[84] So on the morning of October 24, nearly two full days after the ceasefire was supposed to take effect, the Americans slammed on the brakes. The Israelis were told in no uncertain terms to stop military operations. "We cannot," Kissinger said, "make Brezhnev look like a Goddamn fool in front of his own colleagues."[85] The US government had thus shifted course about twelve hours before the famous Brezhnev letter threatening unilateral Soviet intervention was received in Washington—just a bit too late to prevent that threat from being issued.[86]

But the key point to note here is that the Brezhnev threat, and the Soviet moves that had preceded it, was directly provoked by what was viewed as Israel's flouting of the ceasefire. Kissinger himself had no problem recognizing, at the late night meeting where the decision on how to respond to the Brezhnev threat was made, that it was "the Israeli violation" of the ceasefire agreement that "broke the camel's back." It was only then, he pointed out, that "the Soviets decided to move."[87] Indeed, he later admitted to the Israelis that Brezhnev's claim that he had been tricked was "not unreasonable."[88] And he certainly recognized that he had pushed the envelope a bit too far—that he himself was in large measure responsible for creating the situation that had led to the Brezhnev threat. "If the Soviets have decided to go in," Kissinger remarked to Dinitz when he phoned him on the evening of October 24 to tell him about the threat, "I just think we turned the wheel yesterday one screw too much."[89] The "we" is very much worth noting. That single two-letter word is a kind of "smoking gun" here. It shows that the Israelis had not acted on their own, and that Kissinger had given the green light for the Israeli offensive.

It is also important to note that in reacting to the Brezhnev threat the way he did, Kissinger was deliberately engaging in a bit of overkill.[90] "Although at the time all the Russians were going to do was to put a division at the Cairo airport," he later remarked, in ordering the alert he wanted "to teach them that they could not operate far from home."[91] He had learned, he said at the time, "that when you decide to use force you must use plenty of it."[92] The decision to order the alert was in line with the basic philosophy he had outlined a week earlier. "If we get into a confrontation," he had said, "we have to show that we are a giant! We have to win!"[93]

To be sure, the whole "crisis" of October 24–25 was somewhat artificial, since the Americans did not intend to resist the basic Soviet demand that Israel stop its advance. They had actually taken the necessary actions to force Israel into line about twelve hours before the Brezhnev letter was received. But the purpose of the alert was not to confront the Soviets on that issue. It was instead essentially an exercise in image-making. Kissinger wanted—or, more precisely, had come to want—"the most massive Arab defeat possible so that it would be clear to the Arabs that they would get nowhere with dependence on the Soviets," and the green-lighting of the Israeli offensive has to be understood in that context.[94] The whole world needed to be shown that America was the top dog, that the Soviets had been faced down, and that it was the US government that would determine how things ran their course in the Middle East. Egypt was now at Israel's mercy, and Israel was utterly dependent on the United States. The United States, Kissinger said, was thus "in the catbird's seat."[95]

And the Soviets would be playing a purely secondary role. On October 24, for example, Kissinger explained what had been agreed to in Moscow and then outlined how the US government intended to proceed: "The only thing agreed is that the Arabs sit down with Israel, initially with the United States and Soviet Union to get them talking. We privately will tell the Arabs to screw the Russians and come to us for any deals."[96] He of course realized that he should not overdo it. It was important, he thought, to not "humiliate the Soviet Union too much."[97] And he was prepared to throw the Soviets a bone or two to help them save face and keep them from making trouble. But he did want to humiliate the Soviets just the right amount—and above all he wanted to make sure that on the real issues, the United States would be calling the shots.

A SELF-INFLICTED WOUND?

In his Walgreen lectures in 1951, George Kennan suggested that democracies were like those "prehistoric monsters with a body as long as this room and a brain the size of a pin." Their foreign policies had a certain mindless quality. They tended to think too much in terms of abstract moral principles and too little in terms of what would make for a stable international system. They would be much better off, he thought, if they lowered their sights and dealt with other countries in a less ideological and more businesslike way. They should avoid "moralistic slogans" and refrain from picturing their "effort as a crusade"; they should keep their "lines of negotiation to the enemy" open and settle for a reasonable accommodation, rather than insist on total victory. But he understood that the United States, because of its own internal political culture, found it hard to pursue that sort of policy—and he was worried that unless it found a way around that problem, it might be headed for real trouble down the road.[98]

Kennan was by no means the only observer to see things that way, and the failure of détente in the 1970s is often interpreted in those terms. Kissinger, the argument runs, had sought to pursue the kind of policy Kennan had in mind, a policy based on realist principles. But his approach was too subtle, too European, for the unsophisticated Americans, who insisted that the country's foreign policy reflect its moral sensibilities and ideological beliefs. And of course Kissinger himself often took that view. Reading his memoirs, the subtext is clear: it was not his fault if the policy was not successful.

To be sure, a large part of the problem had to do with the external situation, especially in the Middle East. The Soviets were impossible; he had not seen "one shred of evidence" that they "were willing to separate themselves from the hardline Arab program."[99] The Arabs were also impossible; even in February 1973, he claimed, Ismail had merely presented "a polite ultimatum for terms beyond our capacity to fulfill." As for the Israelis, they made their own decisions, and America's ability to influence their behavior was quite limited. But the internal problems, in the final analysis, turned out to be even more daunting. Given the kind of political culture the United States had, it was impossible even for a statesman of his undoubted ability to pursue the sort of realist policy he felt was in America's interest. Indeed, as was pointed out earlier, he went so far as to say as he was about to leave office that the problem had been "almost entirely domestic" in nature.

Our basic claim here is that that whole interpretation of the failure of détente is deeply misleading. It was not because the country would never support a realist policy that things ran their course the way they did in the 1970s. The policy of reaching an accommodation with the Soviet Union was generally welcomed in 1972. If the very idea of improving relations with a major Communist power was simply unacceptable for ideological reasons, the reaction to the détente policy at that point would have been very different. The shift in attitudes at home after 1972 was real enough and obviously played a very important role in the story, but it did not just happen on its own. That shift had a good deal to do with Soviet behavior from 1973 on, or at least with the way it was commonly interpreted. And when you look at how, and especially at when, that shift took place, it is hard to avoid the conclusion that the shift was triggered in large part by the particular interpretation that was placed on Soviet policy during the October War.

The view that the Soviet Union had played a major role in instigating that conflict was very important in that regard, but the events that took place at the end of the war also mattered a great deal. For if the United States had been forced to take the extraordinary step of ordering a worldwide military alert—a step that seemed to suggest that there was a real risk of general nuclear war—then the provocation must have been enormous. The Soviets had actually threatened to send troops to the Middle East, and that suggested that they were as aggressive as ever; détente, therefore, had been a fraud. And it was not just American opinion that was affected by the events of October 1973. The Soviets assumed that Kissinger had not dealt honestly with them and that the Americans had somehow given the green light for the Israeli violations of the ceasefire. What happened at the end of the war thus also tended to discredit détente in Soviet eyes—something that helps explain Soviet policy in the Third World in the mid and late 1970s.[100]

None of this had to happen. If Kissinger had played it straight with the Soviets in October 1973 and had not encouraged Israel to violate the ceasefire he had just negotiated in Moscow, there would have been no Brezhnev threat and no US alert. More generally, if US policy had been different—if the Americans had been more willing to work with the Soviets in dealing with the Arab-Israeli conflict, a policy more in keeping with what was supposed to be the spirit of détente—events might well have run their course in the post-1973 period in a very different way, mainly because feelings within America would have been different, but also because Soviet policy would probably have been different. And what that suggests is that the détente policy as such was not the problem. It was not that a country like the United States was simply incapable, for domestic political reasons, of pursuing a policy based on realist principles. The real problem had to do with the fact that the actual policy the US government chose to pursue at the time was cut from a very different cloth.

The goal in theory might have been to build a world where the United States and the Soviet Union could put ideology aside and deal with each other on a relatively cooperative, businesslike basis. But if Kissinger had taken that goal seriously, would he really have pursued the policy he did in late October 1973? By green-lighting the Israeli ceasefire violations, he was undermining the basic policy his government was supposed to be pursuing. That effect, however, was entirely foreseeable, and that in turn makes you wonder how serious he was in pursuing that policy in the first place—about whether all the talk about building a "lasting structure of peace" was just wool to be pulled over people's eyes for much less noble political purposes.

NOTES

This chapter is derived in part from our article, "A Self-Inflicted Wound? Henry Kissinger and the Ending of the October 1973 Arab-Israeli War," published in *Diplomacy & Statecraft* 32, no. 3 (September 2021): 554–78, copyright Taylor & Francis, available online at https://www.tandfonline.com/doi/abs/10.1080/09592296.2021.1961490. Another version of this paper with links to most of the sources cited is available at http://www.sscnet.ucla.edu/polisci/faculty/trachtenberg/cv/selfinflicted.pdf. An appendix on New Israeli Documents on the 1973 War, discussing recently released Israeli material and containing English translations of extracts from some of those documents, is also available online at http://www.sscnet.ucla.edu/polisci/faculty/trachtenberg/cv/selfinflicted(appendix).pdf. References to those extracts are marked in the notes with an asterisk. The authors would like to thank the Nazarian Center for Israel Studies at UCLA for helping to cover some of their research costs.

1. Address to a Joint Session of the Congress on Return from Austria, the Soviet Union, Iran, and Poland, June 1, 1972, American Presidency Project (APP), https://www.presidency.ucsb.edu/documents/address-joint-session-the-congress-return-from-austria-the-soviet-union-iran-and-poland.

2. See H. W. Brands, "The World in a Word: The Rise and Fall of Détente," *Rhetoric and Public Affairs* 1, no. 1 (Spring 1998): 55.

3. John Lewis Gaddis, "The Rise, Fall and Future of Détente," *Foreign Affairs* 62, no. 2 (Winter 1983): 362.

4. Coalition for a Democratic Majority, Foreign Policy Task Force (Eugene Rostow, chairman), "The Quest for Détente," July 31, 1974, 2. On this document, see Justin Vaïsse, *Neoconservatism: The Biography of a Movement* (Cambridge, MA: Harvard University Press, 2010), 102–3. As Vaïsse notes in that passage, one prominent scholar—Raymond Garthoff—characterized this document as the "first major head-on assault" on the détente policy by neoconservatives. See Raymond Garthoff, *Détente and Confrontation: American-Soviet Relations from Nixon to Reagan* (Washington, DC: Brookings, 1985), 413. See also Eugene V. Rostow, "The Foreign Policy 'Debate,'" *Wall Street Journal*, September 26, 1975, 10. Rostow had served as undersecretary of state for political affairs from 1966 to 1969 and went on in the 1970s to play a key role in the public debate about détente.

5. Robert Conquest, Brian Crozier, John Erickson, Joseph Godson, Gregory Grossman, Leopold Labetz, Bernard Lewis, Richard Pipes, Leonard Schapiro, Edward Shils, and P. J. Vatikiotis, "Détente: An Evaluation," *International Review* 1 (Spring 1974): 2, 22. This assessment was reprinted by the US Senate Armed Services Committee, Subcommittee on Arms Control, in June 1974, and is discussed in Henry Kissinger, *Years of Renewal* (New York: Simon & Schuster, 1999), 247–48. Note also Rostow's claim in 1974 that Kissinger was "'lull[ing] Western public opinion' into a false sense of security." See John Rosenberg, "The Quest against Détente: Eugene Rostow, the October War, and the Origins of the Anti-Détente Movement, 1969–1976," *Diplomatic History* 39, no. 4 (September 2015): 741.

6. Quoted in Murrey Marder, "The Kissinger Years: A Search for Control in a Disordered World," *Washington Post*, November 14, 1976, 27.

7. See Henry Kissinger, *Years of Upheaval* (Boston: Little, Brown, 1982), 235–46, 979–85, 1,030–31; Kissinger, *Years of Renewal*, 97–112, 1,069–78; Henry Kissinger, "Between the Old Left and the New Right," *Foreign Affairs* 78, no. 3 (May/June 1999): 99–116; Henry Kissinger, *Diplomacy* (New York: Simon & Schuster, 1994), 745, 757, 761.

8. Dan Caldwell, "U.S. Domestic Politics and the Demise of Détente," in *The Fall of Détente: Soviet-American Relations during the Carter Years*, ed. Odd Arne Westad (Oslo: Scandinavian University Press, 1997), 105.

9. Julian Zelizer, "Détente and Domestic Politics," *Diplomatic History* 33, no. 4 (September 2009): 653.

10. Gaddis, "Rise, Fall, and Future of Détente," 365. See also David Allen, "Realism and Malarkey: Henry Kissinger's State Department, Détente, and Domestic Consensus," *Journal of Cold War Studies* 17, no. 3 (Summer 2015): 184–219.

11. See, for example, Walter Laqueur, "Détente: What's Left of It?" *New York Times Magazine*, December 16, 1973.

12. Coalition for a Democratic Majority, "Quest for Détente," 3. Even moderate politicians and respectable journalists often took that view. Note, for example, Senator Clifford Case's reference to the "enormous destructive actions that the Soviets took in encouraging [the Arabs to attack Israel in October 1973] in the first place." See US Senate, Foreign Relations Committee, "Détente" (colloquy with Kissinger), September 19, 1974, 266. See also Robert Kaiser, "Détente: It Never Really Took Hold," *Washington Post*, January 15, 1980, A1. The basic point here figured prominently in the conservative critique of détente not just in the 1970s but in the 1980s as well. For one typical example, see James Schlesinger, "The Eagle and the Bear: Ruminations on Forty Years of Superpower Relations," *Foreign Affairs* 63, no. 5 (Summer 1985): 949. "In American eyes," Schlesinger wrote, "an early blow against détente occurred in 1973 with the Yom Kippur War. Soviet attempts to stimulate and to exploit that war were startling to many Americans. The culmination was the Brezhnev letter to Nixon threatening to move Soviet forces into the region and urging, in effect, a Soviet-American condominium over the Middle East. It resulted in the alert of America's military forces and, ultimately, a slow ebbing of the crisis. But the atmosphere of détente never thereafter fully recovered."

13. Message from Brezhnev to Nixon, undated, in United States Department of State, *Foreign Relations of the United States* [*FRUS*], *1969–1976*, vol. 25, *Arab-Israeli Crisis and War, 1973* (Washington, DC: Government Printing Office [GPO], 2011), 735.

14. See, for example, Robert Keatley, "U.S. Stares Down Middle East Threat by Soviet Union as Suspicions of Moscow's Interest in Peace Increase," *Wall Street Journal*, October 26, 1973, 2 (note especially the Muskie comment quoted there); David Binder, "An Implied Soviet Threat Spurred U.S. Forces' Alert," *New York Times*, November 21, 1973, 1; Michael Getler, "Soviet Moves Caused U.S. Military Alert," *Washington Post*, October 26, 1973, A1; Robert Keatley, "Diplomatic Rx: Only Major Accords by Kissinger, Soviet May Salvage Détente," *Wall Street Journal*, March 27, 1974, 1 (note especially the Cranston comment quoted there). The letter containing Brezhnev's threat was leaked to the press in November. See Marilyn

Berger, "Brezhnev Note: 'I Will Say It Straight,'" *Washington Post*, November 28, 1973, A1. Rosenberg, "Quest against Détente," sheds a good deal of light on these issues. This article focuses on the shift in Rostow's views about détente, but other key figures like Albert Wohlstetter and Paul Nitze are also discussed. For a good example of Rostow's views, see his article "The Soviet Threat to Europe Through the Middle East," in Robert Conquest et al., *Defending America* (New York: Basic, 1977), 60–61. In 1973, he wrote that the Soviets had decided that they could "safely carry through the plans for a decisive attack against Israel," which they had "made with [Egyptian] President [Anwar] Sadat in 1972." The Brezhnev threat to intervene at the end of the war was another count in Rostow's indictment of Soviet policy. Richard Pipes, writing in 1981, made the same sort of argument, referring specifically to the "ominous ultimatum" Moscow had issued at the end of the war. See Richard Pipes, *U.S.-Soviet Relations in the Era of Détente* (Boulder, CO: Westview, 1981), xiii.

15. Memorandum of Conversation (Memcon), "Subject: Draft Statement for Senate Foreign Relations Committee Appearance," August 1, 1974, Kissinger Transcripts Collection (KT) 01268, Digital National Security Archive (DNSA), 5. See also Memcon, March 1, 1974, KT01045, DNSA, 4. Note also Kissinger's discussion of this issue at the time in Minutes of the Secretary of State's Staff Meeting, October 23, 1973, in *FRUS, 1969–1976*, vol. 25, 693.

16. See Galen Jackson, *A Lost Peace: Great Power Politics and the Arab-Israeli Dispute, 1967–1979* (Ithaca, NY: Cornell University Press, 2023), chap. 4, and the sources cited there. Note also Galia Golan, "The Soviet Union and the October War," in *The Yom Kippur War: Politics, Legacy, Diplomacy*, ed. Asaf Siniver (New York: Oxford University Press, 2013), 101–18; Victor Israelyan, *Inside the Kremlin during the Yom Kippur War* (University Park: Pennsylvania State University Press, 1995).

17. Transcript of a Telephone Conversation (Telcon), October 24, 1973, 10:20 p.m., US Department of State, Virtual Reading Room, Henry Kissinger Telephone Conversations Collection (DOSKTC). Also in Henry Kissinger, *Crisis: The Anatomy of Two Major Foreign Policy Crises* (New York: Simon & Schuster, 2003), 347.

18. Quoted in Richard Ned Lebow and Janice Gross Stein, *We All Lost the Cold War* (Princeton, NJ: Princeton University Press, 1994), 216.

19. Lebow and Stein, *We All Lost*, 218, 243 (emphasis added). Lebow and Stein were not, of course, the only ones to make this kind of argument. For other examples, see Marvin Kalb and Bernard Kalb, *Kissinger* (Boston: Little, Brown, 1974), 486–87; Edward R. F. Sheehan, *The Arabs, Israelis, and Kissinger: A Secret History of American Diplomacy in the Middle East* (New York: Reader's Digest, 1976), 36–37; Walter Isaacson, *Kissinger: A Biography* (New York: Simon & Schuster, 1992), 528; William Quandt, *Peace Process: American Diplomacy and the Arab-Israeli Conflict since 1967* (Berkeley: University of California Press, 1993), 171–72. In his October 22 meetings with the Israelis, Quandt wrote, Kissinger "was insistent that Israel move into defensive positions and not violate the cease-fire." See also Quandt's review of *FRUS 1969–1976*, vol. 25, in *H-Diplo*, February 17, 2012.

20. For Kissinger's account, see Kissinger, *Years of Upheaval*, 552–613, especially 569; Kissinger, *Crisis*, 308; Kissinger's conversation with James Hoge, September 3, 2003, broadcast on C-SPAN2's BookTV program, especially the part of the video that

begins at 35 minutes and 9 seconds (henceforth cited in the form 35:09) and continues for 4 minutes.

21. Asaf Siniver, "US Foreign Policy and the Kissinger Stratagem," in *Yom Kippur War*, 95.

22. Jussi Hanhimäki, *The Flawed Architect: Henry Kissinger and American Foreign Policy* (New York: Oxford University Press, 2004), 314; Alistair Horne, *Kissinger: 1973, The Crucial Year* (New York: Simon & Shuster, 2009), 290. See also Zach Levey, "Anatomy of an Airlift: United States Military Assistance to Israel during the 1973 War," *Cold War History* 8, no. 4 (November 2008): 492.

23. On the first point, see Siniver, "US Foreign Policy," 95. Siniver first talks about how Kissinger "actively advocated that the Israelis violate" the ceasefire, but in the next paragraph suggests that the green light might only have been "implicit." On the second point, see, for example, National Security Archive Press Release, "Kissinger Gave Green Light for Israeli Offensive Violating 1973 Cease-Fire; U.S.-Israeli Decisions Touched Off Crisis Leading to 1973 U.S. Nuclear Alert; New Documents Correct Previous Accounts in Kissinger Books," October 7, 2003. The press release began by pointing out that newly released documents showed that Kissinger had given the Israelis "a green light to breach a cease-fire agreement arranged with the Soviet Union." But in the next paragraph it went on to note that he had only told the Israelis that he could accept them "taking [a] slightly longer" time to comply with the ceasefire resolution, which was not really at odds with the story Kissinger had himself told in his memoirs. The press release announced the publication of the National Security Archive's Electronic Briefing Book No. 98 (NSAEBB98), "The October War and U.S. Policy." The summaries of the two key documents in the briefing book dealing with this issue (documents 51 and 54) show that the editors still believed Kissinger had inadvertently encouraged the Israelis and soon regretted having done so. On the point about Kissinger quickly changing his mind soon after his return to Washington on October 23, see Craig Daigle, *The Limits of Détente: The United States, the Soviet Union, and the Arab-Israeli Conflict, 1969–1973* (New Haven, CT: Yale University Press, 2012), 318–19. None of this is to say that no scholar has argued that Kissinger deliberately green-lighted the continuing Israeli offensive. See, for example, Tom Blanton's review of three books on Kissinger in *Diplomatic History* 33, no. 4 (September 2009): 772. Blanton says the "Soviets had good reason" to suspect that Kissinger was dragging things out until Israel's gains "could be consolidated." This, he writes, was thus "another case in which Kissinger's duplicity had long-run costs for détente." Kenneth Stein seems more ambivalent. Although he says that Israel violated the ceasefire "with impunity and Kissinger's sanction," he had also just said that Kissinger had only given the Israelis "tacit approval" to continue military operations and that he merely "acquiesced" in the Israeli actions. See Kenneth Stein, *Heroic Diplomacy: Sadat, Kissinger, Carter, Begin, and the Quest for Arab-Israeli Peace* (New York: Routledge, 1999), 92. In neither Stein's nor Blanton's case, however, is much evidence provided to support those views.

24. Hans Morgenthau, "A Talk with Senator McCarthy," *New York Review of Books*, August 22, 1968; Kissinger to Morgenthau, October 9, 1968; Morgenthau to Kissinger, October 22, 1968; Kissinger to Morgenthau, November 13, 1968 (for the

quotation). All of these documents are available online in the Hans Morgenthau Collection, Box 4, Folder 1, Leo Baeck Institute, New York, New York.

25. See Isaacson, *Kissinger*, 119. See also Niall Ferguson, *Kissinger*, vol. 1, *1923–1968: The Idealist* (New York: Penguin, 2015), 670–72, 822.

26. Henry Kissinger, "What Should We Do Now?" *Look*, August 9, 1966.

27. Quoted in Ferguson, *Kissinger*, 672.

28. Memcon, "Subject: Secretary Kissinger's Meeting with Jewish Intellectuals," December 6, 1973 (KT) 00938, DNSA, 2.

29. See Kalb and Kalb, *Kissinger*, 459; Sheehan, *Arabs, Israelis, and Kissinger*, 31.

30. Kissinger, *Years of Upheaval*, 477. For the message itself, see Memcon, "Subject: Middle East Situation," October 7, 1973, in *FRUS, 1969–1976*, vol. 25, 340–41.

31. Amir Oren, "Kissinger Wants Israel to Know: The U.S. Saved You During the 1973 War," *Haaretz*, November 2, 2013.

32. Minutes of the Secretary of State's Staff Meeting, October 10, 1973, in *FRUS, 1969–1976*, vol. 25, 428.

33. Minutes of a Washington Special Actions Group (WSAG) Meeting, "Subject: Middle East," January 14, 1975, in *FRUS, 1969–1976*, vol. 26, *Arab-Israeli Dispute, 1974–1976* (Washington, DC: GPO, 2012), 483.

34. See Message from Meir to Kissinger, undated, in *FRUS, 1969–1976*, vol. 25, 284–85; Memorandum (Memo) from Quandt to Deputy National Security Adviser Brent Scowcroft, "Subject: Arab-Israel Tensions," October 6, 1973, in *FRUS, 1969–1976*, vol. 25, 287.

35. Telcon, October 6, 1973, 8:35 a.m., in Kissinger, *Crisis*, 27. For facsimiles of the original, see DOSKTC and Kissinger Telephone Conversations Collection (KA) 10992, DNSA. Kissinger's reaction was not as idiosyncratic as one might think. At the first meeting of the high-level WSAG held, in Kissinger's absence, after the war broke out, a couple of people, including Schlesinger, assumed that "the Israelis had jumped the gun and had started the fighting." It took a while before anyone at the meeting took issue with that assessment. See Ambassador Alfred Leroy Atherton, Jr., Oral History Interview, Summer 1990, by Dayton Mak, Association for Diplomatic Studies and Training Foreign Affairs Oral History Project, https://www.adst.org/OH%20TOCs/Atherton,%20Jr.,%20Alfred%20Leroy.toc.pdf, 150. The record of the WSAG meeting supports that view. See Minutes of a WSAG Meeting, "Subject: Middle East," October 6, 1973, in *FRUS, 1969–1976*, vol. 25, 295–96. Note also Kissinger's discussion of that initial WSAG view in his interview with James Hoge, 12:40.

36. Telcon, October 6, 1973, 6:55 a.m., in Kissinger, *Crisis*, 18. For facsimiles of the original, see DOSKTC and KA10980, DNSA.

37. Kissinger to Nixon, October 6, 1973, 8:50 a.m. (for delivery at 9:00 a.m.), NSAEBB98, doc. 10.

38. Minutes of a WSAG Meeting, October 6, 1973, in *FRUS, 1969–1976*, vol. 25, 331.

39. Quandt, *Peace Process*, 151. Quandt served under Kissinger at the National Security Council (NSC) from 1972 to 1974.

40. See Jeremy Pressman, *Warring Friends: Alliance Restraint in International Politics* (Ithaca, NY: Cornell University Press, 2008), 100–4.

41. Kissinger-Dinitz meeting, October 7, 1973, 8:20 p.m., NSAEBB98, doc. 18. Israeli documents released in 2014 confirm the point about how important the American attitude was in Israel's deliberations at this time. The new Israeli material was summarized in the Israel State Archive's blog entry for October 6, 2014, "From Low Probability to the Yom Kippur War: Telegrams from Golda's Bureau to the Israeli Embassy in Washington, 5–7 October 1973," http://israelsdocuments.blogspot.com/2014/10/despite-minor-successesthe-situation-is.html.

42. Henry Kissinger, *White House Years* (Boston: Little, Brown, 1979), 1,288 (emphasis in original text).

43. Conversation between Nixon and Kissinger, September 30, 1971, in *FRUS, 1969–1976*, vol. 13, *Soviet Union, October 1970–October 1971* (Washington, DC: GPO, 2011), 1,060; Telcon, October 1, 1971, in *FRUS, 1969–1976*, vol. 13, 1,079.

44. Editorial Note, in *FRUS, 1969–1976*, vol. 14, *Soviet Union, October 1971–May 1972* (Washington, DC: GPO, 2006), 214.

45. This is a major theme in Jackson, *A Lost Peace*.

46. Conversation between Nixon and Gromyko, September 29, 1971, in *FRUS, 1969–1976*, vol. 13, 1,051–55. One can also listen to the tape of this meeting (Tape 580-20) on Luke Nichter's nixontapes.org website; the section of interest begins at 39:50 on this mp3 and goes on for about five minutes. See also Memcon, September 30, 1971, in *FRUS, 1969–1976*, vol. 13, 1,072.

47. Memo from Kissinger to Nixon, "Subject: The Middle East," June 16, 1970, in *FRUS, 1969–1976*, vol. 23, *Arab-Israeli Dispute, 1969–1972* (Washington, DC: GPO, 2015), 441.

48. Nixon's Address before the 24th Session of the General Assembly of the United Nations, September 18, 1969, APP, http://www.presidency.ucsb.edu/ws/index.php?pid=2236; Memo from Harold Saunders of the NSC Staff to Kissinger, "Subject: Soviet Response to Middle East Initiative," July 2, 1970, in *FRUS, 1969–1976*, vol. 12, *Soviet Union, January 1969–October 1970* (Washington, DC: GPO, 2006), 542; Memo for the President's File, September 29, 1971, in *FRUS, 1969–1976*, vol. 13, 1040n8; Editorial Note, in *FRUS, 1969–1976*, vol. 14, 214; Memcon, "Subject: Basic Principles (briefly at beginning); Middle East," May 28, 1972, in *FRUS, 1969–1976*, vol. 14, 1,191–93, 1,195; Memcon, "Subject: Communiqué; Middle East," May 28, 1972, in *FRUS, 1969–1976*, vol. 14, 1,203, 1,211–12. See also Memcon, "Subject: Middle East; Indochina," May 8, 1973, in *FRUS, 1969–1976*, vol. 15, *Soviet Union, June 1972–August 1974* (Washington, DC: GPO, 2011), 437; Memcon, June 23, 1973, in *FRUS, 1969–1976*, vol. 25, 216; Memcon, March 1, 1972, in United States Department of State, *Soviet-American Relations: The Détente Years, 1969–1972* (Washington, DC: GPO, 2007), 601; Memcon, May 20, 1973, KT00732, DNSA, 22; Jackson, *A Lost Peace*, 54–57.

49. Memo from Kissinger to Nixon, "Subject: Memorandum of Conversation with Ambassador Dobrynin, June 11, 1969," June 13, 1969, in *FRUS, 1969–1976*, vol. 12, 179; Memo for the President's File, September 29, 1971, 1,041; Memcon, March 1,

1972, in *FRUS, 1969–1976*, vol. 14, 188; Minutes of an NSC meeting, April 25, 1969, in *FRUS, 1969–1976*, vol. 23, 90.

50. Memo for the President's File by Kissinger, "Subject: President's Meeting with General Secretary Leonid Brezhnev on Saturday, June 23, 1973 at 10:30 p.m. at the Western White House, San Clemente, California," June 23, 1973, in *FRUS, 1969–1976*, vol. 15, 539. See also Message from Dobrynin to Kissinger, undated, in *FRUS, 1969–1976*, vol. 25, 21.

51. On the refugee question, see Memcon, May 28, 1972, 1,189; Memcon, June 23, 1973, in *FRUS, 1969–1976*, vol. 25, 213. As Dobrynin pointed out in that latter meeting, the two sides had reached agreement on this issue in July 1969. On Sharm el-Sheikh, see, for example, Memcon, March 10, 1970, in *Soviet-American Relations*, 134; Memcon, May 18, 1972, in *FRUS, 1969–1976*, vol. 14, 941. On the Golan Heights, see Memcon, April 14, 1969, in *Soviet-American Relations*, 51. On direct talks, see, for example, Memcon, May 28, 1972, 1,206.

52. Memcon, October 15, 1971, in *FRUS, 1969–1976*, vol. 14, 14–15.

53. Memcon, October 30, 1971, in *FRUS, 1969–1976*, vol. 14, 26.

54. Kissinger, *White House Years*, 1,288.

55. For the comment, see Kissinger, *White House Years*, 1,288.

56. Memcon, September 30, 1971, in *FRUS, 1969–1976*, vol. 13, 1,073–74.

57. Memcon, October 30, 1971, 26.

58. Memcon, "Subject: Basic Principles; Middle East; Economic Relations; Announcement of Kissinger Visit," April 23, 1972, in *FRUS, 1969–1976*, vol. 14, 578.

59. Memcon, September 30, 1971, 1,072.

60. Kissinger, *Years of Upheaval*, 215–16 (emphasis in original text).

61. Editorial Note, in *FRUS, 1969–1976*, vol. 25, 85. Note also Kissinger's characterization of the Egyptian proposal in his meeting with the Israeli ambassador, Yitzhak Rabin, the next day. See Memcon, February 27, 1973, in *FRUS, 1969–1976*, vol. 25, 97. On this episode in general, and especially for the point that Kissinger thought the proposals Ismail presented marked an important step forward, see Yigal Kipnis, *1973: The Road to War* (Charlottesville, VA: Just World, 2013), chap. 2, especially 72, 77, as well as Kipnis's chapter in this volume.

62. Memcon, February 25, 1973, KT00681, DNSA, 20. In his talks with the Israelis, Kissinger in fact exaggerated the degree to which the Egyptians were thinking in terms of a separate peace with Israel. The basic point here is also supported by the Israeli sources. "This time it is completely clear," he later told the Israeli ambassador. "The Egyptians are only concerned about themselves and do not tie an agreement with them to the other Arab countries." Quoted in Kipnis, *1973*, 68.

63. Memcon, February 26, 1973, KT00682, DNSA, 8, 11, and especially 22–23. Ismail, in fact, wanted to bring the Israelis in relatively quickly. "But we leave it to your feel," he told Kissinger, "as to the appropriate time—the development of these talks, the atmosphere. Because we won't want to leave the Israeli participation hanging on for a long time. I think that we would like them to come in and start to be in the picture as soon as it is practicable." There were no preconditions mentioned here. See Memcon, February 26, 1973, 4.

64. Memcon, February 26, 1973, 7.

65. Ibid., 14–15, 36.

66. Dr. Muhammad Ghanim, another high Egyptian official who took part in the talks, was quite explicit in this regard. "We feel the basic obstacle to an Egyptian settlement," he said, "is to find how to compromise, how to reconcile the needs of the security of Israel with our sovereignty over Arab land." See Memcon, February 25, 1973, 20. With regard to the rest of the settlement, the Egyptians were clearly open to compromise. As Ismail himself put it: "Well, as long as we put the question of land and sovereignty aside, I think we might be able to achieve some kind of reconciliation on the other elements." See Memcon, February 26, 1973, 32. He reiterated the point in informal conversations with another US official a little later. "The key to a compromise," Ismail said, was "the principle of Egyptian sovereignty in the Sinai." Sovereignty, he said, was "solid enough for them to defend to their own people yet flexible enough to accommodate practical arrangements that may be necessary." "If basic principles were agreed upon," he added, "he was confident that some acceptable formula could be found for the practical arrangements." Roundup of Ismail Comments Made after Kissinger's Talks with Him at Dinner on February 26 and at the Airport on February 27, Henry A. Kissinger Office Files (HAKOFF), Box 135, Folder "Rabin/Kissinger (Dinitz)," [3 of 3], Richard M. Nixon Presidential Library (RMNL), Yorba Linda, California.

67. Memcon, February 26, 1973, 35–37. In a letter to Ismail sent about four months later, Kissinger referred to the procedure Ismail had outlined in February and noted that he had "agreed that this could be a reasonable way to proceed." Kissinger to Ismail (the recipient's name was sanitized out, but it is obvious from the content of the letter and from the withdrawal sheet at the top of the file that Ismail was the addressee), undated (but almost certainly from late June 1973), HAKOFF, Box 130, Folder "Saunders Memoranda—Sensitive, Egypt/Hafez Ismail," RMNL. The fact that this was sent through Central Intelligence Agency (CIA) channels is also clear from the withdrawal sheet. But by the time this letter was sent, it was clear to everyone that the plan could not be put into effect. The US government would have had to put a certain degree of pressure on Israel, and with the Watergate affair coming to a head, Nixon was no longer able to take action of that sort.

68. This is also the conclusion to be drawn from Kipnis's discussion of this episode in *1973*, 64–72.

69. For the argument that Kissinger still sought to limit the Israeli victory, see, for example, Sheehan, *Arabs, Israelis, and Kissinger*, 36. It is important to realize, however, that Kissinger's attitude on this issue had shifted dramatically in the course of the war. In its first phase, his position had been very different, much more in line with what Sheehan and many others have claimed.

70. Memcon, "Subject: Meeting with Jewish Leaders (Philip Klutznik Group)," June 15, 1975, in *FRUS, 1969–1976*, vol. 26, 712.

71. Memcon, October 19, 1973, in *FRUS, 1969–1976*, vol. 25, 622; Memcon, June 15, 1975, 712. See also Kissinger, *Years of Upheaval*, 542. Kissinger was also very irritated by the fact that Nixon had told Brezhnev, just before Kissinger arrived in Moscow, that Kissinger had "full authority" to reach a ceasefire agreement with the Soviets, which, he later wrote, deprived him of "any capacity to stall." See Message

from Nixon to Brezhnev, October 20, 1973, in *FRUS, 1969–1976*, vol. 25, 626; Kissinger, *Years of Upheaval*, 546–47. Note also his discussion of this episode in his 2003 book talk with James Hoge, 19:30 to 20:20. "I wanted to drag out this negotiation" over the ceasefire, he told Hoge, "in order to strengthen our bargaining position" (19:07). He took much the same line in the PBS documentary *The 50 Years War: Israel and the Arabs* (1999), part 2, 22:45 to 23:30.

72. See Memcon, October 22, 1973, in *FRUS, 1969–1976*, vol. 25, 652n3.

73. Kissinger, *Years of Upheaval*, 556–58, 569. Note also Memcon, October 21, 1973, *FRUS, 1969–1976*, vol. 25, 647n2; Memcon, October 22, 1973, *FRUS, 1969–1976*, vol. 25, 657.

74. Kissinger, *Years of Upheaval*, 569.

75. Memcon, October 22, 1973, 658. See also the Israeli account (in English) of a later meeting with Meir and others, October 22, 1973, 3:00 p.m., https://www.archives.gov.il/product-page/2410453.

76. We should also note that Kissinger did not, as is sometimes suggested, impulsively give the Israelis these assurances during his stopover in Israel in order to soothe their ruffled feathers (about being presented with the ceasefire resolution as a great power fait accompli). The message about how the Israelis could have a little extra time to comply with the ceasefire (because of the communications breakdown) had, in fact, already been given to them the previous evening. See Kissinger to Scowcroft, October 21, 1973 (4:05 p.m. Washington time), and Scowcroft to Kissinger, October 21 (8:42 p.m. Washington time), both in HAKOFF, Box 39, Folder "HAK Trip: HAKTO, etc." [3 of 4], RMNL. An extract from the Kissinger cable is in *FRUS, 1969–1976*, 647n2.

77. Matti Golan, *The Secret Conversations of Henry Kissinger: Step-by-Step Diplomacy in the Middle East* (New York: Quadrangle, 1976), 86–87. The Kissinger comment was not quoted in the US record of the meeting. See Memcon, "Military Briefing," October 22, 1973, 4:15 p.m., in NSAEBB98, doc. 56. It is possible, of course, that the remark Golan quoted had been an "off the record" comment. And one US source does provide a certain degree of support for Golan's account. Helmut Sonnenfeldt, who was part of the small group Kissinger took with him on the trip, said flatly that Kissinger told Meir that "you have another 48 hours, and then you've got to stop beating up on the Egyptians, because it'll get us into serious problems with the Soviets if you encircle the Egyptian Third Army and destroy it." But Sonnenfeldt had been less categorical earlier in the interview. "I think Henry," he said, "might also have winked a little bit at [Meir] and indicated that she had just a couple of days, maybe, for Israeli forces to continue, but then they'd have to stop," and he went on to note that he had not been at the Kissinger-Meir meeting. What this suggests is that Sonnenfeldt was probably just speculating about what Kissinger had told the Israeli prime minister, and that his testimony on this point is therefore of only limited historical value. See Helmut Sonnenfeldt Oral History Interview, July 24, 2000, by Charles Stuart Kennedy, Association for Diplomatic Studies and Training Foreign Affairs Oral History Project, https://adst.org/OH%20TOCs/Sonnenfeldt,%20Helmut.toc.pdf, 127, 198–99. It is also worth noting that the recently released Israeli account of this meeting refers to the two-to-three-day period, but does not have Kissinger making the sort

of comment Golan had attributed to him. See Kissinger Meeting with Israeli Military Leaders (with Meir and others present), October 22, 1973, 4:15 p.m., https://www.archives.gov.il/product-page/2410427.

78. Golan had claimed, for example, that Kissinger, prior to his trip to Moscow, had assured the Israelis—who very much wanted to continue their military offensive—that they "had nothing to fear," that "he didn't believe that any agreement would be achieved in Moscow," and that "no big news would come from the meeting in the Kremlin." See Golan, *Secret Conversations*, 75–76. But it had in fact been clear to the Israelis from the outset that the purpose of Kissinger's Moscow trip was to arrange a ceasefire, and Kissinger had by no means promised the Israelis that no ceasefire agreement would be negotiated in Moscow. See Telcon, October 19, 1973, 7:09 and 7:40 p.m., in *FRUS, 1969–1976*, vol. 25, 619–21; DOSKTC. See also Shalev to Gazit, October 18 and 19, 1973, in *Telegrams Sent from the Israeli Embassy in Washington to the Prime Minister's Office during the Yom Kippur War, 5–31 October 1973* [frames 202 and 222]. This collection was posted on the Israel State Archives webpage on the Yom Kippur War, and will henceforth be cited as *Israeli Telegrams*. The URLs are given in the appendix. Kissinger, one should note, dismissed the Golan book as worthless when it came out. When asked for comment, a State Department spokesman said that Kissinger had neither read nor intended to read the book in its entirety, but on the basis of the excerpts he had seen, he considered it "by and large a collection of lies, distortions, and material so taken out of context as to amount to lies." See Bernard Gwertzman, "Israeli Book Gives a Critical View of Kissinger," *New York Times*, March 21, 1976. Quandt's assessment was more judicious. While Golan was "often quite accurate" and provided "new information of real value," he wrote in a review, the book was full of minor errors. One also had to wonder about how solid Golan's account was, since the material it was based on had been confiscated by the Israeli censors before this version of the book was written. See Quandt Review of Golan and Sheehan Books, *Middle East Journal* 31, no. 2 (Spring 1977): 218–19.

79. Telcon, October 23, 1973, in *FRUS 1969–1976*, vol. 25, 683–84. For the Israeli account of the conversation, see *Dinitz to Gazit, October 23, 1973, 1:10 p.m. (reporting on 12:05 p.m. conversation with Kissinger), in *Israeli Telegrams* [frames 276–77]. According to that account, when Dinitz said that there was no way of knowing where the ceasefire line was, Kissinger replied, "If so, and there's no way of knowing, what do you care if a resolution is passed calling for a return to the lines that existed when the ceasefire went into effect?"

80. Memcon, October 22, 1973, in *FRUS 1969–1976*, vol. 25, 663.

81. *Dinitz to Gazit, October 23, 1973, 6:00 p.m. (reporting 3:00 p.m. meeting), *Israeli Telegrams* [frames 281–82]. See also *Shalev to Gazit, October 23, 1973, 6:30 p.m., *Israeli Telegrams* [frames 283–86]. For Nixon's insistence that the offensive cease, see *Dinitz to Gazit, October 23, 1973, 1:15 p.m. (reporting Dinitz's 12:40 p.m. conversation with Scowcroft), *Israeli Telegrams* [frames 277–78].

82. Kissinger-Dinitz telephone conversations, October 23, 1973 (7:20 p.m. and 8:30 p.m.), DOSKTC. For the Israeli account, see *Dinitz to Meir, October 23, 1973 (no time given), *Israeli Telegrams* [frames 291–92]. See also Kissinger, *Crisis*,

322–23 (which did not include the latter part of the transcript of the first of those calls, where Kissinger complained about the Israelis having too much integrity). Another Israeli account of Dinitz's report of his 3:15 p.m. (Washington time) meeting with Kissinger also shows Kissinger pressing the Israelis to accept the new ceasefire and then just pull back 200 to 300 yards. See *Shalev to Gazit, October 23, 1973, 6:30 p.m., *Israeli Telegrams* [frames 283–86]. Note also Memcon, November 1, 1973, in *FRUS, 1969–1976*, vol. 25, 816, for another Kissinger complaint about Israel being too honest. For the point about how his strategy was no longer viable, see Telcon, October 24, 1973, in *FRUS, 1969–1976*, vol. 25, 705. For the point about how the Israelis should have kept their mouths shut, see Minutes of a WSAG Meeting, "Subject: Middle East," October 24, 1973, in *FRUS, 1969–1976*, vol. 25, 711. But even a week later, Kissinger had not totally given up on this strategy, though he now recognized that it might be harder to implement than he had hoped: "Unfortunately the Russians photographed something." See Memcon, November 1, 1973, 815–16. Finally, with regard to the point that the Egyptian violations, which were real enough, were essentially being used by the Israelis as an excuse for continuing with their own offensive, it should be noted that US intelligence at the time seemed to think this was the case. According to the October 23 President's Daily Brief, for example, while "some Egyptian units" had been ordered "to continue combat operations despite the cease-fire," it was not clear "that Egypt 'incessantly and continuously' violated the agreement, as Israel claims." The Israelis, the authors speculated, "may have required little in the way of Egyptian provocation before deciding to press their military advantage." See President's Daily Brief, October 23, 1973, CIA Electronic Reading Room. It was, in fact, quite clear to CIA analysts on October 24 that the Israelis had not been particularly interested in ending the fighting. "The concerted Israeli effort to capture Suez and cut off the Egyptian 3rd Army in the two days since the original cease-fire deadline," they thought, "casts considerable doubt on Tel Aviv's claims that Egypt bears full responsibility for the cease-fire violations." Even on the morning of October 23, it had been clear to the Americans that on the southern part of the Egyptian front Israeli forces had been "ordered to continue fighting"—and not just to fend off Egyptian attacks. Their goal, as the Israelis themselves had made clear, "was to cut off Egyptian forces on the east bank" of the Suez Canal. CIA, Middle East Situation Reports Numbers 71 and 77, October 23 (11:30 a.m.) and October 24 (10:30 p.m.), 1973, in CIA Electronic Reading Room. Both documents are in the CIA collection "President Nixon and the Role of Intelligence in the 1973 Arab-Israeli War," which was released in 2013. Note also Schlesinger's comments in a high-level meeting held the morning after the Brezhnev threat was received. "There are indications," he said, "that the Israelis may have been diddling us yesterday as to who was doing what." They had claimed that "there were flights of Egyptian aircraft designed to coincide with an attempted Egyptian breakout to the east." But it now looked "like the Israelis might have been the ones who were moving, with their aircraft providing cover, and the Egyptians came out to meet them." This, he said, "would support what the Russians were saying to us yesterday about Israel's activities." See Minutes of a Washington Special Actions Group Meeting, October 25, 1973, 10:16 a.m., 2, CIA Electronic Reading Room. Chairman of the Joint Chiefs of Staff Thomas Moorer also felt that the Soviets were justified in blaming the Israelis for violating the ceasefire. See CJCS Memo M-88–73 for the Record, "Subject: NSC/JCS Meeting, Wednesday/Thursday 24/25 October 1973, 2230–0330 (U)," October 24–25, 1973, in *FRUS, 1969–1976*, vol. 25, 739.

83. Memcon, October 24, 1973, in *FRUS, 1969–1976*, vol. 25, 722–23.

84. See especially the record of the meeting at which the decision to order the US military alert was made: CJCS Memo M-88–73 for the Record, October 24–25, 1973, 738–39. The indicators are discussed in most of the scholarly works dealing with the crisis. See, for example, William Quandt, "Soviet Policy in the October Middle East War-II," *International Affairs* 53, no. 4 (October 1977): 596–97; Barry Blechman and Douglas Hart, "The Political Utility of Nuclear Weapons: The 1973 Middle East Crisis," *International Security* 7, no. 1 (Summer 1982): 136–38. On Soviet naval activities at this point, see Lyle Goldstein and Yuri Zhukov, "A Tale of Two Fleets—A Russian Perspective on the 1973 Naval Standoff in the Mediterranean," *Naval War College Review* 57, no. 2 (Spring 2004): 51–52. We now know, incidentally, that the Soviets never intended to push things to the point of a full-scale confrontation with the United States and that the military steps they had taken were essentially for political effect. See Golan, "Soviet Union and October War," especially 112–13; Anatoly Dobrynin, *In Confidence: Moscow's Ambassador to Six Cold War Presidents, 1962–1986* (Seattle: University of Washington Press, 1995), 296; Israelyan, *Inside the Kremlin*, 97, 148, 168, 173, 180–81, 190, 193; Jackson, *A Lost Peace*, 110–16.

85. Telcon, October 24, 1973, in *FRUS, 1969–1976*, vol. 25, 705; Telcon, October 24, 1973, 706. Nixon also had his chief of staff call Dinitz and threaten "drastic action, disassociating self from Israelis" if the Israelis did not stop. And the Israeli ambassador did report that as of 10:38 a.m. Washington time "firing has ceased." The president, Dinitz was told, was "thankful and relieved," although he was probably not sure that this information was to be believed, because the "strong warning [was] reiterated." But Dinitz again assured the Americans that the Israelis had instructed their forces to "do nothing but block and contain Egyptian forces." See Handwritten Note for Scowcroft and "Ambassador Dinitz Situation Report (as dictated by Larry Eagleburger)," October 24, 1973, both in HAKOFF, Box 136, Folder "Dinitz: June 4–October 31, 1973," RMNL. It is, however, not clear whether this US pressure played a decisive part in getting the Israelis to halt their military operations, since they certainly had their own reasons for doing so. See Talia Winokur, "'The Soviets Were Just an Excuse': Why Israel Did Not Destroy the Egyptian Third Army," *Cold War History* 9, no. 1 (2009): 59–78. But the fact that the Americans put great pressure on Israel at this time (and not before) is clear from other sources. Note, for example, Kissinger's remarks in Minutes of a WSAG Meeting, October 24, 714: "We were very tough with the Israelis this morning. We told them this had to stop." For the Israeli account of Nixon's strong warning, see *Dinitz to Gazit, October 24, 1973, 2:00 p.m. (reporting 10:35 a.m. meeting), *Israeli Telegrams* [frames 292–93] (in English). As for the timing, Kissinger later suggested that the Americans all along had wanted to uphold the ceasefire and were spurred into action the previous morning, when he was told that a Brezhnev note had arrived complaining about the Israeli offensive and proposing a new Security Council meeting to deal with the problem. "The urgency

of Brezhnev's appeal," Kissinger wrote, "suggested that the plight of the Egyptian Third Army was far more serious than our own intelligence had yet discovered or the Israelis had told us." The destruction of that army, after the great powers had arranged a ceasefire, was intolerable. Consequently, he then "urgently contacted" Ambassador Dinitz, presumably to make that US position clear. See Kissinger, *Crisis*, 307–8. But the phone conversation with Dinitz, which Kissinger alludes to in this context, was all about how to handle the proposed Security Council resolution—there was not the slightest hint that the Israelis needed to halt their offensive. See Kissinger-Dinitz Telcon, October 23, 1973, 11:04 a.m., DOSKTC.

86. Message from Brezhnev to Nixon, October 24, 1973, 734–35.

87. CJCS Memo M-88–73 for the Record, October 24–25, 1973, 741.

88. Memcon, November 2, 1973, in *FRUS, 1969–1976*, vol. 25, 860–61. On the Soviet belief that they had been deceived, see the sources cited in Galen Jackson, "The Lost Peace: Great Power Politics and the Arab-Israeli Problem, 1967–1979," PhD dissertation, UCLA, 2016, 216n144. Note also Kissinger's comment in a phone conversation with Haig on the evening of October 24 that the Soviets "realize they were taken." The fact that he said "realize," rather than "believe" or "suspect," shows that in Kissinger's view, the Soviets were justified in feeling they had not been dealt with honestly. See Kissinger-Haig Telcon, October 24, 1973, 7:50 p.m., DOSKTC; also in Kissinger, *Crisis*, 340.

89. Kissinger-Dinitz phone conversation, October 24, 1973 (10:00 p.m.), DOSKTC. Kissinger made much the same point in a more indirect way in a meeting the next morning with other top US officials. "The great lesson to be learned from this," he said, "is that when you have a victory, don't turn the screw one time too many." Washington Special Actions Group meeting, October 25, 1973, 10:16 a.m., 3, CIA Electronic Reading Room.

90. Kissinger, in fact, later referred to the alert as a "deliberate overreaction." See Sheehan, *Arabs, Israelis, and Kissinger*, 38; Stein, *Heroic Diplomacy*, 94–95 (quoting from an interview Stein had conducted with Kissinger's assistant, Peter Rodman, in 1992).

91. Memcon, March 31, 1975, in *FRUS, 1969–1976*, vol. 26, 604.

92. CJCS Memo M-88–73 for the Record, October 24–25, 1973, 741.

93. Minutes of a WSAG Meeting, "Subject: Middle East," October 15, 1973, in *FRUS, 1969–1976*, vol. 25, 531.

94. Memcon, June 15, 1975, 712.

95. For the point about Israel's dependence on the United States, see Minutes of the Secretary of State's Staff Meeting, October 23, 1973, in *FRUS, 1969–1976*, vol. 25, 697; Memcon, October 24, 1973, in *FRUS, 1969–1976*, vol. 25, 724. For the point about the United States being in the key position, see Secretary of State's Staff Meeting, October 23, 1973, 697; Minutes of a WSAG Meeting, October 24, 1973, 714; Minutes of a WSAG Meeting, "Subject: Middle East; Vietnam and Cambodia," November 2, 1973, in *FRUS, 1969–1976*, vol. 25, 841.

96. Kissinger Meeting with Clements, Moorer, and Scowcroft, October 24, 1963, CIA Electronic Reading Room.

97. Memcon, October 19, 1973, 622; Memcon, November 2, 1973, in *FRUS, 1969–1976*, vol. 25, 863. See also Jackson, "Lost Peace," 268.

98. George Kennan, *American Diplomacy, 1900–1950* (Chicago: University of Chicago Press, 1951), especially 66, 72–73.

99. Kissinger, *Years of Upheaval*, 551. That claim was repeated many times in that book—and in many of Kissinger's other books as well—but in reality Soviet policy was much more reasonable than Kissinger made out. This is one of the basic themes in Jackson, *A Lost Peace*.

100. For a good summary of the evidence on the Soviet reaction, see Lebow and Stein, *We All Lost*, 243–44. See also Dobrynin, *In Confidence*, 295, 297, 299–301.

Chapter 4

Syria and the 1973 Arab-Israeli War

Raymond Hinnebusch

This chapter examines Syria's role in the October 1973 Arab-Israeli War. It first explores the causes of the war and of Syria's involvement in it by sketching the historical and regional context of the conflict; the domestic origins of the irredentism that drove Syrian behavior; the structural precipitant, namely, the outcome of the June 1967 war; and the calculations and motives of the Arab leaders, particularly Hafiz al-Asad of Syria, who launched the war. It then examines the conduct of the war, including its planning and execution, and the outcome—a shift in the military balance that provoked diplomatic intervention by the United States. Finally, the consequences of the war are sketched. It analyzes why the war led not, as it might have, to a regional peace but instead to a continuing chain of new wars, and shows how the intractable conflict with Israel helped consolidate a national security state in Syria.

THE HISTORICAL CONTEXT OF THE 1973 WAR

A War-Prone States System

The post–World War I "peace to end all peace," as David Fromkin calls it, imposed a states system on the Middle East and North Africa (MENA) region that was structurally prone to war.[1] The area suffered from multiple territorial conflicts and pervasive irredentism, caused by an incongruence between identities and arbitrarily drawn boundaries, which resulted in what Benjamin Miller calls a nation-state imbalance.[2] The most egregious source of instability was the Arab-Israeli dispute. The Zionist project meant that there were two peoples claiming the same land, and conflict between incoming Jewish settlers and the Palestinian community was inevitable.[3]

The first Arab-Israeli war of 1948–1949 transformed this substate, communal dispute into an intractable interstate conflict. Championing the Palestinian cause became an indispensable nationalist credential for aspiring Arab political leaders. For Israel, the war left it without defensible borders, while a portion of what it considered biblical Israel (the West Bank) remained in Arab hands. Continual disputes between Israel and the Arab states over poorly demarcated borders, demilitarized zones, and water rights regularly escalated into military clashes, inflaming and spreading pan-Arab nationalism, which preached the idea of a common Arab nation united against Israel and its Western backers.

The Arab-Israeli conflict made MENA the world's most war-prone region, giving rise to an exceptional number of unstable states that produced an acute security dilemma. The dominant regime type, the military-led authoritarian nationalist republics, of which Syria's Ba'athist regime was typical, legitimized their rule through social reform and Arab nationalism, and the latter required they be seen as trying to deliver on the Arab nationalist agenda. This ultimately led to their involvement in seventeen of the region's nineteen wars that occurred from 1946 to 2010.[4] Despite being a democracy, Israel also was at the center of eight regional wars (counting its assaults on Gaza), three of which were arguably wars of choice (1956, 1967, and 1982). Israel initiated twenty-five of forty-five militarized disputes in MENA, the world's highest frequency of such initiations relative to its period in existence.[5] Arguably, this was due to Israel's special character as an irredentist settler state that was both insecure and expansionist at the same time.

However, war-proneness only translates into war if the power balance incentivizes states to go to war. MENA was particularly susceptible to swings in the power balance because of what the "power transition" school considers to be the most dangerous type of situation, namely when there exists a rising second-rank power with revisionist aims that is approaching the power capabilities of a superior power.[6] In these cases, the latter may try to prevent its eclipse via war, or the former may (mis)calculate that its best chance to change the balance of power has arrived. Thus, Douglas Lemke found that the combination of dissatisfaction and near-power parity increased the chance of war in MENA by 76 percent.[7]

While multiple systemic ingredients for war obtain in MENA, understanding its war-proneness still requires that we look at the agency of state actors and their motivations. In this chapter, the focus is on Syria. But because the war was shaped by its interactions with other key actors—namely, Egypt, Israel, and the United States—these players will also be examined.

The Domestic Origins of Syrian Irredentism: History, Territory, and Identity

Syria's foreign policy was given an enduring revisionist and irredentist thrust by the Western imposition of the Middle East state system and the accompanying frustration of its emerging Arab national identity after World War I. Arab nationalism was a natural reaction to the postwar dismemberment and colonial rule of the country and to the creation of the state of Israel in Palestine, historically part of southern Syria. The truncated state left after the separation of Palestine, Lebanon, and Jordan from Syria was regarded by Syrians as an artificial creation, with identities tending, as a result, to focus on trans-state or supra-state "imagined communities."[8] While pan-Arab nationalism was the dominant identity, the country's dismemberment also fostered an irredentist pan-Syrian nationalism, one that was dissatisfied with the fragmentation of historic, geographical Syria and that had by the 1970s merged with pan-Arabism. The frustration of Syria's identity ushered in an Arab nationalist foreign policy that survived countless changes in leadership.

The historic rejection of the legitimacy of Israel is also deeply rooted in Syrian political culture. Israel, the military superpower of the region, was Syria's main threat and its chief enemy, as manifested in chronic border conflicts. Importantly, Syria's identity locked it into the Arab-Israeli conflict far more deeply than its putative ally, Egypt. Since Egypt had a robust Egyptian nationalism independent of Arab nationalism, Egyptian leaders could accept Israel, even strike a separate peace with it, without suffering fatal legitimacy losses. By contrast, the dominance in Syria of an Arab national identity and the weakness of a separate Syrian identity meant regime legitimacy was contingent on being seen as promoting the Palestinian cause and defending Arab national security against Israel. This sharply constrained the options available to Syrian leaders in any diplomatic dealings with or over Israel.[9]

State Weakness and "Accidental" War

For the first quarter century of its independent existence, weak, unstable Syria was a prize over which stronger states fought. The newly independent state's effort to consolidate public loyalties was compromised when the precarious legitimacy won in the independence struggle was shattered by the loss of Palestine, unleashing two decades of instability in which external forces frequently intervened. Syria was seen as the pivotal state whose choices could decisively affect the balance of power across the region, thus incentivizing intervention by competing rival powers. Domestic instability coincided with perceptions of a rising threat from Israel, stimulated by border skirmishes over the demilitarized zones established between the states at the end of the first Arab-Israeli war. Syria could not do without protective alignments. Hence, in 1958 a sense of external siege and internal polarization, plus widespread pan-Arab sentiment, swept Syrian elites into embracing a brief union with Egypt, the United Arab Republic. The association, however, was soon perceived as Egyptian domination, and was broken up in 1961.[10]

But the ongoing conflict with Israel deepened and intensified Syria's Arab nationalism, a key factor in the rise of the Ba'ath Party to power. The military coup that brought the Ba'ath to power in 1963 ushered in a new era of instability, with dire consequences for Syria. The Ba'ath regime had a narrow support base, owing to its conflicts with the landed oligarchs it overthrew and its Nasserite and Muslim Brother rivals. The regime was also internally split between the party patriarch, Michel Aflaq—who prioritized pan-Arab unionism—and younger radicals, who were more interested in a social revolution in Syria. Ideological and personal rivalries, moreover, were exacerbated by sectarian divisions between Sunni officers and politicos and those of minority sectarian background that had long been disproportionately represented in the party and army. As, in this and subsequent struggles, minority Alawis increasingly won out, thereby disaffecting Syria's Sunni majority, the regime was put under pressure to prove its Arab nationalist credentials.

By the late 1960s, Syria's Arab nationalism was focused on the struggle for Palestine. After the radical minority-dominated faction of the party seized precarious power in a 1966 coup, the regime, driven by ideological militancy and a search for legitimacy, proclaimed a war to liberate Palestine and supported Palestinian fedayeen raids into Israel. This policy, ignoring the unfavorable balance of power with Israel, ended in Syria's 1967 defeat and the Israeli occupation of Syria's Golan Heights.[11] Thus, state weakness and internal conflict led Syria into a disastrous, almost accidental, war.

The 1967 Arab-Israeli War and the Reshaping of Syrian Foreign Policy

Syria was totally unprepared for Israel's 1967 blitzkrieg. After Israel's first strike destroyed its air force on the ground, the Syrian front remained passive, with the army incapable of mobile warfare. When Israel assaulted the Golan Heights, the Syrian army fought back but, lacking air cover, retreated to defend the capital. This became a rout after Damascus radio prematurely broadcast that Quneitra had fallen. Israel sacked Quneitra, expelled 90,000 Syrians, and established military settlements in their place. Quneitra became symbolic of Syria's defeat and of the regime's disgrace. The public blamed the political leadership for recklessly provoking a war and criticized it for prioritizing regime survival over defense of the front by keeping its best units back to defend Damascus. The debacle cost the regime whatever legitimacy it may have had.

Under these pressures, the regime split between the core radical leadership and an alternative faction led by the defense minister, General Hafiz al-Asad. There were mutual recriminations over the disaster, and some tried to have Asad sacked, a threat which spurred him to seek sole authority over the government. The two sides also had incompatible goals and strategies for dealing with the consequences of the war. The radicals insisted on the continued promotion of the Palestinian fedayeen as instruments of a war of liberation, on the model of Vietnam or Algeria. Asad deemed this approach delusional, believing it would only provoke more Israeli attacks, against which Syria was unprepared to defend itself. Asad wanted the guerrillas subordinated to the Syrian military command to ensure they would be instruments of Syrian policy. And whereas the Ba'ath radicals saw the road to Palestine running through revolution in the Arab world—especially in the oil monarchies—and wanted to deepen the class struggle in Syria as a way of mobilizing the masses, Asad advocated the fostering of unity within Syria and in the Arab world against Israel, in the service of what he deemed a more realistic strategy of conventional war to recover the Israeli-occupied territories.

The regime rejected United Nations Security Council (UNSC) Resolution 242, passed in the aftermath of the 1967 war, which called for an Arab-Israeli settlement based on the principle of "land for peace," on the grounds that it ignored Palestinian rights. On this, Asad and his rivals were agreed, as he reaffirmed after seizing power in 1970. Where they differed was that the radicals, thorough "rejectionists," believed any peace settlement with Israel would legitimize what they viewed as the theft of Palestine. For his part, Asad was prepared for an "honorable" settlement, one that included the protection of Palestinian rights, which, in effect, meant the creation of a Palestinian state in the West Bank and an agreement that permitted Palestinians to return to their homes or, alternatively, provided them compensation.

The 1970 Black September crisis in Jordan between the monarchy and the Palestinian fedayeen further drove a wedge in the Syrian leadership. Asad opposed the fedayeen's involvement in the internal politics of the Arab states, including what he referred to as "anarchy" in Jordan and Lebanon. He agreed to intervene in Jordan, via the Syrian-based Palestine Liberation Army, to defend the Palestinians from defeat by the Jordanian regime, but was deterred from providing air support by the threat of a US and Israeli military response, which allowed Jordan to repulse the Syrian-led forces. The radicals charged Asad with defeatism, while he insisted Syria had to avoid provoking Israel when the army was in no condition to fight. When the party leaders stripped him of his post as defense minister, he overthrew them and set out to prepare the way for what would become the 1973 war.[12]

Chapter 4

CAUSES OF THE 1973 WAR

Systemic Causes: The Outcome of 1967

The 1967 war fundamentally altered the Arab-Israeli balance of power and redrew the regional map to Israel's advantage. In upsetting the status quo, the war might have led to an Arab-Israeli peace. Resolution 242, jointly sponsored by the superpowers in the aftermath of the war, provided an internationally accepted framework for a settlement. With its proposed trade of land for peace, the resolution linked "the inadmissibility of the acquisition of territory by war" to a call for all states in the region to be recognized as having the right to live in peace and affirmed that the Arab states would now have to finally accept the existence of Israel. In exchange, Israel would have to withdraw from the territories it had seized.[13] Although Israel denied that the resolution required it to withdraw from *all* the territories, all other states, including the United States, interpreted the resolution to mean virtually complete withdrawal.[14]

The 1967 war also started a transformation in Arab attitudes toward Israel. Despite some short-term inflammation of radical public sentiment, the 1967 defeat, by striking a mortal blow to pan-Arab dreams, started the process of Arab acceptance of the permanence, though not the legitimacy, of Israel. To be sure, the conquest of the 1967 territories further locked the Arab states into the conflict with Israel, in the sense that they could not rest until the occupation of their territory—which touched on vital state and regime interests more directly than the Palestinian cause ever had—was rolled back. Nor could they yet overtly accept a directly negotiated peace settlement, wanting instead a UN-sponsored end to belligerency. But they were under no illusion that they could avoid a formal peace treaty if they were to recover their lost lands. The leading Arab state, Egypt, accepted Resolution 242, which it interpreted to mean total Israeli withdrawal from the lands conquered in 1967 in return for recognition and peace. An irreconcilable, "existential" conflict between the two sides was being transformed into a limited one over territory that was, in principle, more amenable to a compromise settlement.[15]

Why, then, did 1967 lead to more wars, rather than peace? Arguably, this resulted from the unbalanced outcome of the war: Israel, buffered by the occupied territories and buoyed by a sense of overwhelming military superiority, was convinced the Arabs would eventually have to seek peace on Israeli terms and was, in the meantime, satisfied with the status quo.[16] Indeed, the military hegemony Israel achieved in the war gave it cause to feel more secure, and the spectacular success of a "military solution" to its insecurity not only reduced its motivation to reach a permanent settlement with the Arab states, but also whet its irredentist appetite. Israel insisted that a peace settlement would require the Arab states to accept direct negotiations, which would implicitly confer Arab recognition without any necessary quid pro quo. It was also unprepared to return to the 1967 lines. It wanted to keep strategic parts of its conquests that it insisted were needed to give it "secure borders," including the Golan Heights, control of the Jordan River Valley, and parts of the Sinai Peninsula.[17] Additionally, the 1967 victory, in giving Israel control of the occupied territories, radically empowered irredentists intent on settling these territories, which obstructed the potential to trade the occupied lands for peace.[18]

Since Israel had destroyed much of their military forces and occupied Arab lands, the Arabs' bargaining position was weak. In essence, the 1967 war did not result in the compromise negotiated settlement outlined in Resolution 242 because the power asymmetry gave the Israelis no incentive to concede it and the Arab states no capacity to extract it. However, Israel's intransigence predictably stimulated efforts on the part of its Arab neighbors to right the power imbalance by rebuilding the shattered Egyptian and Syrian armies. This ultimately succeeded to the extent that on the eve of the 1973 war, the extremely dangerous power transition scenario obtained. Thus, war in 1967 set the stage for war in 1973.

AGENCY: WHY ASAD WENT TO WAR—HAWKISH IDEOLOGUES VERSUS PRAGMATISTS

Changes in leadership are likely when states lose wars, and this was so in post-1967 Egypt and Syria, where more pragmatic and cautious leaders—Anwar Sadat in Egypt and Asad in Syria—emerged in place of the radical ideologues of the sixties. Radical Arab states that had challenged Israel on behalf of the Palestinian cause, in disregard of the power imbalance against them, were socialized the hard way into the rules of realist prudence needed to survive in a dangerous states system.

That being said, the loss of the Syrian Golan Heights further locked Syria into a struggle with Israel to recover this territory. The recovery of the Golan became the single most important objective in Syrian foreign policy, a matter of national honor and regime legitimacy that was nonnegotiable. This intensified Syria's Arab nationalism, yet in focusing it on the recovery of *Syrian* land, made it more Syria-centric. Syrian Arabism was now expressed in the claim that the Arab states made up a nation with an overriding national interest in the struggle with Israel, and that Syria, as the most steadfast of the frontline Arab states, was entitled to pan-Arab support.

In parallel, however, Asad, as a realist, abandoned Syria's historically irredentist aspirations, notably for the liberation of Palestine. Rejecting what he called the "idealism" of the radicals, he scaled down Syria's goals to fit its capabilities, focusing on the more realistic objectives of recovering the occupied lands, above all the Golan, and achieving "Palestinian national rights," which, in practice, meant a state in the West Bank and Gaza, as part of a comprehensive peace under UN Resolution 242. This implicitly accepted the existence of Israel—as Asad's radical rivals had feared.

Asad's challenge was to achieve this still very ambitious set of goals in the face of the huge power imbalance that weighed in Israel's favor in the aftermath of 1967. While not ruling out diplomacy, Asad was convinced Israel would never withdraw from the occupied territories unless Arab military action upset the post-1967 status quo. The main thrust of his policy after coming to power in 1970 was, therefore, preparation for a conventional war to retake the lost Golan Heights. Toward this end, rebuilding of the shattered Syrian army and forging alliances became his first priorities. He maintained and deepened Syria's close alliance with the Soviet Union to secure arms, and he put aside the radicals' ideological cold war to create new partnerships with the conservative Arab oil-producing states that secured the financing needed for his military buildup. But rebuilding the army was not just a matter of hardware. A key factor in Syria's dismal performance in the 1967 war was the decimation of the officer corps by intra-regime political struggles and purges. Asad put an end to this and professionalized the army. Finally, he struck a strategic alliance with Sadat's Egypt—the most militarily powerful of the Arab states that shared Syria's interest in the recovery of the occupied territories—which was essential to allow a two-front war in which Israel could not, as in 1967, pick off the Arabs one by one.[19]

The "Arab Triangle" as 1973 War Coalition

In this respect, Asad took advantage of and helped in the emergence of a new Arab states system that was crucial to enabling the 1973 war. The 1967 defeat and subsequent death of Sadat's predecessor, Gamal Abdel Nasser, helped transform the Arab system from an Egypt-centered pan-Arab one to what Fouad Ajami called the "Arab Triangle."[20] A militarily preponderant and expansionist Israel had to be contained and rolled back, and this was only possible through inter-Arab cooperation. That the ideological threat that Cairo posed to other Arab states was reduced significantly once Nasser had passed from the scene made this cooperation less risky for the latter. Egypt was still the pivotal Arab state and the natural leader of an Arab coalition against Israel, but it had now to lead by consensus.

Gradually Egypt and Syria, under Sadat and Asad, were thrown together by their common interest in a war for the recovery of the occupied territories, while Saudi Arabia under King Faisal took advantage of their need for financial backing to moderate their policies and achieve full partnership in core Arab affairs. The three leaders began exploring two parallel tracks for the recovery of the occupied territories. Egypt and Syria continued rebuilding their armies with Soviet arms financed by Arab oil money, while Sadat and the Saudis tried to enlist American pressure on Israel for a diplomatic settlement. The alliance of Egypt, Syria, and Saudi Arabia was a precondition, too, for the Arab oil embargo that would be crucial to the Arabs' postwar diplomacy. Thus, Israel's military preponderance sparked an effort on the Arab side to balance it through alliance formation and a military buildup.[21]

International Agency: How US Diplomatic Failures Helped Precipitate the War

If one condition for the 1973 war was the divergence in the attitudes of the Arab states and Israel toward a settlement, another condition was the failure of diplomacy to bridge that gap. Arab hopes that the superpowers might deliver on Resolution 242, which they had helped craft, were gradually disappointed. The Soviets had little leverage over Israel, and the United States, under National Security Adviser Henry Kissinger's influence, gradually abandoned diplomatic efforts to address the Arab-Israeli conflict in a balanced way.[22] Kissinger was opposed to both Resolution 242 and the Rogers Plan—an initiative put forth by Secretary of State William Rogers in 1969 that would have required Israel to withdraw in exchange for peace—because he believed that as long as Egypt and Syria remained aligned with the Soviets, the United States should not use its leverage over Israel to promote such an agreement.

Instead, Kissinger pursued the alternative aim of keeping Israel so militarily strong that the Arabs could not make war. He argued Israel would not make any concessions needed for peace unless it was vastly superior and confident of its security, even though skeptics argued this superiority took away any incentive for Israel to seek a peace settlement. Convinced Israel could defeat any Arab military bid, the administration of President Richard Nixon lacked an incentive to invest political capital in a diplomatic settlement. Thus, several years of Egyptian affirmation of its readiness for peace under Resolution 242, and backdoor efforts by President Sadat to get the United States involved in brokering such a peace—including his expulsion of a large number of Soviet military advisers from Egypt in July 1972—failed to shift US satisfaction with the status quo.

When Kissinger rejected a Soviet proposal that resembled Resolution 242 in June 1973 and ordered substantial new US arms deliveries to Israel, Sadat concluded that the Arabs would have to break the stalemate militarily. He and Asad now agreed that Israel would never negotiate until Arab military action challenged its overwhelming military superiority and shattered its belief that keeping the occupied territories made it more secure. Only costs, such as the significant casualties and the disruption to its economy that it would suffer over the course of an extended war, were likely to shift Israeli calculations. A successful military initiative, launched with Soviet weapons, would also upset Washington's assumption that the status quo served its interests. In parallel, Egypt and Syria were able to leverage the superpower rivalry to attain a sufficiency of Soviet arms deliveries necessary to break the stalemate.[23]

THE 1973 WAR

War Objectives and Planning

Central to the war's conduct was agreement among the frontline Arab states on objectives and plans to coordinate the joint offensive. They were in accord that military action was meant to stimulate international intervention to bring about a political solution. Moreover, they understood that a credible military performance that would recover Arab pride was a political precondition, which would make possible Arab public acceptance of negotiations with Israel. It is true that Syria, unlike Egypt, had not yet accepted Resolution 242, which it saw as implying recognition of Israel without any Israeli concessions in return, but this was only a matter of tactics. Despite claims, perhaps advanced by Egypt, that Sadat had to persuade Asad to abandon his ambition to destroy Israel, the latter realized this was well beyond the Arabs' capabilities. Indeed, this was a main factor precipitating his split with the Ba'athist radicals who had envisioned a long-term guerrilla war to liberate Palestine. Thus, the two leaders were in accord on a conventional war that would militarily compel at least a partial Israeli withdrawal from the occupied territories and gain sufficient bargaining power to eventually achieve total withdrawal via diplomacy.

As for the war's conduct, once the joint Egyptian and Syrian offensives recovered strategic parts of the occupied Sinai and Golan, the Arab armies would dig in to defensive positions with anti-tank guided missiles meant to defeat Israeli armor counterattacks and neutralize the Israelis' advantage in tactical maneuver. In order to offset Israel's air superiority, they would deploy formidable air defense umbrellas with surface-to-air missiles (SAMs) over their positions. If this did not precipitate superpower intervention and a ceasefire, they would conduct a war of attrition aimed at inflicting heavy casualties upon the Israelis and disrupting the country's economy.

An element of surprise was essential to avoid an Israeli preemptive strike and for Egyptian and Syrian forces to each achieve their objectives prior to the Israeli military's full mobilization. Toward this end, they devised a strategic deception plan to condition the Israelis to accept regular troop movements as routine. The Israelis also proved unprepared because of their assumptions that the Arabs were incapable of joint military action or of overcoming Israeli fortifications in the Suez Canal Zone and on the Golan Heights. In the event, the long-term joint planning and preparation of the Egyptian and Syrian armies was in sharp contrast to the shambles of Arab military operations in 1967.[24]

Yet, the strategies of Egypt and Syria did, unbeknownst to Asad, diverge in their priorities in ways that would have major consequences. Asad aimed to recover as much of the Golan as possible militarily before political negotiations started under the auspices of the superpowers and the United Nations. By contrast, Sadat was fixated on getting the United States on his side by breaking with the Soviets and showing Washington he could protect US interests better than Israel. For him, the war was primarily a way to jumpstart US brokerage of a peace settlement. Asad was therefore disquieted when Sadat expelled the Soviet advisers, fearing arms deliveries were thereby jeopardized, and tried to mediate between Cairo and Moscow. As it turned out, the incident increased Soviet arms deliveries to Egypt and Syria, but Asad could not have known that beforehand.

In addition, Sadat misled Asad into thinking Egypt's war plans aimed to take the Sinai's Gidi and Mitla passes, when, in fact, Egyptian generals believed that they were only capable of a limited attack across the Suez Canal, after which they would sit tight in defensive positions and only go farther under the most favorable conditions. This would prove very damaging for Syria because Sadat let Kissinger—and hence the Israelis—know his intentions. In effect, the aim of a two-front war was lost—Israel was able to concentrate on the Golan front for many days without fear of an offensive by Egyptian forces, before dealing with Egypt once Syria had been driven back from the Golan. King Hussein of Jordan was also nominally brought into the war plans, but he assured the United States and Israel that he would do as little fighting as possible, even asking Israeli permission to move a Jordanian unit to help defend the Golan front. The Arabs, in short, were far less united than they appeared.[25]

The Conduct of the 1973 War

On October 6, Egypt and Syria launched a coordinated attack on the Israeli-occupied territories. Egyptian forces—100,000 troops and 1,000 tanks—successfully crossed the Suez Canal, breached Israeli fortifications, and established a bridgehead in the Sinai. There, protected from the Israeli air force by a SAM air defense umbrella, they repulsed Israel's armored counterattack, which suffered serious losses. While this might have made it possible for Egyptian forces to advance to the strategic Gidi and Mitla passes, they stayed in their defensive positions, enabling Israel to turn its full attention to the perilous situation on the Golan front. Egypt missed the opportunity to liberate substantial parts of the Sinai while Israel was preoccupied by the battle with Syria.

Synchronizing its attack with the Egyptian advance in the Sinai, Syria deployed 35,000 troops and 800 tanks to drive the Israelis from the Golan Heights. It aimed to slice through Israeli forces on the Golan, cut their resupply routes, and assume defensive positions to face a counterattack. The Israelis were masters of tank warfare but had only 180 tanks permanently stationed on the Golan. They had, however, established deep fortifications and anti-tank ditches along and behind the 1967 ceasefire line.

The Syrians' three-pronged attack broke through Israeli lines in the center and north, but penetrated farther in the south, taking much of the southern Golan. Airborne commandos captured Mount Hermon, depriving Israel of the ability to monitor the battlefield and allowing Syrian artillery to target Israeli tanks. The Syrians were very close to overrunning Israeli positions, almost reaching the escarpment overlooking the Sea of Galilee and northern Israel. Indeed, at its height the Syrian thrust was thirty-five kilometers inside the Golan. Israel viewed the situation as extremely grave and directed the bulk of its fighting forces to stopping the Syrian advance. In the first day, Syria lost 867 tanks to superior Israeli tactics, but Israel also suffered heavy casualties.

The Syrians continued their attack until the afternoon of October 7, when they halted their advance without having secured the bridges from the Golan. This may have been due to the effectiveness of the Israelis' air force operations, despite their suffering significant losses to Syrian air defense, and the tenacity of Israeli tank units. The pause ended the Syrian attack's momentum, while the failure to take the bridges allowed Israeli reinforcements to arrive on the Golan. Syria attempted to advance again on October 8, but an Israeli counterattack seized and maintained the initiative, putting the Israelis on the offensive by October 9. Israeli aircraft began flying out of Jordanian airspace to attack and destroy Syrian air defense sites, and to provide close air support to advancing Israeli armor on the Golan. During these Israeli-Syrian battles, there were no quick victories, with the two sides engaged in a war of attrition.

Having neutralized Syrian air defenses, Israel began a strategic bombing campaign against targets around Damascus, Syria's only oil refinery, a power installation, and its port facilities. By October 11, the Syrians had lost more than 1,000 tanks; by October 14, Israel had pushed them back across the 1967 ceasefire lines and come within artillery range of Damascus. In a salient near the village of Sasa on the road to Damascus, Syrian forces stubbornly contested the Israeli advance but lost 6,000 men and 800 tanks. Once the situation on the Golan front was stabilized, the Israelis halted their advance and ceased to threaten Damascus, as the Soviets had hinted at direct intervention with ground troops and the United States, according to a senior Israeli source, had threatened to cut off its resupply effort if the Israelis continued.[26]

Meanwhile, from October 7 to 14 Egyptian forces had remained inactive along the Suez Canal. As a result, Asad appealed to Sadat to have the Egyptians take the offensive and force the Israelis to divert resources to the south. On October 14, Sadat, fearing a Syrian collapse would leave him alone militarily and weaken his hand diplomatically after the war, ordered his forces into the Sinai. But this decision now amounted to too little too late, since Israel was now fully mobilized and had blunted the Syrian threat. Egyptian forces were vulnerable to Israeli air strikes once they moved beyond their air defenses on the canal, and the Israelis seized the opportunity to penetrate to the western side of the waterway, thereby encircling the Egyptian Third Army.

By roughly October 20, Sadat, with his armies now threatened by Israeli advances, moved toward accepting a ceasefire proposed by the superpowers without consulting Syria, relying purely on American goodwill to initiate diplomatic negotiations over its terms. Asad, convinced that only the threat of continued military pressure could influence Israel and the United States, was dismayed and alarmed at Sadat's failure to jointly decide on this step. Asad's forces, bolstered by Iraqi and Jordanian units, were now containing Israel in the Sasa salient. On October 20, Asad, who was now preparing a counterattack, rejected the ceasefire proposal. However, on October 22 a superpower-backed Security Council resolution, UNSC Resolution 338, called for a ceasefire and negotiations to implement Resolution 242, and Sadat accepted it. Asad had no choice but to comply, while asserting that Syria accepted UNSC 338 with the understanding that Resolution 242 meant a full Israeli withdrawal and the realization of Palestinian rights.

Tactically, the Syrian army showed motivation, courage, and steadfastness. But it lacked training and experience, and lower commands lacked the ability to take initiative and maneuver as Israeli officers did. Its offense was therefore far less effective than it could have been. However, its defense against the mobilized Israeli army was stubborn. Altogether, Syria and its allies, Iraq and Jordan, lost 1,200 tanks, but unlike in 1967, the Syrian army inflicted serious losses on Israel, including on its vaunted air force. Indeed, its SAM-6s and -7s were very effective, with Israel even losing all eight of its planes in a matter of seconds in one particular engagement. The Syrian army, having acquired new confidence, began a war of attrition on the Golan to keep up the pressure on Israel during the postwar negotiations.[27]

The Outcome of the 1973 War

The 1973 Arab-Israeli War ended with no decisive outcome on the battlefield. At the time of the ceasefire, Israel had seized the initiative and posed threats to both Egypt's army and Syria's capital, but the Arab armies were not defeated and had inflicted significant losses on Israel. Their armies—totally rebuilt, armed, and professionalized since 1967 and possessing new weapons—had, at least temporarily, neutralized Israel's blitzkrieg tactics. They had, thus, successfully broken the political impasse, precipitating international diplomatic intervention, which constituted a political victory for the Arabs in that their grievances now had, it appeared, to be addressed.

The war ended in part because neither side could continue to sustain it once the superpowers decided to end it. Rates of consumption of equipment and ammunition were enormous. Whereas the Arabs lost about 15,000 men, Israel lost roughly 2,800, a very high rate relative to its total population of three million. Israel's air force lost over 25 percent of its combat aircraft. Indeed, only a massive US resupply to Israel prevented a possible defeat and allowed Israel to recover and go on the offensive.[28] However, the American military airlift to Israel had its political costs: it led the Arab oil producers to embargo oil shipments to the United States, precipitating a global energy crisis. The war and the oil embargo brought the Nixon administration to realize that Arab frustration over Israel's unwillingness to withdraw from the territories occupied in 1967 could have major strategic consequences for the United States, and so paved the way for Secretary of State Kissinger's "shuttle diplomacy."

POSTWAR DIPLOMACY: WAR BY OTHER MEANS

Enter Kissinger: Negotiating the End of the War

Kissinger's goals were threefold: to protect Israel, to shift Egypt into the US camp at the expense of the Soviets, and, in turn, prevent a resumption of the war. Soviet arms could not be allowed to prevail, nor to result in an Arab political triumph over Israel—hence the massive US arms deliveries to Israel during the war. Yet the Nixon administration also delayed arms deliveries to Israel to ensure neither side scored a total victory, thereby opening the door to US diplomatic intervention.

While Kissinger had always opposed a comprehensive settlement of the type laid out in Resolution 242, he saw the outcome of the war as an opportunity to broker an alternative agreement that would both ensure Israel's interests and provide Egypt enough to lure it into a separate peace. This would substitute for the comprehensive solution the Arabs expected and that was prefigured in UN resolutions. Kissinger assured the Israelis the United States did not expect them to return to the 1967 lines, although they would have to give up some territory to get Egypt out of the Arab-Israeli military balance. After that, he emphasized, the Syrians and Palestinians would no longer pose a substantial threat to Israel, which meant that the latter would not need to make concessions to them. When asked about his objectives by the Arabs, he insisted he could not predict the outcome of the peace process and that what was important was to maintain the momentum of the negotiations. Yet he famously declared simultaneously that although the Soviets could provide arms, only the United States could deliver a peace settlement that would restore Arab lands. Nixon, too, told Arab leaders that Washington favored an Israeli return to the 1967 borders.

Israel, for its part, was determined that the Arabs would not be rewarded for the war, aimed to divide Egypt and Syria so they could not again mount a two-front campaign, and refused to make concessions to the Palestinians. Kissinger largely agreed with these goals, although he occasionally differed with the Israelis over tactics, particularly when he needed Israel to give small concessions to keep the process from breaking down and to avoid isolating Sadat, as Kissinger lured him, step-by-step, into a separate peace.

What greatly facilitated US aims was Sadat's belief that the United States had "99 percent of the cards," as he often put it, which explains why he tried to convince the Americans that Egypt could serve US interests as well or better than Israel.[29] Additionally, Sadat saw no choice except to rely on Kissinger to extract his Third Army from Israeli encirclement. Once he started down this road, the chances of going back quickly narrowed. Kissinger put forth the idea of a disengagement of forces—which would involve both sides pulling back their troops—as a substitute for substantive implementation of Resolutions 242 and 338, which he said should be postponed to a subsequent Geneva conference. Sadat embraced the idea and let Kissinger know he would not be constrained by any Syrian objections. He made repeated concessions to get the first disengagement agreement on the Egyptian front—known as Sinai I—including giving up all but a symbolic military presence on the east bank of the Suez Canal, Egypt's main war gain and leverage in negotiations. By greatly reducing the threat that Egypt could return to the military option if a comprehensive settlement was not achieved, he sharply undermined the prospects of such an outcome. The more Egypt's military option declined, moreover, the more Israel could redeploy its forces to the Golan front.

However, Kissinger understood that he had to bring Syria into the peace process if Sadat was not to be politically overexposed, especially since Saudi King Faisal was making an agreement on the Syrian front a condition for lifting the oil embargo. Once Sadat accepted Sinai I, he was reluctant to continue peace negotiations before Syria got something too. Thus, Kissinger told Israel that to protect Sadat, Syria would have to be given a token disengagement. Hence began his "shuttle diplomacy" between Israel and Syria.[30]

Asad's Negotiating Aims and Tactics

Although Syria failed to recover the Golan militarily, the Arabs had, as Asad saw it, acquired enhanced political leverage from their credible challenge to the pro-Israeli status quo and from the Arab oil embargo. If Egypt and Syria stuck together and refused to settle for less than a comprehensive peace, he reasoned, they could prevail at the negotiating table. For Asad, it soon became apparent that this meant pushing back against Kissinger's attempt to pull Egypt out of the Arab-Israeli power balance and Sadat's proclivity to go it alone. In Patrick Seale's view, the essence of the postwar diplomatic struggle between Syria and Kissinger was over Egypt. Sadat had promised Asad a concerted strategy—beginning with a promise not to go to the proposed Geneva peace conference until both sides had recovered some territory in disengagement negotiations—but Asad was rightly wary, particularly because Egypt did attend the conference when it met in December.

In February 1974, Asad accepted Kissinger's offer to mediate the Golan Heights disengagement negotiations. Seale reports that at first Asad thought Kissinger's efforts were a serious attempt to broker an acceptable peace, and that disengagement would be a first step toward a full Syrian recovery of the Golan. He hoped that the United States was getting tired of supporting Israel, which, far from being an invincible surrogate capable of protecting US interests in the Middle East, had had to be rescued from near defeat in the war. He differed from Sadat in believing military pressure on Israel had to be sustained to get any concessions from it. Less at Israel's mercy than Egypt (owing to the fact that Israel had trapped Sadat's Third Army), he waged a war of attrition—fighting while talking—on the Golan.

When Kissinger arrived in Damascus, Asad tried to pin him down on the inadmissibility of Israel retaining Syrian territory by conquest and the need to address Palestinian rights, but Kissinger was evasive. Asad wanted an immediate Israeli withdrawal from the Golan, but Kissinger would only offer a limited disengagement of forces agreement. Asad had wanted this before the Geneva conference met in December and, not getting it, had refused to attend. He became increasingly suspicious that Kissinger was seeking to divide Egypt from Syria, and to delay and evade a comprehensive settlement. A key setback for Asad was when Kissinger got Sadat to advise Saudi Arabia to lift the oil embargo—which it did—*before* Syria had achieved a Golan disengagement, thereby weakening his negotiating hand.

In the subsequent negotiations, Asad therefore had to reduce his opening demand to only half the Golan, and conceded an Israeli demand for a list of prisoners. Israel, unwilling to jeopardize its military settlements and insisting the Golan was essential for its security, offered only to divide the salient it had captured beyond the 1967 ceasefire lines, which Asad rejected. Kissinger urged on Israel that the minimum Asad needed was Quneitra and a sliver of territory taken in 1967. The final agreement gave Syria this bare minimum, the symbolic return of Quneitra, with Israel retaining most of the Golan, its military settlements, the strategic hills, and their outpost on Mount Herman.

Disengagement resulted in three zones, including a UN buffer zone that was flanked by Syrian and Israeli zones of restricted forces that would preclude a Syrian return to war on the Golan if the peace process stalled. Although the city of Quneitra was in the UN demilitarized zone, it was returned to Syrian jurisdiction, but not before the Israelis leveled it to the ground. Kissinger promised to work for full implementation of the key UN resolutions, but his actual goal was to avoid this, and he therefore had to head off Nixon's predilection to commit to it. To Kissinger's dismay, Nixon even told Asad that US strategy was to nudge the Israelis back, step-by-step, on the Golan until they reached the edge and tumbled over.[31]

Two-Level Games: Peace Negotiations and Managing Domestic Opinion

During the negotiations, Asad was engaged in something like a "two-level game," as he simultaneously had to deal with politics at home and try to achieve his goals in the peace talks.[32] To strengthen his hand, he informed Kissinger of the domestic constraints on his options. He could not get too far out in front of what was acceptable to his base in the party and army. Unlike Sadat, who took big decisions alone, in Syria Asad's lieutenants were present and had to be convinced too. Asad did not have to deal with a hawkish lobby in the army leadership—Generals Hikmat al-Shihabi, Ali Aslan, and Hasan Turkmani were all cautious professional soldiers—but militants in the party, including military party branches, "constrained him as much as he constrained them," and on Israel they were "implacable," for animosity toward Israel was much stronger in Syria than in Egypt.[33] Thus, the bargaining with Syria was much more tenacious than it had been with Egypt. Nevertheless, at the decision point it was Asad who decided to accept the disengagement deal, dragging his reluctant colleagues along.

Asad's public stature in Syria rose, not just from Syria's credible military performance but also from his tenacious bargaining, successful recovery of Quneitra, and the fact that he did not throw away, as Sadat had, Soviet support in order to establish a diplomatic channel to the United States. Buoyed by this political capital, Asad publicly welcomed the prospect of a real peace on the lines of UN Resolutions 242 and 338. Syria interpreted the latter to include the realization of Palestinian rights, which Asad said would be determined by the Palestine Liberation Organization (PLO), but not as threatening Israel as a state. The settlement would take the form of a peace treaty.[34]

The big discussion in Syrian cafes and homes came to be whether Syria would follow Egypt and realign with the United States to get a full settlement with Israel. Some argued it had less reason to do so, since it was not so impoverished as Egypt and the Americans would deliver less for Syria, meaning it had less to gain by putting all its eggs in the American basket. Some militants in the media were silenced for criticizing what they saw as the pro-American line of the regime, lamenting that "we have known the US is the enemy for a generation, so why does the appearance of Kissinger seem to reverse our earlier resolve and conviction?"[35] Nixon's visit to the country in June angered families of Syrian soldiers killed in the war. The regime justified US-brokered negotiations by pointing to the changed global circumstances. Specifically, it emphasized that US-Soviet détente, which had made Moscow unwilling to commit enough aid to solving Syria's national problem, meant that the Arabs had to maneuver between the superpowers. As the party newspaper, *al-Ba'ath*, put it on June 10, 1974, in international politics there are no permanent friendships or enmities, only interests. Similarly, a party official declared that Syria had to play power politics to survive, and because the United States was a great power, it had to be dealt with.

But in his flirtation with the United States, Asad may have been moving beyond his core party base and, consequently, he needed the support of Syria's merchant bourgeoisie. Kissinger deliberately sent his men with dollars into the *suqs* to make the merchants covetous of an opening to the Western economy. In April, the Syrian media talked about the economic benefits—foreign investment and capital—that would follow accommodation with the West, but warned this was contingent on reaching an acceptable peace with Israel. Syria would not become an American economic dependency, in good part because it had the alternative of Arab capital, owing to the enormous increase in oil prices precipitated by the war. Asad's policy, said the government press, was to make Syria important to both superpowers via Arab alliances, so it could not be ignored.

Public opinion set the parameters of Asad's options. From taxi drivers to professors, Syrians affirmed they wanted peace and a better economic life. But most did not believe Israel would concede the minimum terms Damascus needed in an agreement. Almost all Syrians, whether pro- or anti-regime, opposed a settlement that did not deliver Palestinian self-determination and a full recovery of Arab lands lost in 1967. Even many of the otherwise Western-oriented bourgeoisie were very anti-Israel. Their hope was that the United States would prioritize its own interest in having good relations with the (newly oil-rich) Arabs, and would hence pressure Israel to end its intransigence. Syrians' most optimistic hopes would soon be dashed and their more realistic expectations borne out.[36]

Sinai II and the End of the Syria Track

For Kissinger, the Golan deal was a small price to pay to lure Sadat down the road to a separate peace, for it cleared the way for negotiations for a second disengagement in the Sinai. Israel was candid that the aim of a second agreement with Egypt was to take it out of the Arab-Israeli power balance and to isolate Syria. Kissinger told Israel's new prime minister, Yitzhak Rabin, that Sinai II was designed to protect Israel from having to return to the 1967 borders, and backed Israel's determination to make no concessions on the other fronts—the Golan and West Bank.[37] The disengagement returned to Egypt the Suez Canal, the Sinai oil fields, and the portion of the Sinai on the western part of the Mitla and Gidi passes, but it was demilitarized and monitored by US and UN buffer forces that, in effect, ended any Egyptian potential to use threats of a return to war if peace negotiations broke down. The United States also promised Israel that it would not push for a return of the Golan.

Sinai II was a major victory for Israel. It achieved Egyptian non-belligerency in all but name. Sadat promised Kissinger not to join Syria if it attacked Israel. As a result, Asad accused Kissinger of dividing the Arabs and Sadat of leaving Syria alone facing Israel. He had no interest in a second cosmetic disengagement on the Golan. Against the opposition of much of the US defense establishment, Kissinger gave Israel an enormous arms bonanza, making an Arab return to war much more difficult. He argued that this would increase Israel's flexibility by augmenting its security, but later admitted it actually made the Israelis more obdurate.[38] The move also sparked an arms race between Israel and Syria, which sought Soviet arms to match Israel's new buildup. Effectively, the Syria track in the peace process ended.

The impact of Sinai II was destabilizing, leaving the other Arab states on Israel's borders vulnerable to Israel's great military superiority, with no balancing constraint from Egypt, the strongest Arab power. And it led inexorably to Sadat's subsequent separate deals with Israel, which undermined Syrian diplomatic leverage and shattered the Syrian-Egyptian alliance that was needed to pressure Israel into a comprehensive settlement.[39] Thus, the disunited Arabs frittered away the political leverage the 1973 war had potentially produced. In the longer term, the war profoundly altered the course of Middle East politics, eventually leading to the 1979 Egyptian-Israeli peace treaty and Cairo's realignment away from the Soviet Union and toward the United States, and leaving the Arab world without its historic leading state.[40]

THE CONSEQUENCES OF THE WAR

A Missed Opportunity for Peace

War outcomes can help determine whether there will be a peace settlement or another war.[41] Neorealist theory expects lost wars to socialize states into the rules of the game, inducing greater prudence, reducing ambitions, and subordinating ideology to the calculations of the balance of power.[42] But what about a war that ends with no clear victor?

The fact that there was no clear victor or defeated side in the 1973 war, and that the great post-1967 power imbalance in Israel's favor had been somewhat redressed, seemingly meant that neither side could hope to impose its will by force and, instead, had an incentive to seek a diplomatic solution. The war also stimulated intervention by the superpowers, particularly the United States, which seemed to recognize a unique opportunity to bridge the gap between the two sides. At the same time, the relative Arab success in the war compared to 1967 endowed the frontline states with a legitimacy that made it less politically risky for them to move toward a peace settlement.

Arab summits following the war, led by the "Arab Triangle" powers, legitimized a "comprehensive peace" with Israel in return for its full withdrawal from the occupied territories and the creation of a Palestinian state in the West Bank and Gaza. They also designated the PLO as the sole legitimate representative of the Palestinians in peace negotiations. Arguably, the war gave the Arab states increased leverage to extract the settlement they wanted if they stuck together and played their cards right. Israel, for its part, had an interest in a settlement, albeit a partial one—that is, one with Egypt, since that would leave it free to avoid political settlements on its other fronts—so it also agreed to enter the negotiations process.[43]

The chance for peace was, however, missed, in part because the ostensible US mediator did not seek a comprehensive settlement and, via massive arms deliveries to Israel and the engineering of Egypt's removal from the military equation, restored Israeli superiority. This reduced Israel's incentive to reach a comprehensive peace, leaving Syrian and Palestinian grievances unaddressed. It also radically upset the regional power balance. Indeed, Egypt's opting out of the Arab-Israeli conflict amounted to a form of "buck-passing," a practice that enervates the alliance stability by which weaker states deter powerful ones. In this case, the resulting power imbalance would lead directly to the fifth Arab-Israeli war of 1982, with Israel's invasion of Lebanon, a venture enabled by the neutralization of its southern front. That war would, in turn, lead to a further chain of wars in Lebanon and Gaza.

The Consequences of 1973 for Regional Order: The Collapse of the "Arab Triangle"

The 1973 war initially seemed to revive the pan-Arab system, albeit in new form. The war caused a massive resurgence of Arab nationalism that drove all Arab states to close ranks behind Egypt and Syria. Iraqi and Jordanian forces played crucial roles in containing Israeli counteroffensives against Syria, while Morocco and Saudi Arabia sent token contingents to the front lines, and Algeria and the Gulf states provided financing for Soviet arms deliveries.[44]

The new oil wealth from the price boom unleashed by the oil embargo and production cuts also generated increased interdependence between the Arab states. The expectation that the new wealth would be shared with the states that had fought and sacrificed for the common Arab cause was partly realized in the coming decade by significant transfers to the latter, as well as by labor migration from the frontline states to the labor-scarce Arab oil-producing monarchies and the accompanying transfer of remittances home. Moreover, as the conservative oil monarchies used aid to moderate the radicalism of the nationalist republics, the ideological subversion and media wars typical of the "Arab Cold War" of the 1960s gave way, in inter-Arab affairs, to increased interstate diplomacy and amity.

Yet, just as the 1973 war gave birth to the "Arab Triangle," so did disagreements over the conflict's resolution destroy it, as after the war, Egypt's Sadat took the road to a separate peace at the expense of his Arab partners. Sadat's move had, from at least the middle 1970s, profoundly damaging consequences for the Arab states system. It generated deepened insecurity in the Arab Levant that stimulated a retreat to state-centric self-help policies by the Arab states, most notably Syria, while discrediting the notion within the PLO that Palestinian interests could be peacefully attained.

The first and most destructive symptom of these tendencies was the Lebanese Civil War, unleashed by conflicts over the Palestinians in Lebanon. The Sinai II agreement sparked a showdown between a coalition of Palestinians and radical Lebanese Muslims who wanted to challenge Israel from southern Lebanon on the one hand, and Maronite Christians determined to eradicate this disruptive threat to Lebanese sovereignty on the other. At the same time, Syria, left extremely vulnerable to Israeli power by the collapse of its Egyptian alliance, and seeking to redress the imbalance, tried to use the civil war to impose its leadership in the Levant, especially on Lebanon and the PLO. This precipitated a PLO-Syrian rift that would never be wholly healed.[45]

Meanwhile, Sadat knew Israel was prepared to trade the rest of the Sinai for a peace that would remove Egypt, the strongest Arab state, from the Arab-Israeli power balance. Moreover, he understood that if he stuck with Syria and the PLO in insisting on a comprehensive settlement and a

Palestinian state, he might get nothing, especially since Sinai II had removed Egypt's war option. He therefore entered into negotiations in September 1978 at Camp David for what would be a separate peace treaty. For Israel's new prime minister, Menachem Begin, the Sinai was a price worth paying, since doing so effectively gave Israel the chance to keep the West Bank. While ostensibly the Camp David agreement provided for Palestinian "autonomy," the subsequent failure to realize that objective did not deter Sadat from signing a separate peace with Israel in 1979.[46] As a result, at the Baghdad summit of 1979, Iraq and Syria jointly forced Saudi Arabia and other wavering states to ostracize Egypt from the Arab world. This move, by forcing Egypt into greater dependence on the United States, allowed the virtual neutralization of the core Arab state by a superpower deeply biased toward Israel.[47]

Although Egypt's separate peace with Israel greatly reduced the leverage of Syria and the Palestinians to seek a diplomatic resolution of their grievances, the resulting power imbalance in Israel's favor was insufficient to impose a pro-Israeli peace. Israel therefore tried in 1982 to break the stalemate through its invasion of Lebanon, the aim of which was to establish hegemony over the PLO and Syria. But its failure to do so—and the ability of its enemies to subsequently restore some balance to the military equation via Syria's reach for "strategic parity" through an arms buildup and Hizbollah's asymmetric warfare capability in southern Lebanon—established a certain degree of mutual deterrence.

In parallel, the two Arab-Israeli wars—1973 and 1982—helped initiate a transition toward a more multipolar, state-centric system in which individual state interests eclipsed the putative pan-Arab interest in shaping their foreign policies. On the one hand, the massive insecurity these wars unleashed led individual Arab states to resort to self-help policies, in which they unilaterally and not collectively sought their individual security, most notably in the case of how Syria dealt with Israel. At the same time, the new oil money resulting from the postwar oil price boom allowed states to consolidate themselves, generate new bourgeoisies with a stake in their regimes, and co-opt the middle class, once the constituency of pan-Arabism. The resulting decline of pan-Arabism, in exacerbating the inability of the Arab states to combine their efforts against Israel, further shifted the overall power balance in the latter's favor.

The Impact of the 1973 War on Syria: The Consolidation of Asad's National Security State

The 1973 war, the ensuing diplomacy, and the long-term impact they had on the Arab state system had together a profound impact on Syria. The transformation of the Ba'athist regime under Asad into a huge authoritarian national security state was in good part driven by Syria's beleaguered position in its external environment, specifically by the need to recover the lost Golan from Israel and counter the latter's power. But equally, it was the legitimacy Asad reaped as a result of Syria's credible military performance in the 1973 war that enabled him to concentrate personal power in the presidency.

Asad concentrated power through a strategy of balancing above several regime pillars and rival social forces. Under the radical Ba'athists who preceded him in 1963–1970, the regime had already achieved autonomy from the dominant classes by breaking their control over the means of production and mobilizing workers and peasants through the party. However, the party, initially a stronghold of rejectionism, put ideological constraints on Asad's diplomacy, manifest in the period around the 1973 war. He used his control of the army to free himself of these constraints and built up a personal core of Alawi followers in the security apparatus to give him autonomy from the army. Economic liberalization incorporated segments of the bourgeoisie into his constituency. At the same time, Asad exploited external resources, enabled by the 1973 war—the Soviet arms with which he rebuilt the army and the Arab oil money, a product of the wartime oil price boom, by which the bureaucracy was expanded and the bourgeoisie co-opted—to consolidate his regime.

In the years after 1973, the increased cohesion and stability of his regime gave Asad considerable autonomy from domestic constraints to adapt foreign policy to the external power balance. In his early years in power, and particularly in the immediate postwar decisions thrust upon him by the 1973 war outcome, he sought an intra-elite consensus behind controversial decisions, since his preeminence rested on the support of a personal faction with which he shared power. Thus, in the disengagement negotiations after the 1973 war he took pains to consult the political elite, and in the end was able to pull his reluctant colleagues into the agreement.

The year 1973 was the making of Asad as a wartime and foreign policy leader. Subsequently, foreign policy was no longer subject to bureaucratic politics, in which hawkish or dovish factions had to be consulted because they could veto Asad's decisions. The regime had still to take care not to irreparably damage its legitimacy, which ultimately rested on its claim to be the defender of the Arab cause against Israel. But as long as Asad could justify unpopular decisions—such as the stand Syria took against Iraq in the Iran-Iraq War and again in the 1990–1991 Gulf War—as necessary to the long-term struggle with Israel, he calculated that opposition could be contained at acceptable cost.[48]

The Lessons of 1973: Syria's Operational Code

The outcome of 1973 and the immediate postwar negotiations that took Egypt out of the Arab-Israeli power balance was the immediate and predominant shaper of Syria's foreign policy strategies into the 1990s. Post-1973 Syria under Asad was widely seen to "punch above its weight" in regional politics. This reflected the realist worldview and modus operandi that Asad developed out of his many years of experience dealing with stronger hostile powers, above all in the 1973 war and its aftermath. Asad viewed the world as driven by a Machiavellian struggle for power, where international law was selectively enforced and a state's interests would only be respected if it had the material capacity to defend them. Surviving in a Hobbesian environment like the Levant required a realist matching of ends and means. Thus, Asad scaled down Syria's objectives to achieve what he saw as an honorable peace with Israel—one that would recover the Golan and secure Palestinian rights—and refused any separate peace with Israel that would abandon the Palestinians until the 1990s.

In parallel to scaling down his foreign policy goals, Asad also built up Syria's military capability, establishing a greater congruence between the means and ends needed to make his diplomacy credible and to deter Israeli power. Once Sadat's 1979 separate peace with Israel took Egypt out of the Arab-Israeli power balance, Syria felt extremely vulnerable. For Asad, the threat of an Israel emboldened by the neutralization of its southern front had to be contained, while the peace negotiations could only yield acceptable results once an Arab-Israeli power balance was restored. Asad used the Arab aid Syria received as the remaining frontline state to finance a reach for military parity with Israel, such that he was able to raise a nearly 500,000-man army and receive enormous amounts of Soviet weaponry gratis or on cheap credit.

At the same time, Asad's regional policy was designed to proactively manage the enhanced threats in his immediate environment from the loss of Syria's alliance with Egypt. In Syria's 1976 intervention in the Lebanese Civil War—itself an immediate outcome of the Sinai II agreement—Asad aimed to head off various threats from Lebanon to Syria's position in the struggle with Israel. He blocked a Palestinian defeat of the Maronite Christians to deter the latter's alignment with Israel and prevented the emergence of a radical, Palestinian-dominated Lebanon that could give Israel an excuse to intervene militarily, possibly to seize southern Lebanon, and position itself to threaten Syria's soft western flank. Syria's Lebanon intervention allowed Asad to station his army in the Beqa'a Valley against this danger. Later, however, as the Maronites allied with Israel, Syria tilted toward Palestinian forces confronting Israel in southern Lebanon.

The Lebanon intervention was also part of Asad's attempt to construct a Syrian sphere of influence to substitute for the lost Egyptian alliance in the diplomatic struggle with Israel: whoever controlled Lebanon was also in a strong position to control the PLO and, in turn, the Palestinian card. Syria's bargaining leverage in the Arab-Israeli conflict would be greatly enhanced if it enjoyed the capacity to veto any settlement of the Palestinian problem that left Syria out, or to overcome rejectionist Palestinian resistance to an acceptable settlement. The 1982 Israeli invasion of Lebanon, partly meant to demolish Syria's role in Lebanon, actually gave birth to an increasingly close alliance with Iran that helped substitute for the defection of Egypt from the power balance with Israel.

The suboptimal outcome of the disengagement negotiations had been a cautionary tale for Asad of the pitfalls of negotiating with Israel and relying on US mediation, which together had outmaneuvered him in 1974. Asad realized he could not avoid diplomacy to recover the Golan and tried to seize opportunities to pursue a negotiated settlement, but only if the conditions were right. While he would negotiate if he had enough bargaining cards to give the stronger opponent an incentive to make an acceptable deal, Asad preferred to wait until the balance of power improved when he was not in a strong position, rather than negotiate from weakness and make concessions.

In the meantime, Damascus obstructed all attempts at partial or separate Israeli agreements with other Arab parties that excluded Syria. Its active opposition led to the collapse of both the 1983 Lebanese-Israeli accord and the 1985 Hussein-Arafat bid for negotiations with Israel under the Reagan Plan. Asad also resorted to the use of asymmetric warfare via proxies—Palestinian guerrillas and Hizbollah in southern Lebanon—with the aim of incentivizing Israel to reach a settlement. The unfavorable power balance meant this tactic had to be pursued with caution and behind a military shield that deterred the enemy from bringing its full retaliatory superiority to bear on Syria. With that in mind, the Soviet Union's role as patron-protector had a crucial deterrent effect on Israel's freedom of action against Syria.

Asad nevertheless also sought to reengage the United States in brokering a political settlement and to exploit US fears of Middle East instability to get it to restrain Israel. Thus, in the 1990–1991 Gulf War, Asad joined the US-led coalition against Iraq on the understanding that the United States would broker a new peace process, and after the war Syria attended the Madrid conference. Once the 1993 Israeli-PLO Oslo Accord relieved Damascus of the responsibility to make its own recovery of the Golan contingent on the satisfaction of Palestinian rights, recovery of the full Golan seemed in sight, and Asad concentrated on minimizing the "normalization of relations" and security concessions Israel expected in return. The two sides came very close to a settlement, but a final deal was obstructed by Israel's demands to keep its surveillance station on Mount Hermon and a strip of the Golan that would block Syrian access to Lake Tiberias. This was arguably the last chance to correct the flawed outcome of the post-1973 peace process.[49]

CONCLUSION

The Arab-Israeli wars were ultimately a function of a war-prone regional states system. The 1973 Arab campaign was a response to Israeli territorial expansion and military dominance resulting from the 1967 war, itself a result of irredentism and insecurity on both sides. The year 1973 upset the existing balance of power that so favored Israel, creating potential conditions for an Arab-Israeli peace. However, owing to Arab divisions—which were exploited by Israel and the United States—the outcome was a separate, partial peace that left Syria excluded. Syria's determination to redress this outcome shaped its foreign policy for the next three decades, locking it into an intractable conflict with its powerful neighbor.

NOTES

1. David Fromkin, *A Peace to End All Peace: Creating the Modern Middle East, 1914–1922* (New York: Henry Holt, 1989).

2. Benjamin Miller, "Balance of Power or the State-to-Nation Balance: Explaining Middle East War-Propensity," *Security Studies* 15, no. 4 (2006): 658–705.

3. Deborah Gerner, *One Land, Two Peoples: The Conflict over Palestine* (Boulder, CO: Westview, 1991), 11, 17–18.

4. Raymond Hinnebusch, "War in the Middle East," in *The Routledge Handbook to the Middle East and North African State and States System*, eds. Raymond Hinnebusch and Jasmine Gani (New York: Routledge, 2019), 356–57.

5. Charles S. Gochman and Zeev Maoz, "Militarized Interstate Disputes, 1816–1976," *Journal of Conflict Resolution* 28, no. 4 (December 1984): 585–616; Hinnebusch, "War in the Middle East," 358, 364–67.

6. A. F. K. Organski, *World Politics* (New York: Knopf, 1968).

7. Douglas Lemke, *Regions of War and Peace* (Cambridge: Cambridge University Press, 2002), 118–25.

8. Benedict Anderson, *Imagined Communities: Reflections on the Origin and Spread of Nationalism* (New York: Verso, 1983).

9. Raymond Hinnebusch, "The Foreign Policy of Syria," in *The Foreign Policies of Middle East States*, eds. Raymond Hinnebusch and Anoushiravan Ehteshami (Boulder, CO: Lynne Rienner, 2014), 207–9.

10. Patrick Seale, *The Struggle for Syria: A Study of Post-War Arab Politics, 1945–1958* (London: Oxford University Press, 1965).

11. Avner Yaniv, "Syria and Israel: The Politics of Escalation," in *Syria under Assad: Domestic Constraints and Regional Risks*, eds. Moshe Maoz and Avner Yaniv (London: Croom Helm, 1986).

12. This section drew on the following sources: Moshe Ma'oz, *Syria and Israel: From War to Peacemaking* (New York: Oxford University Press, 1995), 116–19; Patrick Seale, *Asad: The Struggle for the Middle East* (Berkeley: University of California Press, 1989), 117–63.

13. United Nations Security Council Resolution 242, in United States Department of State, *Foreign Relations of the United States, 1964–1968*, vol. 19, *Arab-Israeli Crisis and War, 1967* (Washington, DC: Government Printing Office, 2004), 1,062–63.

14. Charles D. Smith, *Palestine and the Arab-Israeli Conflict* (New York: St. Martin's, 1996), 211–13.

15. Avraham Sela, *The Decline of the Arab-Israeli Conflict: Middle East Politics and the Quest for Regional Order* (Albany: State University of New York Press, 1998), 27–30, 97–109; Smith, *Palestine and the Arab-Israeli Conflict*, 235–37.

16. Shlomo Aronson, *Conflict and Bargaining in the Middle East: An Israeli Perspective* (Baltimore, MD: Johns Hopkins University Press, 1978), 136.

17. Ian J. Bickerton and Carla L. Klausner, *A Concise History of the Arab-Israeli Conflict* (Englewood Cliffs, NJ: Prentice Hall, 1991), 168–69; Ma'oz, *Syria and Israel*, 113–39.

18. Ilan Peleg, "The Impact of the Six-Day War on the Israeli Right: A Second Republic in the Making?" in *The Arab-Israeli Conflict: Two Decades of Change*, eds. Yehuda Lukacs and Abdullah Battah (Boulder, CO: Westview, 1988), 60.

19. This section drew on the following sources: Seale, *Asad*, 185–225; Malcolm H. Kerr, "Hafiz Asad and the Changing Patterns of Syrian Politics," *International Journal* 2, no. 4 (Autumn 1973): 689–706; Raymond Hinnebusch, "Revisionist Dreams, Realist Strategies: The Foreign Policy of Syria," in *The Foreign Policies of Arab States: The Challenge of Change*, eds. Bahgat Korany, Ali al-Din Hilal, and Ahmad Yusuf Ahmad (Boulder, CO: Westview, 1991), 379–80, 391–94; Alasdair Drysdale and Raymond Hinnebusch, *Syria and the Middle East Peace Process* (New York: Council on Foreign Relations Press, 1991).

20. Fouad Ajami, "Stress in the Arab Triangle," *Foreign Policy*, no. 29 (Winter 1977–1978): 90–108.

21. Stephen Walt, *The Origins of Alliances* (Ithaca, NY: Cornell University Press, 1987), 117, 120–21, 265–66.

22. In September 1973, Kissinger also became secretary of state.

23. This section drew on the following sources: Edward R. F. Sheehan, *The Arabs, Israelis and Kissinger: A Secret History of American Diplomacy in the Middle East* (New York: Reader's Digest, 1976), 15–39; Craig Daigle, *The Limits of Détente: The United States, the Soviet Union, and the Arab–Israeli Conflict, 1969–1973* (New Haven, CT: Yale University Press, 2012).

24. Phillip Cane, "The Yom Kippur War: Forty Years Later," *Security and Defence* 4, no. 2 (October 6, 2013); Ma'oz, *Syria and Israel*, 124–28.

25. On Sadat's conduct, see Seale, *Asad*, 194–201.

26. Chaim Herzog, *The War of Atonement, October, 1973* (Boston: Little, Brown, 1975), 136.

27. This section drew on the following sources: Seale, *Asad*, 185–225; Michael C. Jordan, "The 1973 Arab-Israeli War: Arab Policies, Strategies, and Campaigns," *Global Security*, 1997, https://www.globalsecurity.org/military/library/report/1997/Jordan.htm; Riad Ashkar, "The Syrian and Egyptian Campaigns," *Journal of Palestine Studies* 3, no. 2 (Winter 1974): 15–33.

28. Jordan, "1973 Arab-Israeli War."

29. Anwar El-Sadat, *In Search of Identity: An Autobiography* (New York: Harper & Row, 1977), 293.

30. This section drew on the following sources: Seale, *Asad*, 226–49; Sheehan, *Arabs, Israelis, and Kissinger*, 30–128; Matti Golan, *The Secret Conversations of Henry Kissinger: Step-by-Step Diplomacy in the Middle East* (New York: Bantam, 1976).

31. Sheehan, *Arabs, Israelis, and Kissinger*, 133; Seale, *Asad*, 247–48. This section drew on the following sources: Seale, *Asad*, 226–49; Sheehan, *Arabs, Israelis, and Kissinger*, 92–97, 113–28; Ma'oz, *Syria and Israel*, 141–60; Moshe Ma'oz, *Asad: The Sphinx of Damascus: A Political Biography* (New York: Weidenfeld and Nicholson, 1988), 83–108.

32. Robert Putnam, "Diplomacy and Domestic Politics: The Logic of Two-Level Games," *International Organization* 42, no. 3 (Summer 1988): 427–60.

33. Sheehan, *Arabs, Israelis, and Kissinger*, 94.

34. Seale, *Asad*, 250, 256.

35. *Jil al-Thawri* [Revolutionary Generation], June 1974.

36. This section drew on the following sources: Sheehan, *Arabs, Israelis, and Kissinger*, 78–97; Ma'oz, *Syria and Israel*, 130–33; author's field work in Syria, spring 1974; Raymond Hinnebusch, "Does Syria Want Peace? Syrian Policy in the Syrian-Israeli Peace Negotiations," *Journal of Palestine Studies* 26, no. 1 (Autumn 1996): 42–57.

37. Sheehan, *Arabs, Israelis, and Kissinger*, 113–28. On this point, see also, for example, Salim Yaqub, *Imperfect Strangers: Americans, Arabs, and U.S.-Middle East Relations in the 1970s* (Ithaca, NY: Cornell University Press, 2016), 158–59.

38. Sheehan, *Arabs, Israelis, and Kissinger*, 199.

39. Seale, *Asad*, 226–66. The scepticism toward the idea that Kissinger's diplomacy would benefit Israel that was voiced by Matti Golan seems, in retrospect, to have been unjustified.

40. David Wallsh, "Timeless Lessons from the October 1973 Arab-Israeli War," Modern War Institute, October 4, 2017, https://mwi.usma.edu/timeless-lessons-october-1973-arab-israeli-war. This section drew on the following sources: Seale, *Asad*, 244–49, 250–66; Sheehan, *Arabs, Israelis, and Kissinger*, 129–35, 179–200.

41. Some international relations scholars argue that war results from imperfect information. Wars are fought, in other words, to determine which side is stronger—if the parties knew which side was more powerful ex ante, there would be no need to fight a war in the first place. For this argument, see Geoffrey Blainey, *The Causes of*

War (New York: Free Press, 1973); James D. Fearon, "Rationalist Explanations for War," *International Organization* 49, no. 3 (Summer 1995): 379–414.

42. On neorealism, see Kenneth N. Waltz, *Theory of International Politics* (Boston: McGraw-Hill, 1979).

43. Sela, *Decline of the Arab-Israeli Conflict*, 211–13.

44. Ibid., 145.

45. Smith, *Palestine and the Arab-Israeli Conflict*, 242–53; Michael N. Barnett, *Dialogues in Arab Politics: Negotiations in Regional Order* (New York: Columbia University Press, 1998), 191–200; Sela, *Decline of the Arab-Israeli Conflict*, 153–213.

46. On the autonomy talks, see Jeremy Pressman, "Egypt, Israel, and the United States at the Autonomy Talks, 1979," *Diplomacy & Statecraft* 33, no. 3 (September 2022): 543–65.

47. Smith, *Palestine and the Arab-Israeli Conflict*, 256–58.

48. This section drew on the following source: Hinnebusch, "Revisionist Dreams," 388–91.

49. This section drew on the following sources: Hinnebusch, "Does Syria Want Peace?"; Seale, *Asad*, 366–20, 494.

Chapter 5

The Impact of the October 1973 War on the Palestinians

Khaled Elgindy

While the June 1967 Arab-Israeli War is generally acknowledged as having redrawn the geopolitical map of the Middle East and fundamentally transformed the nature of the Arab-Israeli conflict, the impact of the October War of 1973 has gotten much less attention. In reality, the period following the 1973 war remains perhaps the most dynamic and formative period in shaping the nature of Arab-Israeli peacemaking, as well as US and Palestinian official policies and attitudes toward one another over the next half century. Indeed, almost every aspect of the contemporary Middle East peace process and US-Palestinian relations can be traced to the critical years immediately following the 1973 war.

The 1973 war solidified the position of the United States as the undisputed leader of the Arab-Israeli peace process, with all of the political and ideological baggage that this entailed. And no single US policymaker exerted greater influence in shaping that process than Secretary of State Henry Kissinger, as both the architect of the Middle East peace process and the godfather of US Palestinian policy. The process and principles laid out by Kissinger would continue to shape Arab-Israeli peacemaking for most of the next half century, including the preference for a piecemeal peace process over comprehensive settlement negotiations; reliance on American and Israeli preeminence; and, most important, the strategic downgrading of the Palestinian issue. The 1973 war also marked a decisive shift in the diplomatic strategy of the Palestine Liberation Organization (PLO) and its approach toward the United States, as the PLO came to the stark conclusion that the road to Palestinian liberation and eventual statehood necessarily ran through Washington. But as the PLO leadership worked to ingratiate itself with the United States, US officials continued to exclude it from the broader diplomatic process.

These same basic dynamics persisted even after the PLO joined the peace process in 1993. Under the US-dominated Oslo process, the Palestinians were granted a conditional seat at the table in the hope of transforming them into a suitable peace partner. In return, Palestinian leaders ceded a measure of their internal autonomy, with the expectation that the United States would eventually deliver Israeli concessions. In the end, the process succeeded only in institutionalizing Palestinian dependency and weakness.

BACKGROUND (1948–1973)

Israel's creation in 1948 led to the displacement of some 800,000 Palestinians, roughly two-thirds of the Arab population of the former British Mandate of Palestine, an event known among Palestinians as the *nakba*, or "calamity." In the wake of the *nakba*, the Palestinian political and institutional vacuum was largely filled by the Arab states, for which Palestine and the Palestinians became an ideologically and politically potent cause célèbre. Throughout the 1950s and 1960s, key Arab regimes, most notably Egypt, Syria, and Iraq, competed over the sponsorship of various Palestinian political entities as well as paramilitary units, known as fedayeen, both as a means of controlling the nascent Palestinian movement and of burnishing their own nationalist credentials.[1] Even after the emergence of autonomous Palestinian political activism, groups like Fateh and the Marxist-leaning Arab National Movement (ANM)—the parent organization of the Popular Front for the Liberation of Palestine (PFLP) and Democratic Front for the Liberation of Palestine (DFLP)—while remaining broadly pan-Arabist and anti-colonialist in orientation, continued to operate under the tutelage of the Arab states and within the framework of intra-Arab rivalries.

The United States and other Western powers took a very different approach to Israel's creation and the Palestinian problem. Officially, US and international diplomacy continued to be grounded in United Nations (UN) General Assembly Resolution 181, which embodied the UN's decision to partition Palestine into separate Arab and Jewish states, and Resolution 194, which affirmed the right of Palestinian refugees to return to their former homes in Israel. In practical terms, however, both the Western powers and the Soviet Union had acquiesced to the new realities on the ground. As far as US and European officials were concerned, Israel's existence was a political fait accompli, while the "Palestine refugees" were seen primarily as a humanitarian, rather than a political, problem. Indeed, for most of the US policy establishment in the 1950s and 1960s, the idea of Palestinians as a distinct national group was still regarded as highly controversial, if not subversive. Accordingly, US officials generally regarded Palestinian political activity as a ruse devised by Arab states to undermine Israel and as an inherently destabilizing force.[2]

Such perceptions persisted following the creation of the PLO under the auspices of the Arab League in 1964. American officials were initially dismissive of the PLO as yet another ploy in the intra-Arab "struggle for power,"[3] but they eventually came to look at it more seriously.[4] A year after its founding, the State Department banned official contacts with the PLO on the basis of its negation of the Israeli state, while leaving the door open to unofficial dealings with PLO members.[5] By late 1966, however, following the launch of armed guerrilla activity against Israel by Fateh and other fedayeen groups, all Palestinian political factions, including the PLO, were being characterized inside US government circles as "terrorist" organizations, despite the fact that Fateh was not yet part of the PLO and the latter was not yet engaged in armed struggle against Israel.[6]

It was only after the June 1967 Arab-Israeli War that US officials began to look seriously at the Palestinians as political actors in their own right. The 1967 war radically transformed the geopolitical landscape of the region and fundamentally redefined the conflict. Israel's lightning victory over Egyptian, Syrian, and Jordanian forces, which led to its seizure of the remainder of historic Palestine—the West Bank, East Jerusalem, and the Gaza Strip—along with Egypt's Sinai Peninsula and the Syrian Golan Heights, established it as a regional superpower virtually overnight. Diplomatically, UN Security Council Resolution 242, which called on Israel to withdraw from Arab territories occupied during the war in return for peace with Arab states—the so-called land for peace formula—replaced the largely defunct Resolutions 181 and 194 as the framework for a new peace process, which would now be led by the United States. In addition to reframing the conflict as a territorial dispute between sovereign states, Resolution 242 failed to mention the Palestinians, who were discussed only as "refugees," prompting Palestinian political factions to reject it out of hand.[7]

At the same time, the 1967 war convinced the various Palestinian factions and fedayeen groups that they could no longer rely on the Arab states and would need to take matters into their own hands. The March 1968 Battle of Karameh, in which armed Palestinian groups helped stave off invading Israeli troops, marked the beginning of Palestinian political free agency and put Fateh and the fedayeen "on the global map of Third World revolutionaries."[8] By early 1969, Fateh, under the charismatic leadership of Yasir Arafat, had engineered a takeover of the PLO, transforming it into a genuinely autonomous and broadly representative Palestinian decision-making body. At the same time, the meteoric rise of the fedayeen also put the PLO on a collision course with its Jordanian hosts. Now entrenched within the refugee communities in Jordan, where Palestinians made up a numeric majority of the country's population, the increasingly triumphalist factions of the PLO established a virtual "state within a state."[9]

Palestinian guerrilla attacks on Israel from Jordanian territory subjected the kingdom to devastating Israeli reprisals, causing massive human and material losses. Moreover, the presence of an armed Palestinian force with statist ambitions in a country with a Palestinian majority was viewed by the Hashemite monarchy as an existential threat. With the PLO determined to maintain its base of operations in Jordan, King Hussein set out to rein in the Palestinian factions, leading to a bloody civil war in September 1970 and the subsequent expulsion of the PLO from the kingdom, a sequence of events that would come to be known as "Black September."

PLO AND US DIPLOMATIC POSTURES ON THE EVE OF THE 1973 WAR

Despite its defeat in Jordan, the PLO, which had now transferred its operations to the Lebanese capital of Beirut, succeeded in establishing Palestinian nationalism as a force to be reckoned with in the region and beyond. More importantly, the organization had affirmed its role as the main body for Palestinian decision-making.[10] While armed struggle remained central to the PLO's mission and its domestic legitimacy, Arafat's leadership viewed the military and political tracks as inseparable. Indeed, the utility of the former was in opening up space and creating opportunities for the latter. In addition to consolidating Arab state support for Palestinian resistance and political objectives, PLO diplomacy focused on building alliances with other liberation and revolutionary movements, as well as with the global nonaligned movement (NAM). By situating Palestinian liberation within the global context of anti-imperialism and decolonization, the PLO was able to vastly expand its political and diplomatic reach across Africa, Asia, and Latin America, as well as with radical and revolutionary forces in the West—relationships that would prove instrumental to the PLO's international strategy.[11]

When it came to the superpower rivalry, the PLO attempted to walk a fine line. Like other revolutionary Arab regimes, the PLO was officially part of the NAM, though sentiment within the organization was generally more favorable toward the Soviet Union, particularly among leftist factions such as the PFLP, but even within Fateh. The PLO meanwhile continued to view the United States with suspicion, both for its role in Israel's creation and for its reputation among "Third World" liberation movements as a neocolonial power. Nevertheless, Arafat also had a pragmatic side. Starting in late 1969, the PLO leader authorized his security chief, Ali Hassan Salameh, to open a secret channel with the Central Intelligence Agency (CIA) in the hope of establishing a political dialogue with Washington.[12] The PLO-CIA track would blossom many years later, particularly in the realm of intelligence and security cooperation, but much to Arafat's frustration it would remain decidedly apolitical.

The United States, for its part, continued to keep the PLO at arm's length, in part because of its own increasingly conflicted approach to the Palestinians. After the Battle of Karameh, and especially following the Jordan-PLO civil war, a growing number of US officials, particularly in the foreign service and intelligence communities, began to recognize the need to accommodate Palestinian nationalism in some form.[13] Even President Richard Nixon felt the need to acknowledge that "[n]o lasting settlement can be achieved in the Middle East without addressing the legitimate aspirations of the Palestinian people."[14] Thus, while violence may have sullied the image of Palestinians, it also put the issue squarely on the international agenda.

At the same time, most US officials remained highly skeptical and distrustful of Palestinian political leaders. The involvement of PLO factions in political violence, including various acts of terrorism, was no doubt off-putting to US officials. Ultimately, however, Washington's aversion to the PLO was primarily a function of political, rather than moral, considerations. For Israeli leaders, the idea of engaging with the PLO, or for that matter any acknowledgment of Palestinian nationalism whatsoever, was a total nonstarter. And in keeping with their burgeoning "special relationship," US officials remained highly deferential to Israeli needs and priorities. Cold War politics was another key factor. In the Manichean mindset of many US policymakers, the PLO fell squarely in the "radical" camp, alongside regimes in Syria, Algeria, North Yemen, and other Soviet "clients," even though in reality PLO-USSR relations were considerably more nuanced and ambivalent.

Few American policymakers were more hostile to the Palestinians than Kissinger, who was the most important national security official in the US government by the middle of 1973. As Nixon became increasingly consumed by the Watergate scandal, he gradually ceded control of US foreign policy to Kissinger. As a realist, Kissinger viewed geopolitical conflicts strictly through the lens of states and the power dynamics between them. As a result, he had little patience for the notion of a comprehensive peace and even less for the Palestinian question. Moreover, as a dyed-in-the-wool Cold Warrior, Kissinger viewed the Arab-Israeli dispute not as a distinct conflict with its own history and dynamics, but instead as an extension of the global struggle between the United States and the Soviet Union.[15]

The primary goal of Kissinger's Middle East diplomacy, therefore, was to keep the Soviets and their regional clients at bay, while promoting American and Israeli preeminence. All of this precluded a possible role for the PLO, which, for Kissinger, was not only a tool of the Soviet Union—and hence irrelevant to the diplomatic process—but also an "overtly anti-American" force that needed to be marginalized and weakened for Arab-Israeli diplomacy to succeed.[16] While many in western Europe and even within the US government were beginning to come to terms with the need for some sort of political accommodation with the Palestinians, Kissinger remained adamant in his opposition to the idea.

Impatient with the CIA track's failure to open up a political channel, Arafat intensified his overtures to the United States. In July 1973, the PLO chairman sent a message to the Nixon administration promising to "put the lid on" fedayeen operations targeting Americans "as long as both sides could maintain a dialogue,"[17] while also signaling a readiness to live in peace with Israel.[18] The timing was somewhat awkward to say the least. Three months earlier, two American diplomats in Khartoum were murdered by the Black September Organization (BSO), a Fateh terror cell believed to be under Arafat's direction and the same group that had been responsible for the murder of eleven Israeli athletes at the 1972 Olympic Games in Munich.[19] After the Khartoum killings, however, the PLO leadership decided to turn off the "terror tap," effectively ending Fateh's direct involvement in international terrorism.[20]

Be that as it may, Kissinger instructed his people to respond to Arafat with a "nothing message," offering just enough to keep the PLO leader on the hook while offering little in the way of substance. The United States was prepared to be part of "a far-reaching solution of the refugee problem," the message read, while acknowledging that "some Palestinians have an interest in political self-expression of some kind." The carefully worded letter included an additional teaser: "If the Palestinians are prepared to participate in a settlement by negotiation, the US would be pleased to hear their ideas."[21] The PLO's unrequited pursuit of US support would play out more intensively following the October War.

THE 1973 WAR AND ITS AFTERMATH: SHIFTING PERCEPTIONS (1973–1975)

The October 1973 Arab-Israeli War reshuffled the geopolitical deck once again. The surprise attack by Egypt and Syria shattered the aura of Israeli invincibility, giving new impetus to a diplomatic settlement and creating new opportunities for US-PLO engagement. Following the war, UN Security Council Resolution 338 reaffirmed the "land for peace" formula enshrined in Resolution 242 and called for an international peace conference to be held in Geneva in December 1973. In retaliation for the US decision to resupply the Israeli military during the war, the Arab oil-producing states imposed an oil embargo on the United States and its allies. Although the peace process remained officially under the sponsorship of both superpowers, the United States was now the dominant force in the Geneva process and Arab-Israeli peacemaking more generally, both of which were overseen by Kissinger himself.

The war also marked a decisive shift in the PLO's overall diplomatic strategy and its approach toward the United States. The PLO leadership had already begun to shift its focus from armed struggle toward a political settlement after 1970. In the wake of the October War, however, the PLO's determination to enter the diplomatic process increased dramatically, such that it became the core of its state-building project.[22] Moreover, just as Egyptian president Anwar Sadat had concluded that the United States now held "99 percent of the cards," Arafat now similarly believed that the road to a future Palestinian state ran directly through Washington—an assumption that would shape Palestinian politics and diplomacy for the next half century.[23]

On paper, the official Soviet position, which called for a unified Arab stance toward Israel and upheld "the just struggle of the Palestinian Arab people for their legitimate national rights," was considerably more sympathetic to the Palestinians than that of the United States.[24] The Soviets had also provided training and even arms to Arafat's Fateh movement.[25] Despite the PLO's expanding ties to the Soviet Union, however, the relationship remained more a marriage of convenience than one of affection. For the PLO leadership, the Soviet Union represented a useful and mutually beneficial counterweight to the United States. The Soviets, meanwhile, regarded their support for the PLO as a way to burnish their anti-imperialist bona fides, gain access to key Arab regimes, and secure their own role in the Middle East peace process. Even so, with the United States now firmly in control of Arab-Israeli peacemaking, there was little doubt as to which superpower the PLO leadership preferred.

Hoping to earn the PLO a seat at the table at the Geneva conference, Arafat intensified his outreach to Washington immediately after the war. This time, the US administration was more responsive. Kissinger authorized CIA deputy director Vernon Walters to meet with two of Arafat's deputies in Rabat in November 1973 and again in March 1974, the first ever high-level contacts between the United States and the PLO. Arafat hoped to use the dialogue to convince the Americans that he was prepared to make far-reaching compromises, and thereby facilitate his entry into the peace process. By contrast, Kissinger had agreed to engage with the PLO only as a way "to gain some maneuvering room" and limit its ability to create problems for his diplomatic strategy.[26] As a result, Walters was restricted to a "listening brief" and instructed to inform his Palestinian interlocutors that the "United States has no proposals to make."[27] In the end, each side took away from the meeting more or less what it had put into it. Whereas from the US perspective "the meeting yielded no lasting results," the Palestinians drew an entirely different conclusion.[28] As Arafat's envoy confessed to his Moroccan host, King Hassan, the PLO regarded the dialogue with Washington as "historic." He added that "everything the Palestinians had done had been to get the attention of the United States because only it could give them territory."[29]

Indeed, in the immediate aftermath of the war, Arafat went to some lengths to demonstrate the PLO's flexibility. One of the earliest signs that his leadership was moving away from the PLO's traditional maximalist stance came during the Arab summit in Algiers in November 1973. The Algiers Declaration omitted two previously sacred clauses regarding the Palestinian struggle, which had emphasized the "indivisibility of Palestine" and the sanctity of "armed struggle" as the only path to liberate Palestine. While the Israelis dismissed the new language as a restatement of PLO policy to destroy Israel in two phases instead of one, the assembled Arab delegates "saw it for what it was: a step toward accepting Israel."[30] To further ingratiate himself to the Americans, Arafat intensified the PLO's clandestine security cooperation with the CIA. Specifically, he agreed to extend Fateh's help in providing security for American diplomats stationed in Lebanon, and to supply valuable intelligence on a wide range of anti-American threats, including an assassination attempt on Kissinger in December 1973 and other terror plots by rogue Palestinian factions.[31]

In the run-up to Geneva, Arafat sent his clearest message yet to the Americans. Communicating through a third party, the PLO leader privately assured US officials that the PLO "in no way seeks the destruction of Israel, but accepts its existence as a sovereign state; the PLO's main aim at the Geneva conference will be the creation of a Palestinian state out of the 'Palestinian part of Jordan' [the West Bank] plus Gaza."[32] This was the first, albeit unofficial, endorsement by the PLO leadership of a peace settlement based on a two-state solution, fifteen years before it became official PLO policy and a quarter century before either the Israelis or the Americans came around to the idea. From the standpoint of internal Palestinian politics, Arafat's gestures were highly risky as well. The PLO factions remained deeply divided over the Geneva process, and the idea of relinquishing any part of the Palestinian homeland in return for a "mini-state" in the West Bank and Gaza remained highly contentious. Indeed, for some Palestinian groups such a compromise was treasonous.

Kissinger had no intention of bringing the PLO or the Palestinians, both of which were fundamentally incompatible with his Middle East diplomacy, into the negotiations. After all, the Israelis were categorical in their rejection of any form of Palestinian participation at any stage of the peace process, and as Kissinger later observed, they "resisted any reference to Palestinians no matter how hedged and qualified."[33] To the extent that the Palestinians factored into Kissinger's thinking—which was very little—it was not as a distinct national group with a discernable set of political demands or grievances but as perennial spoilers, a diplomatic "nuisance" that threatened to disrupt the peace process and thus needed to be brought under control or otherwise neutralized. "Once [the PLO are] in the peace process, they can radicalize all the others," he said. "They'll raise all the issues the Israelis can't handle, and no other Arab can raise any other issues once the PLO is raised."[34] In his view, the "Palestinian problem" was not, as most of the world believed, a matter that concerned Israel, but an issue to be resolved by and within Jordan, and the solution lay with Jordan's King Hussein, rather than with the PLO.[35] As such, he insisted, the Palestinians should be treated "not as an international but as an inter-Arab concern."[36]

Kissinger had other concerns as well. He worried about the potential domestic political fallout from trying to involve the Palestinians in the peace process. As he put it, "In the United States anything including the PLO would run us into trouble with the Jews in the maximum conditions for irresponsibility."[37] Moreover, in keeping with his Cold War mindset, the primary goal of US mediation was not to address the underlying grievances or root causes of the conflict, but to support Washington's Israeli ally against the Soviet Union's "radical" Arab clients, such as Syria and the PLO, while working to pry other Arab states, and especially Egypt, away from USSR influence and to keep the Soviets from having any meaningful role in the peace process.[38] Such views were certainly not uncommon in US government and political circles at the time. But as attitudes toward the Palestinians in Washington generally began to soften in the early and mid-1970s, Kissinger's views remained largely impervious to change.

The December 1973 Geneva conference was therefore largely for international, and especially Arab and Soviet, consumption. As Kissinger later explained, "We had no incentive to participate in a diplomacy—much less a multilateral conference—in which the Soviet Union would appear as the lawyer for the Arab side and maneuver us into a position where we would be either isolated at the side of Israel or obligated to deliver Israeli acquiescence to a program incompatible with its long term survival."[39] Instead, the real process would be conducted by Kissinger himself through "step-by-step diplomacy."

In contrast to the Arab and Soviet positions, which favored a unified Arab stance toward Israel and pushed for a prominent role for the PLO at Geneva, Kissinger's piecemeal approach was designed to deal with the Egyptian, Jordanian, and Syrian tracks separately. The question of Palestinian participation would be decided after the launch of the Geneva conference, preferably at the end of the process.[40] In the first phase, Kissinger focused on brokering disengagement agreements between Israel, Egypt, and Syria, with the aim of securing further interim deals that might eventually lead to separate peace deals between Israel and each of its Arab neighbors. Egypt was especially crucial to Kissinger's plan, since it was the largest and most militarily capable Arab state and Sadat had signaled his intention to turn away from the Soviet Union when he expelled a large number of USSR military personnel from the country in July 1972.

Even after the PLO was excluded from the Geneva conference, Arafat continued to push his pragmatic agenda, both internally and externally, while working to enhance the international standing of both the PLO and the Palestinians. In doing so, he hoped to make it impossible for the US administration to continue ignoring them. In November 1973, the European Community called for respecting the "legitimate rights of the Palestinians" and, for the first time, acknowledged the Palestinians as a party to the conflict.[41] Months later, Soviet foreign minister Andrei Gromyko held his first public meeting with Arafat.[42]

In June 1974, Arafat pushed the Palestine National Council, the PLO's parliament-in-exile, to adopt a new political program calling for the establishment of a "fighting national authority" on any liberated part of Palestinian territory. Although rejected by hard-line PLO factions like the PFLP and the Syrian-backed Al-Saiqa, the measure was widely regarded as a win for PLO moderates, including in Washington.[43] Despite its "heavily qualified language," White House national security staffer William Quandt explained to his superiors, the new PLO statement amounted to a recognition "that it was prepared to settle for a Palestinian state consisting only of the West Bank and Gaza."[44] Indeed, even hard-liners inside the PLO leadership, according to an internal assessment by the CIA, were showing "elements of rather startling pragmatism."[45]

Such assessments were indicative of the profound shift that had occurred with regard to the Palestinians within the US national security and intelligence establishments in the aftermath of the October War. As US intelligence analysts closely monitored the intense internal debate between PLO "moderates" and "rejectionists," many urged the administration to take advantage of Arafat's gestures.[46] By early 1975, there was strong support within the State Department for engaging with the PLO.[47] As the American ambassador to Lebanon, G. McMurtrie Godley, argued to Kissinger in January 1975, "however inconvenient its existence or repugnant its behavior, [the] PLO has become a reality," and it enjoyed the sympathy and support of millions of Palestinians and Arabs across the region.[48] Moreover, continuing to exclude the Palestinians from the peace process, a US national intelligence estimate warned, would likely result in increased terrorism and violence.[49] Even Congress, where pro-Israel and anti-PLO sentiment ran especially high, was beginning to show signs of change, as a number of senators and representatives spoke openly for the first time about Palestinian rights and past suffering.[50] A handful of lawmakers went so far as to meet with Arafat—helping to boost the Palestinian leader's legitimacy and opening up new channels of communication with Washington—and urged the administration to do the same.[51]

Kissinger remained unmoved, however. If anything, the PLO's growing international acceptability became a source of endless frustration and alarm for Kissinger, who still clung to the idea that Jordan, rather than the PLO, should speak for the Palestinians. In a meeting with American Jewish leaders in early 1974, he warned that "if the Israelis don't make some sort of arrangement with Hussein on the West Bank in six months, Arafat will become internationally recognized and the world will be in a chaos."[52] Kissinger's timing was off by just a few months. In October, the Arab League unanimously recognized the PLO as "the sole legitimate representative of the Palestinian people."[53] Kissinger blasted the decision as a "fit of emotional myopia" by the Arab states, and lamented that it had "deprived Hussein of his negotiating role on the West Bank," as well as granted authority to "the one group Israel was least likely to accept, as interlocutor."[54]

The high point of Arafat's international campaign, however, came a few weeks later when the UN General Assembly—over strong US objection—voted to grant observer status to the PLO as the official "representative of the Palestinian people," while affirming the "right of the Palestinian people to self-determination."[55] Arafat's diplomatic victory at the United Nations was yet another major setback to Kissinger's vision for the peace process, and it resulted in a tension for US policy that would play out consistently over the next several decades. Without mentioning the PLO by name, the US representative to the United Nations, John Scali, castigated those engaged in a "deliberate policy of terror," while insisting that the "sole alternative to the sterile pursuit of change through violence is negotiation."[56]

The irony, of course, was that it was precisely Washington's exclusion of the PLO from the peace process that had brought Arafat to the United Nations in the first place. "I am a rebel and freedom is my cause," declared Arafat in his now famous address before the UN General Assembly. Though the thrust of his message was ultimately a political appeal, he stated: "Even as today we address this General Assembly from an international rostrum we are also expressing our faith in political and diplomatic struggle as complements, as enhancements of armed struggle." To drive the point home, the PLO chief ended his speech on a dramatic note: "Today I have come bearing an olive branch and a freedom-fighter's gun. Do not let the olive branch fall from my hand."[57]

Despite Washington's continued hostility toward the Palestinian leader, US officials continued to engage with the PLO. Upon Arafat's arrival in New York City, roughly a week before the landmark UN vote, not only did US officials do nothing to prevent the PLO leader's speech, they also afforded him all of the pomp and circumstance of a head of state, including a Secret Service security detail and official motorcade. Arafat's red-carpet treatment, which occurred shortly after the Arab oil embargo had been lifted and in the midst of highly sensitive Egyptian-Israeli disengagement talks, may have been a gesture to Egyptian, Saudi, and other Arab leaders, who had persistently badgered Kissinger on the need to talk to the PLO. But there were other reasons for affording Arafat such a warm welcome. On the day of his speech, a meeting took place at the Waldorf Astoria between a senior CIA official and Salameh. Although records of the meeting remain classified, what is known is that an agreement was reached to formalize existing US-PLO understandings on security and intelligence sharing, as well as the training of Palestinian forces providing security for US diplomats in Beirut. Arafat hoped that by ingratiating himself with the Americans and elevating the PLO's status, he would force US officials to take up the Palestinian issue and make it impossible for Washington to continue ignoring the PLO politically. He was wrong on both counts.

OPENING A WINDOW AND CLOSING THE DOOR

In the wake of the historic UN vote, developments on the American-Palestinian front evolved quite rapidly—but in two different directions. Even as Washington became more open and attuned to the perspectives and aspirations of Palestinians, the door to their inclusion in the political process was simultaneously being closed. Despite the apparent deepening of US-PLO ties, the United States continued to keep the PLO at arm's length.

No sooner had Arafat's delegation departed New York City than the State Department put forward new guidelines instructing government officials to avoid any statement or action "implying official [US government] recognition of [the] PLO as quote [the] sole legitimate representative of [the] Palestinian people unquote or in any other capacity."[58] A month later, the Immigration and Naturalization Service issued a blanket ban on visas to "past and present members" of the PLO. The ban was so broad and sweeping that it drew protests from the State Department for effectively painting all Palestinians with the brush of "terrorism," which was deemed "highly questionable and offensive."[59] Although Kissinger later authorized an exemption for the PLO's

UN personnel, other PLO officials were effectively prohibited from traveling to the United States. There were other exceptions as well, but they were similarly short-lived. In late 1976, as a gesture to Sadat, Kissinger agreed to allow the PLO to open an "information office" in Washington. Following a complaint from the Israeli ambassador, however, he promptly had the office shut down and its officers deported.[60]

American official ambivalence was on full display in late 1975. By March of that year, Kissinger's step-by-step approach had reached a dead end. A year of on-and-off shuttle diplomacy had failed to secure a second Israeli disengagement deal with Egypt, an outcome for which both Kissinger and President Gerald Ford blamed Israel, due to its refusal to consider a meaningful withdrawal in the Sinai. In an attempt to pressure the Israelis to soften their stance, Ford declared a "reassessment" in US-Israel relations, which included the suspension of US weapons transfers, a downgrading of diplomatic ties, a threat to abandon step-by-step diplomacy in favor of a comprehensive US peace plan, and even the prospect of some form of Palestinian participation in the peace process.[61] When faced with intense opposition from the American Jewish community and Congress, however, the administration eventually backed away from its threats.[62]

At the same time, the broader policy community—both inside and outside of government—was involved in its own reconsideration of US Middle East policy, particularly with regard to the Palestinians. Even Congress's historically icy relationship to the Palestinian question was beginning to thaw somewhat. In the fall of 1975, the House of Representatives held a series of unprecedented hearings on the "Palestine Issue," which covered the whole range of issues—from the origins of the conflict, to the nature of Palestinian politics, to the shortcomings of existing US policy—and brought Palestinian voices to Capitol Hill for the first time in more than half a century.[63]

The administration was showing signs of change as well, using the autumn 1975 congressional hearings as a platform to announce a new approach to the Palestinians. Testifying before the House Committee on International Relations, Deputy Assistant Secretary of State Hal Saunders reiterated the US position that "the legitimate aspirations or interests of the Palestinians must be taken into account." But for the first time he also acknowledged that the fate of the Palestinians was not merely a humanitarian matter, but also a "political factor which must be dealt with" in the context of negotiations. Saunders added, "In many ways, the Palestinian dimension of the Arab-Israeli conflict is the heart of that conflict." The statement called for "bringing issues of concern to the Palestinians into negotiation," but stopped short of calling for direct Palestinian participation in the peace process, maintaining the old formula of allowing the Arab states to represent Palestinian interests, which the Israelis were of course free to reject.[64] Outraged over Saunders's testimony, the Israeli leadership protested the new policy, prompting Kissinger to publicly disavow the statement—despite having vetted it beforehand.[65]

At the same time, an interagency working group made up of State Department, CIA, and other analysts was launched to study various aspects of the issue, from the status of West Bank land and Israeli settlements to the possibility of bringing the Palestinians, and perhaps even the PLO, into the peace process. The working group also commissioned two Washington think tanks to conduct their own studies of the issue. The better known of these, published by the Brookings Institution in December 1975, called for what was then considered a radically new approach to the peace process based on a comprehensive peace settlement and an end to the step-by-step approach, as well as some form of Palestinian self-determination.[66]

Washington's newfound openness to the Palestinian question did not, however, translate into a more accommodating policy toward the PLO or the Palestinians. In fact, the opposite occurred. In an attempt to push the stalled Egyptian-Israeli disengagement talks forward, and with both the Israeli government and pro-Israel forces in Washington calling the bluff on the Ford administration's threats, Kissinger concluded he could catch more flies with honey than with vinegar. As a way to incentivize the Israelis to agree to a more substantive withdrawal from parts of the Sinai, Kissinger promised that the United States would not "recognize or negotiate with" the PLO until it recognized Israel's right to exist and accepted Security Council Resolution 242, and further promised to "consult fully" with Israel beforehand.[67] The pledge, which was contained in a secret memorandum of agreement (MOA) signed by the two sides in September 1975, notably made no mention of terrorism, which was only added as a third condition a decade later.

Arafat was in no position to accept the conditions, however. Having already incurred the wrath of the hard-line Palestinian factions for his gestures to Washington and implicit acceptance of Israel, formal recognition of Israel—whose leaders in any case did not even recognize the existence of a Palestinian nation—was not on the table. The same went for Resolution 242, which had neglected even to mention the Palestinians, much less their right to self-determination.[68] Kissinger had downplayed the significance of the MOA as little more than a codification of existing US policy.[69] In reality, however, it came to be seen as a "no contact" policy that effectively tied the hands of subsequent administrations.[70] At the same time, in a separate letter from Ford to Israeli prime minister Yitzhak Rabin, the United States promised always to consult with Israel before putting forward any peace proposal of its own, the so-called no surprises pledge.[71]

Some have taken Kissinger's willingness to engage with the PLO as a sign that, while he was clearly no fan of the organization, he was not implacably opposed to the Palestinians or their aspirations, and might even have accepted a deeper political role for the PLO had it, for instance, shown a greater willingness to compromise.[72] For example, it is clear Kissinger did not view the MOA as a blanket ban on US dealings with the PLO. This was particularly true of the highly valued US-PLO security dialogue, which he considered to be exempt from the pledge and took on even greater importance after the start of the Lebanese Civil War in 1975.[73] Moreover, Kissinger repeatedly assured Arab leaders that the United States had not ruled out recognizing the PLO or even the possibility of a future Palestinian state.[74]

But the notion that Kissinger was prepared to countenance a PLO role—or any type of Palestinian participation in the peace process during his tenure—simply does not jibe with the totality of the historical record, including Kissinger's own copious memoirs, to say nothing of the lasting impact of his policies. As he wrote after leaving office, "The idea of a Palestinian state run by the PLO was not a subject for serious discourse."[75] To the extent that Kissinger was prepared to deal with the PLO, his purposes were strictly utilitarian or tactical in nature. The goal of the US security dialogue with the PLO, apart from its obvious intelligence and security value—as Kissinger frequently reminds us—was mainly to neutralize its troublemaking ability and keep it from disrupting his step-by-step diplomacy. Likewise, Kissinger's assurances to Arab leaders mainly served as a way to placate them and keep them engaged in the process.[76]

It is true that Kissinger expressed a certain inevitability about a PLO role in the peace process. "We can't refuse forever to talk to the PLO," he told his colleagues in late 1975, just weeks after his pledge to the Israelis. "We could co-exist with the PLO. It is indeed historically inevitable."[77] The question, however, was not if, but when, how, and under what conditions the PLO would be allowed to join the political process. And on this, Kissinger left little doubt. "We cannot deliver the minimum demands of the PLO so why talk to them," he told a group of US ambassadors in August 1976. "They are a Soviet trojan horse because they would give the Soviets leverage over the negotiations if they got into them prematurely. We can bring them in at the end of the process after the others have been satisfied and the PLO has been weakened."[78]

In contrast to his ad hoc, tactical dealings with the PLO, Kissinger's hostility to PLO participation in the political process was deliberate and strategic—something he stressed repeatedly both in real time and in later reflections. Indeed, as a non-state actor with close ties to the Soviets, and whose very existence posed a direct threat to two important US allies, the PLO was everything Kissinger loathed. "We had as little desire to involve Arafat as we had to share the table with Gromyko, for we viewed the PLO as a potentially disruptive force," he explains in his memoirs.[79] As such, the PLO was antithetical to Kissinger's vision of peace. Clinging to the view of the PLO as inherently radical and fundamentally incapable of compromise, he dismissed Arafat's repeated gestures of moderation as insincere.[80] Kissinger's abiding belief in the PLO's dogmatism was ultimately shaped by his own ideological rigidity, as he continued to insist that "involving the PLO was incompatible with the interests of any of the parties to the Middle East conflict," a rather remarkable claim in light of the fact that the Arab states, the Soviets, much of western Europe, and large swaths of the US foreign policy and intelligence communities had voiced their support for bringing the PLO into the political process.[81]

Nor was Kissinger's desire to weaken the PLO merely theoretical. As the Lebanon war raged on, the US administration happily accepted the assistance of Fateh security forces in coordinating the evacuation of American citizens from Beirut in the summer of 1976, for which they earned public expressions of gratitude from both Ford and Kissinger.[82] In a letter to Arafat delivered through Egyptian intermediaries, the secretary of state noted his desire "to inform the Palestinian leadership of his appreciation of the great and constructive role undertaken by the Palestinians."[83]

But this did not prevent Kissinger from using the Lebanese crisis as an opportunity to tame the PLO. His hope was that a Syrian intervention in Lebanon would weaken Fateh and keep the PLO divided, allowing him to continue promoting Jordan as the representative of the Palestinians.[84] The goal, as Kissinger put it, was "to help weaken the PLO without losing the PLO."[85] Whether he genuinely believed he could undermine the PLO in the political and diplomatic realms without seriously diminishing its security value to the United States, or was simply prepared to sacrifice the latter in order to attain the former, remains unclear. What we do know, however, is that the PLO's exclusion from the peace process helped to embolden Palestinian rejectionists at the expense of Arafat and other moderates. As a heavily redacted CIA analysis concluded at the time, "Yasir Arafat's relatively moderate policies favoring Palestinian participation in Middle East peace negotiations have so far brought few tangible gains for the Palestinians." As a result, "PLO leaders are also taking pains to polish their activist image in order to detract from the appeal of the rejectionists."[86]

LASTING LEGACY

The dynamics and trends established after 1973 would continue to shape US-Palestinian relations for the next several decades, both before and after the PLO's formal entry into the peace process in 1993. Despite the passage of several decades and successive US administrations from both parties, the peace process engineered by Kissinger in the 1970s would become the template, in both procedural and ideological terms, for all future US peacemaking in the Arab-Israeli arena. In addition to solidifying US "ownership" over the Arab-Israeli negotiations, Kissinger's policies succeeded in keeping the PLO out of the peace process for nearly two decades, as well as in prioritizing separate peace deals between Israel and each of its Arab neighbors over a comprehensive peace settlement, all of which was designed to prioritize US and Israeli interests over those of the Arab states and their backers. Even President Jimmy Carter's administration, despite its preference for a comprehensive peace and persistent attempts to bring the PLO into the peace process, ultimately reverted to the Kissinger model, thanks to both the 1975 MOA and Egypt's decision to pursue a separate peace with Israel in 1978.[87]

The Camp David Accords, which in addition to producing the first formal peace treaty between Israel and an Arab state also included a separate framework for limited Palestinian autonomy in the West Bank and Gaza, was a testament to Carter's diplomacy, but also to Kissinger's astute political engineering. The Camp David autonomy plan itself became a precedent for dealing with the Palestinian track, both as a model for a future interim arrangement and in marking a return to the old framework of determining the fate of Palestinians without their participation. Moreover, Kissinger's strategic exclusion of the PLO was not solely a function of what the group said or did but also reflected a particular mindset, a philosophy that explicitly and fundamentally devalued—even pathologized—the politics and aspirations of the Palestinians. While Kissinger's enduring disdain for all things Palestinian was certainly not invented by or unique to him—and may well have been an inescapable outcome of the "special relationship" and the Israel-centric lens through which most US policymakers and politicians viewed the issue—he succeeded in elevating this mindset into an article of faith of the US-led Middle East peace process, of which the formal exclusion of the PLO was only one part.

In the end, the way in which events ultimately unfolded aligned rather neatly with Kissinger's original vision. After Egypt, Jordan became the second Arab country to sign a peace treaty with Israel in 1994. Syria and Israel came exceptionally close to a conflict-ending agreement in 2000, but ultimately fell short of that goal. At the same time, the "no surprises" pledge, which became a staple in all subsequent US-sponsored negotiations, from Carter's Camp David summit to the Obama administration's talks of 2014, helped to ensure that the United States and Israel, as the two most powerful actors in the process, remained in political lockstep. Meanwhile, Kissinger's MOA, which was later expanded and codified into US law and inspired several generations of anti-PLO legislation, succeeded in delaying the PLO's entry into the diplomatic process before eventually subduing it. The PLO finally joined the peace process in 1993, much as Kissinger had hoped, from a position of weakness.

On the other side of the equation, the PLO leadership, with very few exceptions, has since the mid-1970s remained remarkably consistent in its commitment to a US-led peace process, even when the United States could not deliver. Israel's disastrous invasion of Lebanon in 1982, in which a US-brokered ceasefire failed to prevent the massacre of some 1,000 to 3,000 Palestinian refugees at the hands of an Israeli-allied Lebanese militia, marked one of the bloodiest episodes in the history of the Israeli-Palestinian conflict, as well as the first instance of a US-brokered deal between the PLO and Israel.[88] The Lebanon debacle left the PLO badly weakened and internally divided but otherwise did nothing to diminish the PLO's faith in Washington, which only intensified throughout the 1980s.

President Ronald Reagan's administration, for its part, kept up the pretense of shunning the PLO, though there was hardly a moment in which it was not engaged with it in one back channel or another.[89] Reagan did eventually open an official dialogue with the PLO after Arafat had met US conditions in late 1988, though it ultimately went nowhere, as neither Reagan nor his successor, George H. W. Bush, could yet countenance a direct role for the PLO in the peace process. The 1991 Madrid peace conference, which brought the Palestinians into the diplomatic process for the first time—without the PLO—had the look and feel of a multilateral process, but in reality, it consisted of separate bilateral tracks, including a joint Palestinian-Jordanian delegation.

The start of the Oslo process in 1993 fundamentally transformed US-Palestinian relations, though most of the underlying dynamics remained the same. On the one hand, the PLO's direct incorporation into the peace process necessitated a degree of normalization in US-Palestinian ties and even fostered a budding bilateral relationship of sorts. On the other hand, given the depth of the US-Israel special relationship and the enduring influence of the pro-Israel forces in Congress, the US-Palestinian relationship remained highly precarious, conditional, and ultimately reversible. Although it did not begin as a US initiative, the Oslo process that the United States inherited and quickly came to dominate was based on a familiar model. Building on the earlier Camp David Accords, Oslo called for limited Palestinian autonomy for a five-year interim period, while putting off the core issues of the conflict to the end of the process. Moreover, the process itself—a set of interim deals with no clearly defined endgame and a focus on incremental progress and confidence-building measures, all under permanent US stewardship—was quintessentially Kissingerian.

At the same time, the Oslo process represented a somewhat odd convergence of interests between the United States and the PLO. For the PLO, which was badly weakened and virtually bankrupt in the aftermath of the 1991 Persian Gulf War, Oslo was a lifeline that would help ensure its survival and allow it to establish a foothold in the homeland on which to build the long-awaited Palestinian state. Meanwhile, President Bill Clinton's administration saw the Oslo process as a vehicle not just for resolving the conflict but also for transforming the Palestinians into a suitable peace partner. Moreover, the return of the peace process to Washington, much like Kissinger's diplomacy in the 1970s, was seen as a way of projecting American power and influence, as the world's sole remaining superpower, in the Middle East and beyond, as well as promoting Israeli normalization and integration in the region.

The establishment of official US-PLO ties after Oslo, however, did not lead to a normalization of relations between the two sides. Instead, the process reflected, and ultimately reinforced, the highly asymmetrical political and power dynamics that existed between the Palestinians on the one hand and Israel and the United States on the other, particularly in light of prevailing notions about the defective nature of Palestinian politics among decision-makers on both ends of Pennsylvania Avenue. The vast corpus of anti-PLO legislation accumulated over the years remained on the books, while Congress enacted temporary presidential waivers in order to allow the peace process to continue, all of which remained conditional on Palestinian compliance with its obligations under Oslo.

The fact that Oslo was not simply a process of conflict resolution between two parties but also a process of "state-building" for the Palestinians meant that outside actors, including the United States, foreign donors, and even Israel, now had a direct say in—and in many ways an effective veto over—key aspects of Palestinian political life.[90] As a result, the Oslo process became as much a tool for transforming Palestinian politics as for altering the dynamics between Israelis and Palestinians. If the Palestinians' entry into the peace process was predicated, as Kissinger had wanted, on the PLO being tamed, the Oslo process would help ensure that its successor, the Palestinian Authority (PA), would be fully domesticated.

For its part, the Palestinian leadership was willing to give up a degree of control over internal Palestinian politics and decision-making in the hope that the United States would ultimately prevail on Israel to end its occupation of the West Bank and Gaza, and thereby enable the creation of a Palestinian state. Instead of leading to independence, however, Oslo effectively deepened and institutionalized Palestinian dependence on the United States, which was no longer simply the chief mediator but also the PA's main political sponsor and largest single donor, as well as on Israel.[91] Moreover, as the two most powerful actors bound by a special relationship, the United States and Israel had both the ability and the incentive to shift as many of the political risks and costs onto the Palestinians as possible, especially when things went wrong.

The collapse of US-sponsored negotiations at Camp David and the subsequent outbreak of the Al-Aqsa Intifada in 2000 were a reminder of just how precarious and conditional the relationship was. Despite explicit promises by Clinton to Arafat not to blame the Palestinians in the event of the summit's failure,[92] and although it was clear that both sides had contributed to the failure of negotiations and the escalating violence, the Clinton administration did not hesitate in placing the blame for both on the Palestinians, while echoing Israeli claims that there was "no partner" on the Palestinian side.[93]

The view that Palestinian intransigence and militancy were the primary drivers of the conflict, rather than Israel's continued occupation, intensified under President George W. Bush, particularly in the wake of the 9/11 terror attacks. Bush demanded the Palestinians "elect new leaders . . . not compromised by terror," while effectively green-lighting Prime Minister Ariel Sharon's military assault on Palestinian governing and security institutions.[94] The election of Mahmoud Abbas, who brought an end to the intifada and was even more committed to the PLO's American strategy than his predecessor, did little to alter these dynamics, as the Palestinians learned following Hamas's surprise election victory in 2006. Unwilling to accept any role for Hamas in the Palestinian government, the Bush administration and Israel led an international blockade of the PA, in effect forcing Abbas to choose between international isolation and undoing the results of a democratic election, ultimately leading to civil war and the division of the PA in 2007.[95]

Meanwhile, attempts by the Palestinian leadership to break free from this arrangement or otherwise enhance its domestic or international standing, such as its bid to gain membership in the United Nations in 2011–2012 or seek reconciliation with Hamas, have typically been met with sanctions and other punitive measures, including new laws conditioning US financial assistance to the Palestinians and the continued operation of the PLO mission in Washington on the Palestinians refraining from joining any other UN agencies or taking any action against Israel at the International Criminal Court.[96] While these measures were enacted by Congress rather than the administration, a direct ideological line can be drawn straight from Kissinger's 1975 MOA through the anti-PLO laws of the 1980s and 1990s to recent laws such as the Taylor Force Act and the Anti-Terrorism Clarification Act of 2018.

In the end, the Palestinian leadership understood it was too weak and dependent on the United States to pull away completely. The closest the Palestinian leadership has ever come to abandoning its American strategy, following President Donald Trump's decision to recognize Jerusalem as Israel's capital in late 2017, was ultimately short-lived. Abbas responded by severing political and security ties with the United States and Israel, marking a historic low in Palestinian-American relations. Once Trump was defeated in 2020, however, Abbas quickly announced the resumption of PA security coordination with Israel, along with other gestures to the incoming administration of President Joe Biden.

CONCLUSION

The post-1973 period was undoubtedly the most dynamic and most formative in terms of US-Palestinian relations and the Arab-Israeli peace process. As the United States emerged as the preeminent player in Arab-Israeli peacemaking, the PLO leadership came to the realization that the road to Palestinian statehood ran exclusively through Washington. It was also in this period that the basic principles of a US-led peace process, with all of its attendant baggage, were laid down. In particular, the three pillars of Kissinger's diplomatic strategy—maintaining US and Israeli preeminence, incremental progress over comprehensive peace, and the pathologizing of Palestinian politics and aspirations—would shape US Middle East diplomacy well after the Palestinians joined the peace process. Even the idea of a two-state solution, first floated by the PLO leadership in the mid-1970s, a quarter century before either the United States or Israel came around to the idea, emerged during this period—though it may have now finally have reached its sell-by date.

Looking back at the last half century of Arab-Israeli peacemaking and American-Palestinian relations, it is hard to escape a basic paradox. On the surface, both the US-led peace process and the PLO's "US strategy" were highly successful, in that both have largely achieved what they set out to do. The diplomatic process that Kissinger engineered, with considerable help from Congress and the pro-Israel lobby, effectively kept the PLO and the Palestinians out of the peace process for the better part of two decades, and thereafter tamed it. On the other side of the ledger, the PLO succeeded in eventually joining the US-led peace process and in enlisting American support for Palestinian statehood.

And yet all of these today seem like pyrrhic victories. In many ways, the process Kissinger created worked *too* well, first by delaying the PLO's entry into the peace process and then by attempting to tame it. The Oslo process has effectively institutionalized Palestinian weakness and dependence on the United States and Israel in ways Kissinger could only have dreamed of. At the same time, a weak and divided Palestinian leadership proved not to be an asset to the peace process, as Kissinger had insisted, but a source of chronic violence and instability. For most of the last fifty years, the Palestinian leadership, from Arafat to Abbas, has wagered on the United States as the only party capable of compelling Israel to end its occupation and allowing the emergence of an independent Palestinian state. The lopsided power dynamics that Kissinger was so keen to enshrine in the peace process, however, effectively reversed that formula. Instead of the United States delivering Israel, the US-led peace process ended up delivering the Palestinians to Israel. Not only has the Palestinians' overreliance on American deliverance failed to bring about liberation, it has also come at the expense of Palestinian agency and initiative, as well the leadership's domestic legitimacy and internal Palestinian political cohesion. In the end, the peace process succeeded in making Palestinian leaders more pliant, but left them too weak to serve as effective peace partners or to address the myriad challenges facing the Palestinian people.

NOTES

1. See Yezid Sayigh, *Armed Struggle and the Search for State: The Palestinian National Movement, 1949–1993* (New York: Oxford University Press, 1997), 73–78. See also Moshe Shemesh, *The Palestinian Entity, 1959–1974: Arab Politics and the PLO* (London: Frank Cass, 1996).

2. Central Intelligence Agency (CIA), Central Intelligence Bulletin, February 15, 1958, https://www.cia.gov/readingroom/docs/CENTRAL%20INTELLIGENCE%20BULL%5B15772438%5D.pdf. See also Telegram from the Embassy in Jordan to the Department of State, August 12, 1957, in United States Department of State, *Foreign Relations of the United States [FRUS], 1955–1957*, vol. 13, *Near East—Jordan, Yemen* (Washington, DC: Government Printing Office [GPO], 1988), 156–58; Letter from Under Secretary of State Christian Herter to the Ambassador in Lebanon (Robert McClintock), February 13, 1958, in *FRUS, 1958–1960*, vol. 13, *Arab-Israeli Dispute; United Arab Republic; North Africa* (Washington, DC: GPO, 1992), 18–20; Telegram from the Embassy in Jordan to the Department of State, January 5, 1956, in *FRUS, 1955–1957*, vol. 13, 12–15; Memorandum (Memo) from Assistant Secretary of State for Near Eastern and South Asia Affairs Phillips Talbot to Secretary of State Dean Rusk, "Subject: Suggested Reply to Memorandum of Israeli Ambassador [Regarding] Arab-Israel Situation," May 1, 1961, in *FRUS, 1961–1963*, vol. 17, *Near East, 1961–1962* (Washington, DC: GPO, 1994), 92–96.

3. Circular Airgram (CA-10209) from the Department of State to Certain Posts, "Subject: Guidance on U.S. Contacts with the Palestine Liberation Organization," March 30, 1965, in *FRUS, 1964–1968*, vol. 18, *Arab-Israeli Dispute, 1964–1967* (Washington, DC: GPO, 2000), 426–27.

4. Research Memo (RNA-12) from Deputy Director of the Bureau of Intelligence and Research George C. Denney Jr. to Acting Secretary of State George Ball, "Subject: The Search for a 'Palestine Entity,'" May 11, 1964, in *FRUS, 1964–1968*, vol. 18, document 54.

5. Circular Airgram (CA-10209), March 30, 1965, 426–27.

6. Intelligence Memo No. 2205/66, "Palestine Arab Terrorist Organizations," December 2, 1966, in *FRUS, 1964–1968*, vol. 18, 698–700. See also CIA, Central Intelligence Bulletin, January 20, 1967, https://www.cia.gov/readingroom/docs/CIA-RDP79T00975A009600030001-2.pdf.

7. For the text of Resolution 242, see United Nations Security Council Resolution 242, in *FRUS, 1964–1968*, vol. 19, *Arab-Israeli Crisis and War, 1967* (Washington, DC: GPO, 2004), 1,062–63.

8. Sayigh, *Armed Struggle*, 147. See also W. Andrew Terrill, "The Political Mythology of the Battle of Karameh," *Middle East Journal* 55, no. 1 (Winter 2001): 91–111.

9. Yezid Sayigh, "Armed Struggle and State Formation," *Journal of Palestine Studies* 26, no. 4 (Summer 1997): 17–32.

10. Yezid Sayigh, "The Armed Struggle and Palestinian Nationalism," in *The PLO and Israel: From Armed Conflict to Political Solution*, eds. Avraham Sela and Moshe Maoz (New York: St. Martin's, 1997), 30.

11. Paul Thomas Chamberlin, *The Global Offensive: The United States, the Palestine Liberation Organization, and the Making of the Post-Cold War Order* (New York: Oxford University Press, 2012), 22.

12. Kai Bird, *The Good Spy: The Life and Death of Robert Ames* (New York: Broadway, 2015), 105.

13. Paper Prepared by the National Security Council Staff, November 13, 1970, in *FRUS, 1969–1976*, vol. 23, *Arab-Israeli Dispute, 1969–1972* (Washington, DC: GPO, 2015), 623–32.

14. Second Annual Report to the Congress on United States Foreign Policy, February 25, 1971, American Presidency Project (APP), https://www.presidency.ucsb.edu/documents/second-annual-report-the-congress-united-states-foreign-policy.

15. Henry Kissinger, *White House Years* (Boston: Little, Brown, 1979), 369.

16. Henry Kissinger, *Years of Upheaval* (Boston: Little, Brown, 1982), 625, 503, 624–29.

17. Memorandum of Conversation (Memcon), August 3, 1973, in *FRUS, 1969–1976*, vol. 25, *Arab-Israeli Crisis and War, 1973* (Washington, DC: GPO, 2011), 248n2.

18. Kissinger, *Years of Upheaval*, 626.

19. Intelligence Memo, "The Seizure of the Saudi Arabian Embassy in Khartoum," June 1973, in *FRUS, 1969–1976*, vol. E-6, *Documents on Africa, 1973–1976* (Washington, DC: GPO, 2006), document 217.

20. Sayigh, *Armed Struggle*, 311.

21. Paper for Response to Palestinian Approach, Attached to Memcon, August 3, 1973, 249.

22. Philipp O. Amour, "Palestinian Politics in Transition: The Case of the October War," in *The Yom Kippur War: Politics, Legacy, Diplomacy*, ed. Asaf Siniver (New York: Oxford University Press, 2013), 140.

23. For the Sadat quote, see, for example, Anwar El-Sadat, *In Search of Identity: An Autobiography* (New York: Harper and Row, 1977), 293.

24. Quoted in John C. Reppert, "The Soviets and the PLO: The Convenience of Politics," in *The International Relations of the Palestine Liberation Organization*, eds. Augustus Richard Norton and Martin H. Greenberg (Edwardsville: Southern Illinois University Press, 1989), 115.

25. Reppert, "Soviets and the PLO," 115.

26. Kissinger, *Years of Upheaval*, 628.

27. Ibid., 628.

28. Backchannel Message from Deputy CIA Director Vernon Walters to Kissinger, November 4, 1973, in *FRUS, 1969–1976*, vol. 25, 882–86. See also Kissinger, *Years of Upheaval*, 629.

29. Backchannel Message from Walters to Kissinger, November 4, 1973, 885n7.

30. Jonathan J. Goldberg, *Jewish Power: Inside the American Jewish Establishment* (Reading, MA: Basic, 1997), 247.

31. Bird, *Good Spy*, 353–54.

32. CIA, Central Intelligence Bulletin, December 14, 1973, https://www.cia.gov/readingroom/docs/CIA-RDP79T00975A025800090001-6.pdf.

33. Kissinger, *Years of Upheaval*, 758.

34. Memcon, June 22, 1976, in *FRUS, 1969–1976*, vol. 26, *Arab-Israeli Dispute, 1974–1976* (Washington, DC: GPO, 2012), 1,043.

35. Kissinger, *Years of Upheaval*, 503, 1,139.

36. Ibid., 628.

37. Memcon, June 22, 1976, 1,037.

38. Malcolm H. Kerr, "America's Middle East Policy: Kissinger, Carter and the Future," IPS Papers No. 14 (Washington, DC: Institute for Palestine Studies, 1980), 15.

39. Henry Kissinger, *Years of Renewal* (New York: Simon & Schuster, 1999), 353.

40. Kissinger, *Years of Upheaval*, 758.

41. Anders Persso, *The EU and the Israeli–Palestinian Conflict, 1971–2013: In Pursuit of a Just Peace* (Lanham, MD: Lexington, 2015), 75.

42. CIA, Central Intelligence Bulletin, March 6, 1974, https://www.cia.gov/readingroom/docs/CIA-RDP79T00975A026200120001-7.pdf.

43. Sayigh, *Armed Struggle*, 322. See also Goldberg, *Jewish Power*, 247.

44. Chamberlin, *Global Offensive*, 239.

45. CIA, Central Intelligence Bulletin, December 14, 1973, https://www.cia.gov/readingroom/docs/CIA-RDP79T00975A025800090001-6.pdf.

46. See, for example, CIA, Central Intelligence Bulletin, February 25, 1974, https://www.cia.gov/readingroom/docs/CIA-RDP79T00975A026200040001-6.pdf; "Arafat's Latest Efforts to Out-maneuver Fedayeen Diehards," May 2, 1974, https://aad.archives.gov/aad/createpdf?rid=98875&dt=2474&dl=1345.

47. James R. Stocker, "A Historical Inevitability? Kissinger and US Contacts with the Palestinians, 1973–76," *International History Review* 39, no. 2 (2017): 327.

48. Quoted in Osamah Khalil, "Oslo's Roots: Kissinger, the PLO, and the Peace Process," September 3, 2013, https://al-shabaka.org/briefs/oslos-roots-kissinger-plo-and-peace-process.

49. Special National Intelligence Estimate (SNIE 30/3–73), "The Arab-Israeli Situation and the Oil Crisis," December 5, 1973, in *FRUS, 1969–1976*, vol. 25, 1,027.

50. J. William Fulbright, "The Clear and Present Danger" (speech), November 2, 1974, https://www.speeches-usa.com/Transcripts/jw_fulbright.html; "Israel in the US Senate," *Journal of Palestine Studies* 4, no. 4 (Summer 1975): 167–69.

51. For example, Senator James Abourezk of South Dakota met with Arafat in 1973 and Senator Howard Baker of Tennessee did the same in 1975. See James G.

Abourezk, *Advise and Dissent: Memoirs of South Dakota and the U.S. Senate* (Chicago: Lawrence Hill, 1989), 240; Frank Starr, "The Words That Arafat Won't Say," *Chicago Tribune,* June 30, 1975.

52. Memcon, February 8, 1974, in *FRUS, 1969–1976*, vol. 26, 116.

53. "PLO Sole Legitimate Representative of the Palestinian People—LAS Rabat Summit; Resolution on Palestine, Seventh Arab League Summit Conference, October 28, 1974," available at United Nations: The Question of Palestine, https://www.un.org/unispal/document/auto-insert-194621.

54. Kissinger, *Years of Upheaval*, 787.

55. See UN General Assembly Resolution 3236, "Question of Palestine" (A/RES/3236), and Resolution 3237, "Observer Status for the Palestine Liberation Organization" (A/RES/3237), November 22, 1974, https://documents-dds-ny.un.org/doc/RESOLUTION/GEN/NR0/738/39/IMG/NR073839.pdf?OpenElement. For an explanation of the US rationale in opposing both measures, see "Palestinian Resolution at UNGA," November 20, 1974, https://aad.archives.gov/aad/createpdf?rid=246419&dt=2474&dl=1345.

56. UN General Assembly, "President: Mr. Abdelaziz Bouteflika (Algeria), Agenda Item 108, Question of Palestine (continued)," November 21, 1974, https://www.un.org/unispal/document/auto-insert-186778.

57. "The Speech of Yasser Arafat," Palestine at the United Nations, *Journal of Palestine Studies* 4, no. 2 (Winter 1975): 181–92.

58. "Contacts with PLO Representatives," November 26, 1974, https://aad.archives.gov/aad/createpdf?rid=256045&dt=2474&dl=1345.

59. "Visa Ineligibility: Palestine Liberation Organization," December 22, 1974, https://aad.archives.gov/aad/createpdf?rid=272586&dt=2474&dl=1345. See also "Visas and Status of PLO UN Observers," April 15, 1975, https://aad.archives.gov/aad/createpdf?rid=28906&dt=2476&dl=1345; "PLO Plans for New York Observer Office," March 5, 1975, https://aad.archives.gov/aad/createpdf?rid=212692&dt=2476&dl=1345; "Visa Ineligibility: Palestine Liberation Organization," January 16, 1975, https://aad.archives.gov/aad/createpdf?rid=126377&dt=2476&dl=1345.

60. Ambassador Robert B. Oakley, Oral History Interview, July 7, 1992, by Charles Stuart Kennedy and Thomas Stern, Association for Diplomatic Studies and Training Foreign Affairs Oral History Project, https://www.adst.org/OH%20TOCs/Oakley,%20Robert%20B.toc.pdf, 62; Bernard Gwertzman, "U.S. Orders P.L.O. Representative to Leave Country," *New York Times*, November 24, 1976. See also Memo from Quandt to National Security Adviser Zbigniew Brzezinski, "Subject: Full Set of Notes from Landrum Bolling," September 19, 1977, in *FRUS, 1977–1980*, vol. 8, *Arab-Israeli Dispute, January 1977–August 1978* (Washington, DC: GPO, 2013), 498–517; Sameer Abraham, "The PLO at the Crossroads: Moderation, Encirclement, Future Prospects," *Middle East Report* 80 (September–October 1979): 54–65; "U.S. Rebuffs Washington PLO Office," *Palestine* 2, no. 1 (February 1977): 1, 4–6, 16.

61. Stocker, "A Historical Inevitability?" 330.

62. Martin Indyk, *Master of the Game: Henry Kissinger and the Art of Middle East Diplomacy* (New York: Alfred A. Knopf, 2021), 493. See also Ahron Bregman,

Cursed Victory: A History of Israel and the Occupied Territories (New York: Pegasus, 2014), 94–95; Goldberg, *Jewish Power*, 239.

63. House of Representatives, "The Palestine Issue in the Middle East Peace Efforts" Hearings, Committee on International Relations, 94th Congress, https://babel.hathitrust.org/cgi/pt?id=pur1.32754077071516&seq=1.

64. On Saunders's testimony, see Marwan R. Buheiry, "The Saunders Document," *Journal of Palestine Studies* 8, no. 1 (Autumn 1978): 28–40.

65. See Bernard Gwertzman, "U.S. Seeks Talks on P.L.O., Denies a Change in Policy," *New York Times*, December 31, 1976.

66. "The Brookings Report on the Middle East," *Journal of Palestine Studies* 6, no. 2 (Winter 1977): 195–205.

67. Memoranda of Agreement, September 1, 1975, in *FRUS, 1969–1976*, vol. 26, 828–32.

68. See, for example, Statement of Farouk Khaddoumi, UN Security Council 1879th Meeting, The Middle East Problem including the Palestinian Question, January 26, 1976, https://documents-dds-ny.un.org/doc/UNDOC/GEN/NL7/600/24/PDF/NL760024.pdf?OpenElement, 24–25.

69. Kissinger, *Years of Renewal*, 456.

70. Oakley Oral History Interview, 64; Nicholas A. Veliotes Oral History Interview, January 29, 1990, by Charles Stuart Kennedy, Association for Diplomatic Studies and Training Foreign Affairs Oral History Project, https://www.adst.org/OH%20TOCs/Veliotes,%20Nicholas%20A.toc.pdf, 91.

71. Indyk, *Master of the Game*, 533.

72. See, for instance, Stocker, "A Historical Inevitability?"

73. Bird, *Good Spy*, 176. See also, Gordon Thomas, *Gideon's Spies: The Secret History of the Mossad* (New York: Thomas Dunne, 2007), 281–82.

74. For example, see Memcon, December 17, 1975, National Security Archive Electronic Briefing Book No. 193, https://nsarchive2.gwu.edu/NSAEBB/NSAEBB193/HAK-12-17-75.pdf, 5–6.

75. Kissinger, *Years of Upheaval*, 625.

76. Bird, *Good Spy*, 174; Memcon, December 17, 1975, 5–6; Kissinger, *Years of Upheaval*, 625.

77. Memcon, "Subject: The Middle East," November 28, 1975, in *FRUS, 1969–1976*, vol. 26, 871.

78. Memcon, "Subject: Guidance for Ambassador Eilts and Pickering," August 7, 1976, in *FRUS, 1969–1976*, vol. 26, 1,058–59.

79. Kissinger, *Years of Upheaval*, 1,036.

80. Ibid., 629.

81. Ibid.

82. Office of the White House Press Secretary, "Question and Answer Session with the President," June 20, 1976, https://www.fordlibrarymuseum.gov/library/document/0248/whpr19760620-004.pdf.

83. James M. Markham, "Peace Force in Beirut," *New York Times*, June 22, 1976. See also Bird, *Good Spy*, 176–77.

84. "U.S. Rebuffs Washington PLO Office," 1, 4–6, 16. See also Stocker, "A Historical Inevitability?" 331.

85. Memcon, June 22, 1976, 1,046. See also Kissinger, *Years of Renewal*, 1,053.

86. CIA Directorate of Intelligence Memo (OCI No. 0424/75), "Internal Politics of the Palestine Liberation Organization," February 6, 1975, https://www.cia.gov/readingroom/docs/CIA-RDP80R01731R002300100002-8.pdf, 3.

87. Jimmy Carter, *White House Diary* (New York: Farrar, Strauss and Giroux, 2010), 352.

88. Sayigh, *Armed Struggle*, 551. See also John Boykin, *Cursed Is the Peacemaker: The American Diplomat Versus the Israeli General, Beirut 1982* (Belmont, CA: Applegate, 2002), 268; Thomas L. Friedman, *From Beirut to Jerusalem* (New York: Picador, 1989), 161. See also Seth Anziska, "A Preventable Massacre," *New York Times*, September 16, 2012.

89. Veliotes Oral History Interview, 127; Ward Sinclair and Lou Cannon, "Reagan Unaware of Contacts with PLO, Aides Say," *Washington Post*, February 20, 1984. See also Kathleen Christison, *Perceptions of Palestine: Their Influence on U.S. Middle East Policy* (Berkeley: University of California Press, 2001), 205; "Cases of United States Visas Granted to Officials of the PLO During the Reagan Administration (Ability of Civil And Criminal Actions Against Yassir Arafat's Palestine Liberation Organization [PLO])," Hearing before the Subcommittee on Security and Terrorism of the Committee on the Judiciary, United States Senate, 99th Cong., 2nd sess., April 23, 1986.

90. See Khaled Elgindy, *Blind Spot: America and the Palestinians from Balfour to Trump* (Washington, DC: Brookings Institution, 2019), 135–52. See also Jamil Hilal, "PLO Institutions: The Challenge Ahead," *Journal of Palestine Studies* 23, no. 1 (Autumn 1993): 46.

91. Scott Lasensky, "Chequebook Diplomacy: The US, the Oslo Process and the Role of Foreign Aid," in *Aid, Diplomacy and Facts on the Ground: The Case of Palestine*, eds. Michael Keating, Anne Le More, and Robert Lowe (London: Royal Institute for International Affairs/Chatham House, 2006), 47. See also Scott Lasensky, "Underwriting Peace in the Middle East: US Foreign Policy and the Limits of Economic Inducements," *Middle East Review of International Affairs* 6, no. 1 (March 2002): 94–95.

92. Madeline Albright, *Madame Secretary: A Memoir* (New York: Miramax, 2003), 493.

93. For more on the reasons behind Camp David's failure, see Deborah Sontag, "And Yet So Far: A Special Report; Quest for Mideast Peace: How and Why It Failed," *New York Times*, July 26, 2001. See also Robert Malley and Hussein Agha, "Camp David: The Tragedy of Errors," *New York Review of Books*, August 9, 2001; Robert Malley and Hussein Agha, "Camp David and After: An Exchange (2. A Reply to Ehud Barak)," *New York Review of Books*, June 13, 2002; Charles Enderlin, *Shattered Dreams: The Failure of the Peace Process in the Middle East, 1995–2002* (New York: Other, 2003); Clayton E. Swisher, *The Truth about Camp David: The Untold Story about the Collapse of the Middle East Peace Process* (New York: Nation,

2004); Aaron David Miller, *The Much Too Promised Land: America's Elusive Search for Arab-Israeli Peace* (New York: Bantam, 2008), 288–89.

94. Remarks on the Middle East, June 24, 2022, APP, https://www.presidency.ucsb.edu/documents/remarks-the-middle-east.

95. See David Rose, "Gaza Bombshell," *Vanity Fair*, April 2008.

96. See Public Law 112–74, December 23, 2011, Consolidated Appropriations Act 2012, https://www.govinfo.gov/content/pkg/PLAW-112publ74/pdf/PLAW-112publ74.pdf; Public Law 114–113, December 18, 2015, Consolidated Appropriations Act 2016, https://www.congress.gov/114/plaws/publ113/PLAW-114publ113.pdf.

Chapter 6

The Cold War and Oil

Paving the Way to a US-Led Peace Process

Jeremy Pressman

The 1973 Arab-Israeli War and Arab oil embargo set the stage for intensive US diplomacy to resolve the Arab-Israeli conflict, a sharp turn from US policy prior to the war. The two events raised significant concerns in the United States over the Cold War and over Western energy needs. Consider US secretary of state Henry Kissinger's pithy summary of where things stood at the end of the war: "The conflict at the end of October had found us on one side, the Arabs with Soviet backing on the other side, and the oil embargo. We were a potential enemy to the Arabs."[1]

Conflict resolution, soon embodied in the peace process, was thought to be a pathway to avoid a repeat of 1973. Resolving the Arab-Israeli conflict would remove a potential spark for dangerous US-Soviet confrontations that could give the Soviets greater access to the Middle East. It would also mean less friction between the United States, or the West generally, and friendly Arab states, especially oil-exporting ones like Saudi Arabia. In short, US officials believed Arab-Israeli wars challenged US global strategic needs and US energy interests; preventing such wars was thus in the US national interest.

What is equally important is that over time the same factors—the Cold War and Arab oil—that made the peace process a high priority either disappeared with the collapse of the Soviet Union or, in the case of oil, changed so dramatically that they could no longer undermine US national interests to the same degree. The seeming urgency for a diplomatic resolution coming out of 1973, at least based on these two factors, largely evaporated. In turn, this helps explain why the United States stopped using its material leverage to press Israel on the peace process.²

This chapter is based on primary US documents and secondary sources. One should note that the two top US officials involved, President Richard Nixon and Kissinger, both have reputations that make relying on their statements especially challenging: for major corruption in the former case and for misrepresenting the historical record in the latter.³ But they, and especially Kissinger, were the key US decision-makers. Given that caveat, I have done my best to reconstruct the record of high-level US thinking at the time.

From September 1970 to October 1973, the United States was satisfied with the quiet and stability on the Arab-Israeli front, what William Quandt, a former US official and author of *Peace Process*, referred to as "The Deceptive Calm." US interest in the conflict, he writes, waned: "In the absence of acute crises, American policymakers paid comparatively little attention to the area."⁴ The war in Vietnam consumed much domestic and foreign policy attention. Especially from 1971 to 1973, "the Arab-Israeli conflict was absent from the headlines, [and] American diplomats remained uncharacteristically quiet and passive."⁵ There was no "sense of urgency" in US diplomacy.⁶ It was "no war, no peace."⁷

From a bureaucratic perspective, Kissinger, the national security adviser, undermined the Arab-Israeli diplomatic proposals put forward by Secretary of State William P. Rogers during the Nixon administration's first term.⁸ (Kissinger himself became secretary of state in September 1973 just before the war.) That war broke out in 1973 could thus be seen as evidence of the dangers of assigning Arab-Israeli diplomacy a low priority. De facto quiet or calm is not a permanent state of affairs.

On October 6, 1973, Egypt and Syria launched a surprise attack on Israel in order to shake up the status quo, drawing the Soviet Union and the United States into the fray. During the war, the United States launched a massive military resupply effort to help Israel. Initially, the flow of arms from the United States to Israel was small. During the October 9–12 period, Israel's requests for military arms increased, but Washington did not increase the flow.⁹ But on October 10, the same day US arms began reaching Israel, the United States learned the Soviet Union was resupplying Syria with "more than 200 tons of military equipment."¹⁰ Soviet leaders also put seven airborne divisions on high alert.

In response to these Soviet moves and repeated Israeli requests for arms, on October 16, Kissinger privately told his colleagues the United States should send 25 percent more arms to Israel than the Soviet Union sent to its Arab allies in order to "outmatch" Moscow.¹¹ He reiterated that a massive US arms resupply of Israel was intended to send a strong message to the Soviet Union and the world that the United States was the stronger superpower. In a meeting with Portugal's ambassador to the United States, Joao Hall Themido, Kissinger detailed the Soviet arms effort, adding, "It could cause grave consequences if Soviet arms should prevail over U.S. arms in the Middle East. ... The U.S. has the capacity to double what the Soviets put in." The sense one gets is that the US message was for the world, not just the direct war participants and the Mideast region; the Soviet resupply effort "could have too many consequences everywhere."[12]

Kissinger's concern was based on at least two fears. First, he worried that if the Soviets prevailed in the Middle East, they would use this same approach of massive weapons transfers in other parts of the world. In this way of thinking, arms equal influence. Second, he believed the US-Soviet arms balance in the Arab-Israeli conflict would affect the resolution of that conflict. By preventing the Soviets from using arms transfers to determine the outcome of the October War, "the Arab states will learn that they must deal with the United States in order to achieve a settlement."[13] For Kissinger, the road to Middle East peace had to run through Washington, with Moscow on the sideline.[14]

The US-Israeli negotiations over arms shipments were intertwined with competing understandings of how the fighting should end. Whereas the United States favored a relatively rapid ceasefire, it seemed Israel wanted to continue fighting until it attained a larger military victory. The United States was waiting to launch a massive resupply effort until Israel accepted the idea of a ceasefire. Delays in ramping up the weapons shipments seem to have led Israel to become more open to a ceasefire.[15] At the same time, the US government also became concerned about (partially) standing aside and potentially handing the Soviet Union and its Arab allies a military and/or psychological victory. Thus, on October 13, Nixon authorized a direct airlift of weapons to Israel and, by the next day, US C-5 transport planes were landing in Israel to deliver arms. In a phone call, the president told the secretary of state he wanted a major US effort: "[I]f we are going to do it, don't spare the horses."[16]

The US airlift was "in full swing," abandoning any pretense that the US shipment of arms to Israel could be done without much fanfare.[17] According to Quandt, on October 16, Kissinger privately told top US national security officials that "the Soviets must see that the United States could deliver more than they could."[18] On October 19, Nixon requested $2.2 billion in aid for Israel from Congress.

Within a few days, the war produced a dangerous superpower crisis, one of the few—unlike the Berlin airlift, Cuban missile crisis, and Taiwan Straits crises—that occurred in the second half of the Cold War. The US-Soviet disagreement revolved around ending the fighting and the implementation of the ceasefire called for in United Nations Security Council (UNSC) Resolution 338, which was passed on October 22. As the fighting dragged on, the Egyptian and Soviet governments became increasingly concerned for the survival of Egypt's Third Army, as Israel continued to tighten its position around Egypt's trapped military personnel.

On October 24 at 10:00 p.m., Nixon received a deeply alarming message from Soviet general secretary Leonid Brezhnev. One US official called the letter "a real piss-swisher."[19] After expressing his concern that Israeli forces were still fighting rather than adhering to the ceasefire, Brezhnev invited Nixon to "urgently dispatch to Egypt Soviet and American military conti[n]gents" to implement the UNSC resolution. If Washington would not join him, Brezhnev continued, the Soviet Union "should be faced with the necessity urgently to consider the question of taking appropriate steps unilaterally. We cannot allow arbitrariness on the part of Israel."[20] It was a threat of unilateral Soviet military intervention in the Middle East.

Both at the time and in his memoirs, Nixon called this moment "the most difficult crisis we have had since the Cuban confrontation of 1962."[21] In the Oval Office after the war, Nixon told Israeli prime minister Golda Meir that it "was pretty hairy," though how involved Nixon himself actually was in US decision-making in late October is an open question, given that the Watergate scandal was his main focus at that point.[22] For his part, Kissinger later wrote that Brezhnev's letter "was one of the most serious challenges to an American President by a Soviet leader."[23]

On October 25, the United States responded to Brezhnev by saying that the idea of sending US and Soviet forces to Egypt was "not appropriate" and denying significant ceasefire violations were taking place. Nixon wrote, "[W]e must view your suggestion of unilateral action as a matter of the gravest concern involving incalculable consequences." Nixon only expressed support for greater international supervision of Egyptian and Israeli military forces that might include some Soviet and US noncombat personnel. Nixon warned Brezhnev that the future of détente was at stake:

> You must know, however, that we could in no event accept unilateral action. This would be in violation of our understandings, of the agreed Principles we signed in Moscow in 1972 and of Article II of the Agreement on Prevention of Nuclear War. As I stated above, such action would produce incalculable consequences which would be in the interest of neither of our countries and which would end all we have striven so hard to achieve.[24]

In concrete terms, the United States raised the alert status of the US military to DEFCON 3 and of the Strategic Air Command to DEFCON 4. At Nixon's behest, Kissinger requested internal contingency planning for US military intervention in the Middle East, likely for the purpose of countering a possible Soviet military move in the region.[25]

The superpower crisis quickly deescalated. Brezhnev accepted Nixon's idea to send observers.[26] But for a brief moment, the Soviet stance seemed not only to risk an open US-Soviet fight but also, and perhaps more likely, to open the door to deeper Soviet involvement in the Middle East, something the United States strongly opposed. As Kissinger later wrote, "[A] principal purpose of our own Mideast policy was to reduce the role and influence of the Soviet Union, just as the Soviets sought to reduce ours."[27] After the war, Osamah Khalil writes, Kissinger "sought Moscow's co-operation at the UN Security Council whilst attempting to limit Soviet involvement in a settlement."[28]

This US-Soviet interaction occurred in tandem with the Arab oil embargo and production cuts. As Fiona Venn notes, changes in geopolitics and the world oil market, most of which were separate from the Arab-Israeli conflict, fed into the oil confrontation of 1973. The war broke out at a time when multinational oil companies and oil-exporting states were already negotiating over the price of oil and the share of the sales that each should collect. Just before the war, the United States was importing 1.2 million barrels of oil per day from the Arab oil-exporting countries.[29] Already in 1972, the Saudi oil minister, Sheikh Ahmed Zaki Yamani, warned the United States that Saudi Arabia might use oil pressure to advance its political interests.[30] In the spring of 1973, Saudi King Faisal had talked about using oil as a weapon against the West, specifically to press for an Israeli withdrawal from Arab territory.[31] In a drawn-out war, the oil pressure might make the United States think twice about sending arms to replenish Israeli stocks.[32]

On October 17, Arab oil ministers met in Kuwait and said they would cut production until Israel withdrew to the June 4, 1967, lines, though they stopped short of actually taking that step at that point. But such a step came soon enough. On October 15, Kissinger was still trying to keep the US aid program to Israel under wraps to prevent an Arab move on oil.[33] However, in response to Nixon asking Congress for the $2.2 billion in aid for Israel, Saudi Arabia announced an oil embargo against the United States and the Netherlands, and cut Saudi oil production by 10 percent.[34] The Organization of Arab Petroleum Exporting Countries (OAPEC) instituted the embargo and, with the exception of Iraq, cut production. For its part, Iraq nationalized Dutch and US holdings.[35] As a result, in the last three months of 1973 oil prices increased fourfold.[36] The pressure continued after the war, with agreement on further cuts on November 4.[37] OAPEC ministers who met in Vienna on November 18 decided not to end the embargo.[38]

After the war, Nixon made ensuring the United States had enough oil "a high priority."[39] On November 29, Kissinger met with the Washington Special Actions Group (WSAG), a group of high-level US officials, offering an explicit link between oil and the US push for peace negotiations: "Our position with the Saudis is that they have demonstrated their power. They have moved us off our position of letting things take their natural course. We have assumed a major responsibility for the [Arab-Israeli] negotiations, which they wanted."[40] Kissinger, in other words, was acknowledging that a significant shift in American policy had taken place, such that before the war the United States was "letting things take their natural course," whereas after the conflict it was pressing hard for a diplomatic process.

Eventually, the OAPEC states, except Libya, temporarily ended the embargo in March 1974—and then more permanently in June and July—after the United States helped negotiate ceasefire agreements between Israel and Egypt and Syria. David Painter contends that US economic and military support for Saudi Arabia was a factor in OAPEC's decision as well. Riyadh also pledged to raise production by one million barrels a day.[41]

The result of the war and embargo was US wariness about the potential impact of future Arab-Israeli fighting. Already near the end of the first week of the fighting, Kissinger publicly stated that one of the two US principal objectives was "the promotion of a more permanent, more lasting solution in the Middle East."[42] Kissinger, who had not devoted his energy to Arab-Israeli matters prior to 1973, "set out to become the peacemaker," in Quandt's words. To Kissinger, Quandt writes, "the October war was a vivid example of the volatility of the Arab-Israeli conflict."[43]

As Kissinger privately told Egyptian officials, "The great achievement in the present crisis is that it has changed the situation."[44] The situation, he told the foreign ministers of Algeria, Kuwait, Morocco, and Saudi Arabia, "is totally different now from what it was between 1967 and 1973." The United States, Kissinger said, would now have more influence and more arguments to press Israel for an Arab-Israeli settlement. Washington would, Nixon added, launch "a diplomatic initiative in which we will use our full weight."[45] As Fouad Ajami later noted, Kissinger "told the Egyptians, folks, I only handle crises when they're hot. Oil was hot, and oil brought him to the region. That's why he went, that's what the entire shuttle diplomacy was about, a way of ending the oil embargo."[46]

For Nixon, the US-Soviet crisis also meant that the United States had to become actively engaged in Arab-Israeli negotiations. As the president said at a press conference, the United States could not let an Arab-Israeli war jeopardize US-Soviet détente.[47] On November 1, he told Meir: "[W]e are going to try very hard to get a reasonable peace settlement. Your interests require it. Our interests require it. The world's interest requires it. These US-Soviet confrontations are not pleasant."[48]

Due to these factors, after the war the United States, in Quandt's words, "committed its top diplomatic resources to a sustained search for a settlement of the Arab-Israeli conflict."[49] If Washington could resolve the dispute, then it could not trigger another superpower crisis or another US-Arab energy row. On October 26, Nixon said publicly: "[I]t is indispensable at this time that we avoid any further Mideast crisis so that the flow of oil to Europe, to Japan, and to the United States can continue."[50] Despite détente—a partial desire by US and Soviet officials to cooperate on some issues—the war showed local conflicts could spark a superpower confrontation, which could weaken the United States directly (if actual US-Soviet fighting occurred) and/or indirectly (if it bolstered the Soviet position in the Mideast). As Venn writes, a clear victory for a Soviet-allied country "would heighten the likelihood of other radical states in the region building closer links with Moscow."[51]

One way to think about the situation is as a struggle for the allegiance of the Arab states. That Israel was in the US camp was unquestioned. But could the United States make inroads in the Arab world? Allying with and arming the Arab states had been the Soviet way into the region. If the United States could woo key Arab leaders, however, the Soviets would be frozen out. Egyptian president Anwar Sadat's move in July 1972 to expel the large number of Soviet military advisers from his country had been an important signal that change was possible.

The particular way that the 1973 war ended was, likewise, a similarly important signal. Recall that the Israeli armed forces had encircled Egypt's Third Army, that Egypt could not resupply that army, and that Sadat was growing increasingly concerned about its survival by October 25–26. The United States, through Kissinger, played the key external role in mediating this impasse, albeit with the help of an important concession from Sadat that paved the way to a resolution. Israel agreed to allow one nonmilitary resupply convoy to access the Third Army, while Egypt agreed to send a major general to meet with an Israeli counterpart at Kilometer 101 in the Sinai Peninsula. On this small agreement, the Soviets were irrelevant.

At that moment, Kissinger sensed the growing US advantage. As he said at a meeting of the WSAG on November 2: "But now we are in the catbird seat. Everyone is coming to us on their knees begging us for a settlement. We can reduce Soviet influence in the area and can get the oil embargo raised if we can deliver a moderate program, and we are going to do it."[52] The core of that "moderate" program was the US-led peace process with the Arab states—though there was to be no official US engagement with the Palestinian national movement. As Kissinger later wrote, "We had managed to achieve a cease-fire and were beginning to move into a pivotal position as the arbiter of the peace process."[53] By "we," Kissinger meant the United States, without the Soviet Union.

The postwar Arab-Israeli negotiations also highlight the centrality of oil and the Soviet Union to US officials. The Egyptian-Israeli disengagement agreement and the negotiations that led to it reveal US officials repeatedly underscoring the connection between Arab-Israeli peace and the twin goals of improving US energy security and avoiding another US-Soviet crisis. Egypt and Israel signed the agreement, also known as Sinai I, on January 18, 1974. For Nixon and Kissinger, the agreement was an opportunity to end the oil embargo and eliminate the potential for Arab-Israeli crises to spark US-Soviet ones.

Once Egyptian-Israeli talks were underway, Kissinger made clear to Nixon the larger potential impact on the energy side. "[A] quick agreement," he said, "is essential to get the oil embargo and production restrictions lifted."[54] In January, Kissinger traveled to Cairo and met with Sadat. Sadat promised to resolve the oil crisis, at least the immediate one: "Sadat told me that if a disengagement agreement can be reached this week he will use his personal influence—particularly with King Faisal and [Algerian] President [Houari] Boumedienne—to see that the oil embargo is brought to an end shortly after agreement is reached."[55] A few days later, on January 19, Kissinger sent a message to Nixon stating he had Sadat's "assurance" the embargo would be lifted in a matter of days.[56] Nixon, in turn, told a congressional delegation that the Egyptian-Israeli disengagement agreement had created a "chance" to lift the embargo.[57] But more was needed, Nixon added: "The U.S. will use its constructive influence toward a long-term settlement."[58] Thus, the oil issue was moving on two tracks as a result of the 1973 war: a short-term effort to end the existing oil crisis and a long-term effort to prevent the oil crisis from occurring again by improving US ties with Egypt and Saudi Arabia.

Nixon and Kissinger also tied the Sinai I agreement to the US-Soviet dimension. "We have now disengaged the military forces of the two sides and averted a possible resumption of the war and a possible great power confrontation," Kissinger declared.[59] The secretary of state told the cabinet: "If the Soviet presence had moved into the Middle East, we would have had a serious problem."[60] "[W]e are seeking . . . also to keep the Soviets out," said Nixon in a private meeting with Kissinger and congressional leaders.[61] In another private setting, Kissinger agreed, saying: "[W]e have to keep the Soviets from disrupting everything."[62] During the Syrian-Israeli talks, Kissinger spoke of keeping Soviet officials in the dark so they could not meddle in the negotiations.[63]

Privately, Kissinger did not think the United States needed to negotiate a comprehensive settlement on all fronts. If he could get Egypt and Israel to make peace, and thereby remove Egypt from the Arab military equation, that would be enough to stymie pan-Arab military plans versus Israel. Toward that end, a Syrian-Israeli disengagement agreement would be useful because it would provide cover for Egypt to move toward a peace treaty with Israel.[64] At the same time, Kissinger told the Israelis that the breakdown of the Syrian-Israeli talks would allow the Soviets to "inject themselves into the picture in a most unfavorable way," and might lead the Arabs to reinstitute the oil embargo.[65] For Kissinger, there was a direct tie between the peace process on the one hand and the energy crisis and Soviet matters on the other.

Top American officials, in other words, saw the regional dynamics in the Middle East impacting the US position at the global level. The US government did not want another Arab-Israeli war to cause wider strategic problems, as happened in October 1973, when the fighting had caused major Cold War and energy crises. But US officials also felt that the process could move the opposite way, from the strategic level to the regional one. For example, Kissinger wanted "to change the situation where the Soviet Union was the supporter of the Arabs and we were the supporter of Israel."[66] The United States wanted to pry away Soviet allies, which meant getting the Arab states to be open to close ties with the United States, even if they did not disown the Soviet Union.[67] The 1973 war had exposed the stark divide between the pro-US and pro-Soviet camps. Kissinger wanted to blur that divide, and the peace process was the vehicle through which to do so.

Some scholars, such as Robert Vitalis, reject the argument that the oil embargo represented a real threat to the United States, both in 1973 specifically and more broadly as a political weapon whose use could be replicated in the future. In *Oilcraft*, Vitalis argues that the global energy market, not US force projection capabilities and military meddling in the Persian Gulf, is what has ensured that oil has kept flowing. Dangers like insufficient supply and interrupted access were illusory. Oil exporters needed the revenue that came from sales, and oil importers needed the oil to fuel their economic growth and way of life. Moreover, the price spikes and US gas lines in 1973 had little to do with the war and embargo. Instead, they had much more to do with macroeconomic changes and long-running tensions between the countries that possessed oil and the multinational companies that extracted and transported it.[68]

But even if ones adopts Vitalis's perspective and accepts that US decision-makers in 1973–1974 were operating on the basis of a misperception, I would argue that the energy issue was nevertheless crucial. After all, that misperception ultimately drove US policy. Indeed, Vitalis himself anticipated such an objection: "Some might argue that, regardless, a political consequence of the boycott is the U.S. engagement in the 'peace process,' the return of Sinai to Egypt, and so on."[69] Vitalis does downplay the value of the peace process. He notes that the peace process was not designed to lead to a Palestinian state but rather to prevent its emergence. In the interest of conflict resolution or genuinely addressing Palestinian self-determination, he sees it as counterproductive.[70]

Did the war shape the specific diplomatic strategy that the United States adopted in its Arab-Israeli diplomacy? The war and larger considerations about US-Soviet relations meant the peace process was not unilateral US diplomacy or complete deference to Israeli inaction, as had been the case before the 1973 war. Washington needed Arab engagement not only to deal with the oil question, but also to woo them away from Moscow. Involving Arab actors shaped the nature of the diplomatic process and helped stymie Soviet goals for a greater Middle East presence and role. It was overdetermined that the United States did not view the Soviet Union as a true diplomatic partner. Even with détente, the United States did not want the Soviet Union to be accorded co-equal status, despite rhetorical commitments prior to the war like the joint communiqué from the June 1973 US-Soviet summit.

Lastly, the United States needed some peace, not a comprehensive peace. Roland Dannreuther argues that the US focus was more on having a process than on achieving peace. I would phrase it differently: The Nixon administration was interested in a peace process for Israel and Egypt, but not for Israel and the other key Arab players, especially the Palestine Liberation Organization.[71]

In the decades that followed the October 1973 war, two crucial things changed, which weakened the US need for a successful and final peace process outcome. The Arab oil-exporting states realized that although an embargo hurt their customers, it also hurt their own economies because it shut down their most important revenue stream, energy sales. It was far from a one-sided or cost-free means of pressuring Israel's allies in the United States and elsewhere. Moreover, OAPEC's power to set oil prices eroded in the 1980s with the rise of market forces and international petroleum exchanges.[72]

In addition, when the Cold War ended in 1989, the United States and Soviet Union were no longer engaged in a global military competition. By the end of 1991, the Soviet Union had collapsed entirely. The concern about an Arab-Israeli war potentially sparking a destabilizing global confrontation between the United States and Soviet Union was totally off the table.

Maybe that explains why the US use of material leverage versus Israel faded away during diplomatic disagreements after the end of the Cold War. When Kissinger wanted to press Israel due to its continued ceasefire violations in October 1973, he warned the Israeli government that the United States would pursue another UNSC resolution with measures to enforce it. During President Gerald Ford's administration, the United States called for a "reassessment" of US-Israeli relations when it felt Israel's policy was not forthcoming.[73] The administration of President George H. W. Bush deducted US aid in response to Israeli settlement expansion, which was seen as an obstacle to a negotiated peace. But by the twenty-first century, US policy toward Israel consisted mainly of inducements. Even President Barack Obama's tough love approach toward Israel involved mainly rhetorical admonishment, not material sanctions. When push came to shove, the less-pressing need in the

United States for a full resolution of the Arab-Israeli conflict, combined with US domestic political factors, meant US talk, not material threats and action.

NOTES

1. Memorandum of Conversation (Memcon), "Subject: Bipartisan Leadership Meeting on the Egyptian-Israeli Disengagement Agreement," January 21, 1974, in United States Department of State, *Foreign Relations of the United States* [*FRUS*], *1969–1976*, vol. 26, *Arab-Israeli Dispute, 1974–1976* (Washington, DC: Government Printing Office [GPO], 2012), 97.

2. The United States government never used much material leverage versus Israel in order to advance Arab-Israeli negotiations. My point is that its use went from a little to near zero.

3. For example, on Kissinger see George Lardner Jr., "Kissinger Overstated Clearance on Memoirs, U.S. Official Says," *Washington Post*, June 10, 1980; Geoffrey Robertson, "The Truth According to Kissinger," *The Guardian*, July 4, 1999.

4. William B. Quandt, *Peace Process: American Diplomacy and the Arab-Israeli Conflict since 1967* (Berkeley: University of California Press, 2005), 103.

5. William B. Quandt, *Decade of Decisions: American Policy toward the Arab-Israeli Conflict, 1967–1976* (Berkeley: University of California Press, 1977), 129. Chapter 5 of this book is titled "Standstill Diplomacy, 1971–1973."

6. Quandt, *Decade of Decisions*, 200.

7. Quandt, *Peace Process*, 107.

8. Walter Isaacson, *Kissinger: A Biography* (New York: Simon & Schuster, 1992), 511.

9. The October 9–12 timeframe is from Quandt, *Peace Process*, 109.

10. Quandt, *Peace Process*, 111. See also Quandt, *Decade of Decisions*, 179.

11. Quandt, *Decade of Decisions*, 179, 188, 196–97; Transcript of a Telephone Conversation (Telcon), October 16, 1973, Kissinger Telephone Conversations (KA) 11269, Digital National Security Archive (DNSA), 1. The United States was tracking the exact number of US and Soviet flights bringing arms to their Israeli and Arab allies, respectively, and the tonnage of equipment. See, for example, Minutes of a Washington Special Actions Group (WSAG) Meeting, October 17, 1973, Kissinger Transcripts Collection (KT) 00854, DNSA, 6.

12. Memcon, "Resupply Flights through Lajes to Israel," October 15, 1973 (KT) 00846, DNSA, 1, 2.

13. Memcon, "Subject: Middle East," October 16, 1973, (KT) 00849, DNSA, 2.

14. On the US desire to keep the Soviet Union out of the peace process and out of the region, see Galen Jackson, "Who Killed Détente? The Superpowers and the Cold War in the Middle East, 1969–77," *International Security* 44, no. 3 (Winter 2019/2020): 129–62. See also the sources cited in endnote 27 below.

15. Quandt, *Decade of Decisions*, 181–82.

16. Telcon, October 14, 1973 (KA) 11237, DNSA, 1.

17. Quandt, *Peace Process*, 114.

18. Ibid., 116.

19. Memorandum (Memo) for the Record, "Subject: NSC/JCS Meeting, Wednesday/Thursday, 24/25 October 1973, 2230–0330 (U)," October 24–25, 1973, in *FRUS, 1969–1976*, vol. 25, *Arab-Israeli Crisis and War, 1973* (Washington, DC: GPO, 2011), 737.

20. Message from Brezhnev to Nixon, undated, in *FRUS, 1969–1976*, vol. 25, 734–35.

21. The President's News Conference, October 26, 1973, American Presidency Project, https://www.presidency.ucsb.edu/documents/the-presidents-news-conference-84.

22. Memcon, November 1, 1973, in *FRUS, 1969–1976*, vol. 25, 830.

23. Henry Kissinger, *Years of Upheaval* (Boston: Little, Brown, 1982), 583.

24. Message from Nixon to Brezhnev, October 25, 1973, in *FRUS, 1969–1976*, vol. 25, 748–49.

25. Quandt, *Decade of Decisions*, 198–99; Memo for the Record, October 24–25, 1973, 741–42.

26. Telcon, October 25, 1973, in *FRUS, 1969–1976*, vol. 25, 752.

27. *Kissinger, Years of Upheaval*, 600. See also Jussi M. Hanhimäki, *The Flawed Architect: Henry Kissinger and American Foreign Policy* (New York: Oxford University Press, 2004), 304; Isaacson, *Kissinger*, 525, 529, 537, 539, 545, 547, 550, 569.

28. Osamah Khalil, "The Radical Crescent: The United States, the Palestine Liberation Organization, and the Lebanese Civil War, 1973–1978," *Diplomacy & Statecraft* 27, no. 3 (September 2016): 500.

29. Fiona Venn, *The Oil Crisis* (London: Pearson Education Limited, 2002), 5, 8–9, 20.

30. Venn, *Oil Crisis*, 17.

31. Quandt, *Peace Process*, 99–100. See also Robert B. Stobaugh, "The Oil Companies in the Crisis," in *The Oil Crisis* (New York: W. W. Norton, 1976), ed. Raymond Vernon, 182–83; Daniel Yergin, *The Prize: The Epic Quest for Oil, Money, and Power*, part 7, "The Tinderbox," July 25, 2019, at 15:58, https://youtu.be/-_proohDhmI.

32. Venn, *Oil Crisis*, 18.

33. Telcon, October 15, 1973 (KA) 11254, DNSA, 1. That evening, Kissinger told former secretary of state Dean Rusk that he did not expect joint Arab action "to cut all the oil." Telcon, October 15, 1973 (KA) 11261, DNSA, 1–2.

34. Quandt, *Peace Process*, 117; Quandt, *Decade of Decisions*, 188, 190. See also Memo Prepared in the Office of Economic Research, Central Intelligence Agency, October 19, 1973, in *FRUS, 1969–1976*, vol. 36, *Energy Crisis, 1969–1974* (Washington, DC: GPO, 2011), 620–25.

35. David S. Painter, "Oil and Geopolitics: The Oil Crises of the 1970s and the Cold War," *Historical Social Research* 39, no. 4 (2014): 190; Venn, *Oil Crisis*, 18.

36. Venn, *Oil Crisis*, 1.

37. Ibid., 18.

38. Clyde H. Farnsworth, "New Arab Oil Cut to Europe Voided: Exporters Cancel 5% Drop for December—Embargo on Dutch and U.S. Kept," *New York Times*, November 19, 1973.

39. Venn, *Oil Crisis*, 20.

40. Minutes of a WSAG Meeting, "Subject: Middle East and Indochina (see separate minutes for Indochina portion)," November 29, 1973, in *FRUS, 1969–1976*, vol. 25, 1,006.

41. Painter, "Oil and Geopolitics," 193. Libya ended its embargo in July 1974.

42. Quandt, *Decade of Decisions*, 181.

43. Quandt, *Peace Process*, 183.

44. Memcon, October 29, 1973, in *FRUS, 1969–1976*, vol. 25, 784.

45. Memcon, October 17, 1973 (KT) 00852, DNSA, 8, 9.

46. Yergin, *Prize*, part 7, at 23:44. See also Venn, *Oil Crisis*, 84, 89.

47. President's News Conference, October 26, 1973.

48. Memcon, November 1, 1973, 833. A few months later, Nixon privately told congressional leaders that "another war would be dangerous to world peace" and, with regard to the United States and Soviet Union, "neither side wants a confrontation there." See Memcon, January 21, 1974, 101.

49. Quandt, *Decade of Decisions*, 202.

50. President's News Conference, October 26, 1973. See also Quandt, *Decade of Decisions*, 205.

51. Venn, *Oil Crisis*, 79.

52. Minutes of a WSAG Meeting, "Subject: Middle East; Vietnam and Cambodia," November 2, 1973, in *FRUS, 1969–1976*, vol. 25, 841.

53. Kissinger, *Years of Upheaval*, 614.

54. Memo from Kissinger to Nixon, January 6, 1974, in *FRUS, 1969–1976*, vol. 26, 3.

55. Memo from Deputy National Security Adviser Brent Scowcroft to Nixon, January 13, 1974, in *FRUS, 1969–1976*, vol. 26, 5.

56. Telegram from Kissinger to Scowcroft, January 19, 1974, in *FRUS, 1969–1976*, vol. 26, 92.

57. Memcon, January 21, 1974, 100.

58. Ibid., 101.

59. Memcon, "Subject: Secretary Kissinger's Report on Egyptian-Israeli Disengagement Agreement," January 23, 1974, in *FRUS, 1969–1976*, vol. 26, 103.

60. Memcon, January 23, 1974, 104. Kissinger added, "We are not trying to freeze out the Soviet Union. It's just that we intend to play a role in the Middle East." That seems disingenuous, as the United States wanted to limit the Soviet political-military presence in the region *and* run the peace process unilaterally, even if the Soviets ostensibly were allowed to play a supporting role. On this point, see also Jackson, "Who Killed Détente?"

61. Memcon, "Subject: Middle East," March 8, 1974, in *FRUS, 1969–1976*, vol. 26, 165. On April 25, Kissinger similarly told the leaders of several American Jewish organizations: "Our whole strategy for four years was to create a situation where the Arabs become frustrated with the Soviet Union and turn away from the Soviet Union." See Memcon, April 25, 1974, in *FRUS, 1969–1976*, vol. 26, 201. See also Letter from Nixon to Meir, April 30, 1974, in *FRUS, 1969–1976*, vol. 26, 212.

62. Memcon, April 25, 1974, 203.

63. Memo from Scowcroft to Nixon, May 6, 1974, in *FRUS, 1969–1976*, vol. 26, 224; Memo from Scowcroft to Nixon, May 6, 1974, in *FRUS, 1969–1976*, vol. 26, 225. See also Hanhimäki, *Flawed Architect*, 329–30.

64. Memcon, February 8, 1974, in *FRUS, 1969–1976*, vol. 26, 115. This comment was at odds with what Kissinger—while invoking Nixon—told Syrian president Hafiz al-Asad about the US "determination and commitment to make a major effort to achieve Syrian-Israeli disengagement as rapidly as possible as a further initial step toward a just and durable peace settlement in the Middle East." See Telegram from the Department of State to the Embassy in Lebanon, February 11, 1974, in *FRUS, 1969–1976*, vol. 26, 123. However, Sadat—according to Kissinger—reaffirmed Kissinger's original point: "Sadat said that once Syrian-Israeli disengagement is achieved, he is prepared to embark on a serious negotiation with the Israelis on a second phase." See Memo from Scowcroft to Nixon, May 5, 1974, in *FRUS, 1969–1976*, vol. 26, 222.

65. Memo from Scowcroft to Nixon, May 2, 1974, in *FRUS, 1969–1976*, vol. 26, 216. At Kissinger's request, Nixon reinforced the secretary of state's arguments to the Israelis. See Letter from Nixon to Meir, May 4, 1974, in *FRUS, 1969–1976*, vol. 26, 219.

66. Memcon, March 8, 1974, 163.

67. For an example of Kissinger's approach to wooing the Arab states away from Moscow and toward Washington, see Memcon, March 1, 1974, in *FRUS, 1969–1976*, vol. 26, 137–59.

68. Robert Vitalis, *Oilcraft: The Myths of Scarcity and Security That Haunt U.S. Energy Policy* (Stanford, CA: Stanford University Press, 2020).

69. Vitalis, *Oilcraft*, 183n5.

70. I take a different position on the Palestinian dimension. See Jeremy Pressman, "Egypt, Israel, and the United States at the Autonomy Talks, 1979," *Diplomacy & Statecraft* 33, no. 3 (2022): 543–65; Jeremy Pressman, "Explaining the Carter Administration's Israeli-Palestinian Solution," *Diplomatic History* 37, no. 5 (November 2013): 1,117–47.

71. Roland Dannreuther, "Understanding the Middle East Peace Process: A Historical Institutionalist Approach," *European Journal of International Relations* 17, no. 2 (June 2011): 187–208.

72. Venn, *Oil Crisis*, 60–61.

73. Letter from Ford to Israeli Prime Minister Yitzhak Rabin, March 21, 1975, in *FRUS, 1969–1976*, vol. 26, 553.

Conclusion

Jerome Slater

THE ROOTS OF THE OCTOBER 1973 WAR

In the June 1967 Arab-Israeli War, Israel captured the Sinai Peninsula and the Gaza Strip from Egypt, the Golan Heights from Syria, and the West Bank and East Jerusalem from Jordan, thus seizing all of the remaining territory that had been allocated for a Palestinian state in the 1947 United Nations (UN) partition plan. In the immediate aftermath of the war, the Israeli government decided that in the context of overall peace settlements it would return the Sinai—but not Gaza—to Egypt and the Golan Heights to Syria. No decision was reached about the West Bank—the cabinet was divided over what to do—but East Jerusalem would not be returned to Jordanian control.

In the following year, Israel's position hardened, and in October 1968 the government reached a secret decision that explicitly rescinded Israel's initial postwar policies.[1] In particular, even if a peace agreement could be reached with Egypt, Israel would retain Gaza, parts of eastern Sinai bordering on Israel, and Sharm El-Sheik, the strategic location overlooking the Gulf of Aqaba, Israel's opening to the Red Sea and the Pacific Ocean.

In the next three years, exchanges of artillery attacks between Israel and Egypt escalated into what became known as "the Canal War."[2] In the course of the war, Israeli war planes—mostly provided by the United States—bombed military and industrial targets in the Egyptian heartland, including the suburbs of Cairo, in some estimates killing some 10,000 Egyptian civilians in the process.[3] A major study of the war concluded: "One of the major purposes of the raids, Defense Minister Moshe Dayan announced, was to bring home to the Egyptians their military vulnerability and inferiority and thereby 'topple' [Egyptian president Gamal Abdel] Nasser."[4]

AN AVOIDABLE WAR

One of the central themes of several of the writers in this book—especially Galen Jackson and Marc Trachtenberg, Yigal Kipnis, and William Quandt—is that the 1973 war was eminently avoidable, and would have been but for the intransigent policies of both Israel and the United States.[5]

During the run-up to the war, the Soviet Union made a number of reasonable and fair proposals to President Richard Nixon's administration that the two superpowers collaborate to—in effect—impose a peace settlement between Israel and Egypt. As developed in this book (and my own earlier work), there is substantial evidence that Nixon himself, though blowing hot and cold, was on several occasions open to such a collaboration, but was thwarted by the hard-line policies of Henry Kissinger, his national security adviser and, after September 1973, secretary of state. As Jackson and Trachtenberg put it in their chapter in this volume: "The evidence now available makes it abundantly clear that the Soviets had tried hard to work with the Americans in reaching a settlement that would have made the war unnecessary, had very much wanted to avoid a new Middle East war, and had warned US leaders repeatedly that if nothing were done an armed conflict was unavoidable."

Among the Soviet efforts to settle the Arab-Israeli conflict and avert a possible superpower confrontation was a secret 1971 offer to Israel to resume diplomatic relations and guarantee its security in the context of a general settlement based on the restoration of the pre-1967 boundaries. Israel was not interested, and the Nixon administration continued to resist any compromise settlement that was rejected by Israel or which preserved a Soviet role in Middle East diplomacy focusing on a political solution to the Arab-Israeli conflict.

In the course of its prewar diplomatic efforts, on several further occasions the Soviets proposed fair compromises—compromises that would be consistent with, and indeed further enhance, Israeli national security—on all the central issues of the Arab-Israeli conflict: territorial and border issues; a gradual withdrawal of Israeli forces from its 1967 conquests, backed by a variety of security measures, including the establishment of demilitarized zones, the deployment of a UN peacekeeping force in Sinai, and a commitment by Egypt to prevent Palestinian guerrilla attacks on Israel; free passage for Israeli shipping through the Suez Canal and Straits of Tiran; and an end to the economic boycott of Israel by its Arab enemies.

All of these proposals were rejected by the Nixon administration. Later, Kissinger admitted that Soviet complaints about being excluded from diplomacy were "perfectly true," for the central US policy in the Arab-Israeli conflict was to ensure the exclusion of the Soviet Union from any important political, military, or diplomatic role in the Middle East.[6] Moreover, until the 1973 war Israel was convinced that the Arabs had no military option and that the diplomatic stalemate worked in its favor.

As a result of US and Israeli intransigence—as well as the exclusion of the Palestinian issue from the prewar diplomacy—the early 1970s became a tragedy of lost opportunities to avert the 1973 war (and subsequent ones as well) and to have reached a comprehensive settlement of the Arab-Israeli conflict.[7]

THE WAR

In view of the deadlock, on October 6, 1973, Egypt and Syria launched attacks on the Israeli military positions in the Sinai and Golan Heights. Both states launched only limited attacks, the goal of which was to convince Israel that its security required that it withdraw from the occupied territories. Neither country had the intention of invading Israel itself—that is, Israel within its pre-1967 boundaries. Not only did the Egyptians and Syrians know that they lacked the military capabilities to do so, but they also realized that even such a "success" might lead to the Israeli use of nuclear weapons, which they knew or assumed Israel had.

The initial Egyptian goal was to cross the Suez Canal and establish its forces on the east bank, though later they advanced another thirty miles toward the Sinai mountain passes.[8] Similarly, Syria's political goals and military actions in the war were carefully limited. In the opening days of the war, the Syrian army seized the thinly defended Golan Heights—Israeli forces were then mainly deployed in the Sinai—and was then in a position to invade Israel's Jordan Valley and Galilee areas. However, even before Israeli reinforcements turned the tide, the Syrian forces stopped near the pre-1967 border. As Quandt writes, it was later revealed that Syrian president Hafiz al-Asad, probably in part because he feared a nuclear response by Israel, had issued strict orders to the army leaders that they were not to cross into Israel.[9]

Egypt's initial military successes in the Suez Canal area were soon reversed, as Israeli forces not only pushed the Egyptian forces back across the canal, but threatened to advance into the Egyptian heartland. They stopped only after US and Soviet pressure forced the Israeli government to agree to a ceasefire.

CONSEQUENCES OF THE WAR

An argument can be made that at least some of the consequences of the war were positive. As Risa Brooks argues in her chapter in this volume, despite their ultimate defeat the early military prowess of its military forces restored Egyptian pride and paved the way for the 1979 Israeli-Egyptian peace treaty, in which Israel—now convinced that the costs of holding on to all of its 1967 territorial acquisitions was too high—agreed to withdraw its military forces and settlers from the Sinai in exchange for an end to Egyptian economic, political, and military pressures against the Jewish state.

Further, the final military defeat of the Egyptian and Syrian forces and the emergence of Israeli nuclear deterrence—soon followed by the formal withdrawal of Egypt from the overall Arab-Israeli conflict and the de facto withdrawal of Syria as well—persuaded the other Arab states that Israel could not be militarily defeated.[10] As a consequence, there followed, in time, the 1994 Israeli-Jordanian peace treaty and the 2020 Abraham Accords, the latter of which normalized relations between Israel and a number of key Arab states.

Similarly, the disastrous defeat of the Arab states in the 1973 war played a major role in convincing Palestine Liberation Organization (PLO) leader Yasir Arafat that the Palestinians could not rely either on their military forces or on those of the Arab world as a whole to resolve the conflict with Israel. Consequently, Arafat realized that the best hope for the Palestinians would be a compromise two-state peace settlement. Over the next few years, the PLO's strategy gradually changed to give priority to negotiations over guerrilla warfare and terrorism, culminating in November 1988 with the official PLO announcement that it recognized Israel, accepted its right to exist, and would seek only the creation of a Palestinian state in the West Bank and Gaza, with Arab East Jerusalem as its capital. Further, the organization agreed that the new state would be largely demilitarized, welcome the stationing of international peacekeeping forces along its borders, and end terrorism and all forms of attack on Israel from its territory.

Despite these arguably positive consequences of the 1973 war, in my view they were outweighed by the negative ones—beginning most obviously with the tragic human costs to all the participants.

Beyond that (as argued above), had US and Israeli policies been less intransigent, a peace deal could have been reached not only between Israel and Egypt, but also between Israel and Syria.[11] This seems especially likely in light of the evidence that the Soviet Union was prepared to use its influence with the Arab world and join forces with the United States in efforts to prevent new Arab-Israeli wars.

In addition, while the longer-range consequences of the Arab oil embargo imposed during the 1973 crisis were complicated, paradoxically one of them was to convince the Arab oil-producing states that using the "oil weapon" had been too politically dangerous and costly to their own economies to be repeated in the future. As a result, Jeremy Pressman argues in his chapter in this volume that the net effect of the embargo was to reduce the likelihood that it would be repeated. Thus, the embargo actually lessened the incentive of the US government over the long term to impose pressures on Israel to reach a two-state settlement.

Another negative consequence—not only of the October 1973 war but of the overall Arab-Israeli conflict since 1948—Raymond Hinnebusch argues, was to increase nationalism and authoritarianism in Syria, which under the Asad regime became a hard-line dictatorship. The consequences are still playing out in contemporary civil war–torn Syria.

Though not discussed in this book, some Israeli analysts argue that another consequence of the war was to increase militarism and religious fanaticism in Israel. For example, the establishment of messianic Jewish settlements in the West Bank began in 1974.[12] The consequences of the rise of the settler movement in Israel are still a major political factor in the conflict today.

Finally, while yet another Arab defeat—together with the emergence of the Israeli nuclear deterrent—convinced most of the Arab world to abandon the hope of militarily defeating Israel, the formal or de facto peace settlements that followed, from the Israeli-Egyptian peace treaty through the Abraham Accords, could only be reached because the Arab states effectively abandoned the Palestinians to their fate. With no effective Arab or US pressures to induce Israel to agree to end its occupation and repression of the Palestinians, the two-state settlement idea is effectively dead, and the prospects for justice for the Palestinians have never been more remote.

NOTES

1. Avi Shlaim, *The Iron Wall: Israel and the Arab World* (New York: W. W. Norton, 2014), 271–72.

2. The conflict is also frequently referred to as the "War of Attrition."

3. Jerome Slater, *Mythologies Without End: The US, Israel, and the Arab-Israeli Conflict, 1917–1920* (New York: Oxford University Press, 2020), 158.

4. Lawrence L. Whetten, *The Canal War: Four-Power Conflict in the Middle East* (Cambridge, MA: MIT Press, 1974), 90.

5. See also Slater, *Mythologies Without End*, 152–64.

6. Quoted in Slater, *Mythologies Without End*, 164.

7. In addition to my book, *Mythologies Without End*, and the chapter by Jackson and Trachtenberg in this volume, see Daniel Kurtzer et al., *The Peace Puzzle: America's Quest for Arab-Israeli Peace, 1989–2011* (Ithaca, NY: Cornell University Press, 2012). This book, which includes three former high-ranking US diplomats and two leading academic scholars among its coauthors, reached similar conclusions about the tragedy of lost opportunities resulting from the rigidities of both Israeli and US policies.

8. According to the chapter written by Risa Brooks in this volume, this decision was reluctantly taken by Sadat, at the urgent request of the Syrian government, which hoped to force Israeli troops to divert from the Golan Heights to the Sinai front.

9. For a list of the sources of these assessments, see Slater, *Mythologies Without End*, 161.

10. See Slater, *Mythologies Without End*, 193–94.

11. In practice, one could argue that despite the absence of a formal agreement between the two countries, a de facto peace between Syria and Israel has existed for some time. As Israeli prime minister Benjamin Netanyahu said in July 2018, "We haven't had a problem with the Assad regime. . . . For 40 years, not a single bullet was fired on the Golan Heights." Quoted in Slater, *Mythologies Without End*, 207.

12. See Benjamin Beit-Hallahmi, *Despair and Deliverance: Private Salvation in Contemporary Israel* (Albany: State University of New York Press, 1992).

Index

Abbas, Mahmoud, 142–43
Abraham Accords, 168
Aflaq, Michael, 96
Agranat Commission, 31n85, 31n90
Ajami, Fouad, 100, 156
Algeria, 97, 156
Allon, Yigal, 6, 9–11
Amer, Abdel Hakim, 38–39, 41, 46, 48–49
anarchy, 97
Al-Aqsa Intifada, 141–42
Arab-Israeli War. *See specific topics*
Arabs: Arab Cold War, 113; Arab National Movement, 124; Arab Socialist Union, 52n17; Arab Triangle, 100–101, 112–14; to Brezhnev, vii–viii; to Dayan, 19; Egypt and, 26–27, 102–6; in geopolitics, 106–7; intelligence on, 15, 102–3; Israel and, ix, 2, 13–14, 18, 62–63, 78, 110–11, 117, 138–39, 151–60, 165–69; in Jordan, 99; to Kissinger, 152–53; Kuwait and, 155; leadership of, 1; MENA to, 93–94; in Middle East, 64; military of, 98–99, 101–2; nationalism of, 102; OAPEC, 155–56, 160; oil from, xi, xv–xvi, 101, 129; in Palestine, 105, 169; pan-Arabism, 95, 113–14, 158–59; radicalism to, 97, 99–100, 131; to Sadat, 101–2; Suez Canal to, 46, 103; Syria and, 24–25; USSR and, xiii, 72–76, 163nn60–61, 168. *See also specific topics*
Arafat, Yasir, 125–30, 132–40, 142–43, 146n51, 149n89, 168
al-Asad, Hafiz: Faisal and, viii; leadership of, 13, 22–23, 97, 99–100; national security state of, 114–18; negotiations with, 109–11; to Netanyahu, 170n11; reputation of, 21, 24, 93, 169; Sadat and, 100–101, 108; U.S., to, 105
Aslan, Ali, 109
authority: authoritarianism, 114–15; of Kissinger, 86n71; in Middle East, 133–34; Palestinian Authority, 141–42; of Sadat, 53n37, 53n42; sovereignty and, 40–41; of UN, 73–74, 97, 109, 155

El-Badri, Hasan, 46

Bar-Joseph, Uri, 55n69
Bar-Lev, Chaim, 37
Bar-Lev Line, 37–38, 45
Begin, Menachem, 27, 114
Biden, Joe, 142
Black September Organization, 128
Blanton, Tom, 82n23
Brezhnev, Leonid: Arabs to, vii–viii; détente to, 80n14; Egypt to, 75–76; foreign policy of, 65–66; Israel to, xii, 59; Meir and, 60; Middle East to, 58; Nixon and, xvi, 13, 57, 80n12, 86n71, 154; reputation of, xiv; to Schlesinger, 88n82
Bush, George H. W., 140, 160
Bush, George W., 142

Camp David, x, 114, 139–42
Carter, Jimmy, 139
cease-fire agreement, 59–60, 72–73, 88n82, 157
Central Intelligence Agency (CIA): foreign policy and, 1; government and, 86n67; intelligence from, 128; Kissinger and, 129–30; Palestine to, 127, 136; USSR to, 22
Christians, 116
CIA. See Central Intelligence Agency
Civil Defense, 11
civil-military relations, 36, 38–41, 45–46
Clinton, Bill, 141–42
Cold War: Arab Cold War, 113; oil and, 151–61, 163n48, 163nn60–61, 164n64; politics of, 57, 100, 127, 131. See also specific topics
communism, 77–78
containment, 18–19
Cuban missile crisis, vii–viii, xiii

Daigle, Craig, 29n31
Dannreuther, Roland, 160
Dayan, Moshe: Arabs to, 19; Dinitz on, 16; in diplomacy, 9–10, 17–18; Elazar and, 15–16, 20–21; foreign policy and, 23; Galili and, 9, 12; intelligence from, 74–75; Kissinger and, 10–11; Meir and, xiii, 11–12, 14–15, 17–18, 30n70; Rabin and, 31n89; scholarship from, 165; Syria to, 32n96; U.S., and, 14, 31n87; Zamir and, 20
Democratic Front for the Liberation of Palestine (DFLP), 124
détente: to Brezhnev, 80n14; geopolitics of, 57–58, 110; to Meir, 156; scholarship on, xi, 80n12; to U.S., xiv, 77–78
DFLP. See Democratic Front for the Liberation of Palestine
Dinitz, Simcha: on Dayan, 16; in diplomacy, ix, xii, 63; Kissinger and, 75, 88n79, 88n82, 91n89, xviin8; after Rabin, 13–15; UN and, 90n85
diplomacy: civil-military relations and, 45–46; Dayan in, 9–10, 17–18; Dinitz in, ix, xii, 63; Dobrynin in, 65; in geopolitics, 112–14; international agency and, 101–2; with Ismail, H., 28n26, 29n30; with Israel, x, 11, 51n11, 88n82; Israeli Security Theory in, 37; in Jordan, 27; Kissinger in, viii–ix, xii, xv, 7, 22, 57–61, 70–72, 83n35, 101, 106–11, 163nn60–61; of Meir, 1–2, 24, 29n49; in Middle East, xi, 156; negotiations in, 1–2; with PLO, 126–34; political analysis of, 9–14, 25–27; political control and, 40; politics of, 12–13, 24–25; pragmatism, 99–100; of Rabin, 5; with Sadat, 158; shuttle, 106, 108, 135, 156; Sinai II, 111, 113; sovereignty and, 8; Suez Canal in, 26; with Syria, 27, 106–12; unilateralism and, 159–60; by U.S., x–xi, 51n14, 138–44, 170n7
Dobrynin, Anatoly: in diplomacy, 65; on Sadat, xviin7; scholarship from, 85n51; on USSR, xi

Eban, Abba, 12
economic liberation, 40
economics, 48–49, 100–101
Egypt: allegiances with, 15–16; Arabs and, 26–27, 102–6; Bar-Lev Line to, 37–38; to Brezhnev, 75–76; demands of, 9, 66–68; economy of, 40; foreign policy of, 2–3, 54n57; in geopolitics, 154; intelligence on, 90n85; Israel and, vii–viii, xi–xii, 3–4, 7–8, 17, 26–27, 32n109, 33n110, 44–45, 55n69, 168; Jordan and, 139; Kissinger and, x, 2, 85n62; Marwan on, 7; media in, 39; Meir on, 5; Middle East and, 75; military effectiveness of, 36, 42–48; military of, 21, 35–41, 48–50, 51n11, 53n42, 54n56, 59, 74, 102–3; to Nixon, 4–5; operational planning by, 46–47; politics in, 17–18, 23–24; protests in, 52n17; Sadat for, 51n14, 100, 157, xviin5; Saudi Arabia and, 100–101, 134; in Six-Day War, 24; sovereignty of, 4, 10, 13, 21–22; Suez Canal to, ix, 73, 107, 111, 167; Syria and, ix, xv, 1, 12–14, 17, 19–20, 95, 116, 125, 165, 167; United Arab Republic and, 96; U.S., and, xii, xiv–xv, 7, 94, 110, 112, 136; USSR and, xiii–xiv, 18, 32n100, 45–46, 63, 88n82, 131–32, 154; in War of Attrition, 18. *See also specific topics*
Elazar, David: Dayan and, 15–16, 20–21; foreign policy of, 31n86, 31n89; Israel to, 18–19; reputation of, 10; Sadat and, 15; Zamir and, 10
embargoes, 100–101, 155–56, 159, 169
energy, 106, 155–57

Fahmi, Ismail, 25
Faisal (king), viii, 100–101, 107–8, 155
Fateh, 124–30, 138
Fawzi, Mohammed, 40, 53n42
Ford, Gerald, 57, 135–36, 138, 160–61

foreign policy: of Brezhnev, 65–66; CIA and, 1; civil-military relations and, 45–46; containment, 18–19; Dayan and, 23; decision-making in, 21; Eban on, 12; of Egypt, 2–3, 54n57; of Elazar, 31n86, 31n89; to Galili, 11–12; implementation stages, 8–9; of Nixon, 6, 32n104, 58, 163n48, 166, xviiin14; with Palestine, 5–6; political analysis of, 7–9, 14–16; pragmatism, 99–100; of Rabin, 111; of Sadat, 107–8; of Saudi Arabia, 156; scholarship on, 76–77; of Syria, 96–97; of U.S., viii, 71–76; of USSR, ix, xiv, 47

Gaddis, John Lewis, 57–58
Galili, Yisrael: Dayan and, 9, 12; foreign policy to, 11–12; Galili document, 24; Kissinger and, 12; Meir to, 10–11
al-Gamasy, Mohammed Abdel al-Ghani, 32n108, 41, 43–45, 55n71
Gawrych, George, 37
geopolitics: Arabs in, 106–7; of autonomy, 26–27; of communism, 77–78; of détente, 57–58, 110; diplomacy in, 112–14; of economic liberation, 40; Egypt in, 154; of energy, 106; history of, 79n4, 93–97; Iran in, 64; Israel in, 72–76, 124–26; in Middle East, 164n64; of 1967 War, 96–102; of nuclear war, viii, 90n84; of oil, 22–23, 111; Palestine in, 123–24, 128–34, 143–44; Syria in, 112–18; of Vietnam War, 61, 73, 97, 152; of war, 52n21
Ghanim, Muhammad, 86n66
Godley, G. McMurtrie, 132–33
Golan, Matti, 87n77, 88n78
Gromyko, Andrei, 63–66, 71, 132
Gulf War, 115, 140–41

Haig, Alexander, 63, 91n88
Hamas, 142

Hassan (king), 130
Heikal, Mohamed, 53n42
Hizbollah, 114, 117
Hoge, James, 86n71
Hussein (king), 5–6, 70, 131

ICC. *See* International Criminal Court
identity, 95
ideology, 96
implementation stages, 8–9
integration, 45–46
intelligence: on Arabs, 15, 102–3; CIA, 1, 22, 86n67, 127–30, 136; from Dayan, 74–75; on Egypt, 90n85; on internal relations, 120n41; in U.S., 132–33
internal relations, 120n41
international agency, 101–2
International Criminal Court (ICC), 142
Iran, 64, 115
Iraq, 105, 115, 140–41
irredentism, 95
Ismail, Ahmed, 41, 43–45
Ismail, Hafiz: diplomacy with, 28n26, 29n30; Kissinger and, 4, 6–7, 22–23, 32n102, 66–71, 85n61, 85n63, 86nn66–67; Meir and, 3; Nixon and, 4, 67; reports from, 5; to Sadat, 10; scholarship from, x; on Syria, 5–6
Israel: Allon on, 11; Arabs and, ix, 2, 13–14, 18, 62–63, 78, 110–11, 117, 138–39, 151–60, 165–69; archives from, viii–ix, 84n41, xviin3; Bar-Lev Line to, 37–38; to Brezhnev, xii, 59; cease-fire to, 59–60, 72–73, 88n82; diplomacy with, x, 11, 51n11, 88n82; domestic instability in, 95–96; Egypt and, vii–viii, xi–xii, 3–4, 7–8, 17, 26–27, 32n109, 33n110, 44–45, 55n69, 168; to Elazar, 18–19; elections in, 13–14, 23, 32n102; to Ford, 135; in geopolitics, 72–76, 124–26; goals of, 12–13; Golan on, 88n78; in ICC, 142; Israel Defense Forces, 15–18, 20–21, 31n89, 32n96;
Israeli Security Theory, 37; Jericho missiles for, xiii; Jordan and, xv, 125–26; Kissinger and, xi, 9–14, 17, 29n31, 30n65, 72–76, 87n76, 135–36; Middle East and, 66–67, 98–99; military of, 8–9, 16, 32n96, 36; Nixon and, 25, 74; in Oslo Accord, 117–18; Palestine and, 22, 68, 97; political analysis of, 17–18; politics in, 24; to prisoners of war, 108–9; to Rogers, 53n42; in Rogers Plan, 27n7; to Sadat, 113–14; SAMs and, 102–4; scholarship on, 60–61; Suez Canal to, 8; Syria and, xiii, 21, 25, 31n89, 70, 96–97, 164n64, 169, 170n11; U.S., and, xii–xiii, 14, 21–22, 29n31, 90n85, 98–99, 101–2, 107–11, 123–24; to USSR, 81n14, 82n23; in War of Attrition, 18; Zionist project for, 93–94. *See also specific topics*

Jarring, Gunnar, 23
Jericho missiles, xiii
Jordan: Arabs in, 99; diplomacy in, 27; Egypt and, 139; Hussein for, 5–6, 131; Iraq and, 105; Israel and, xv, 125–26; Palestine and, x, 25, 69–70, 127; Syria and, 5–6, 67–68, 97, 131–32

Kennan, George, 76–77
Kennedy, John F., vii, viii
Khalil, Osamah, 155
Khrushchev, Nikita, vii
Kissinger, Henry: Arabs to, 152–53; authority of, 86n71; CIA and, 129–30; Dayan and, 10–11; demands of, 9; Dinitz and, 75, 88n79, 88n82, 91n89, xviin8; in diplomacy, viii–ix, xii, xv, 7, 22, 57–61, 70–72, 83n35, 101, 106–11, 163nn60–61; Egypt and, x, 2, 85n62; Galili and, 12; Godley and, 132–33; Haig and, 63, 91n88; in history, 68–70; implementation stages to, 8–9;

Ismail, H., and, 4, 6–7, 22–23, 32n102, 66–71, 85n61, 85n63, 86nn66–67; Israel and, xi, 9–14, 17, 29n31, 30n65, 72–76, 87n76, 135–36; Khalil on, 155; leadership of, 1–2; Meir and, xi, 6–8, 12, 14, 27, 28n26, 29n28, 62, 72–73, 87n77; Middle East and, 13–14, 127–28, 130–31; MOA of, 136–37, 139, 142; Nixon and, viii, xiv, 2–3, 5, 7, 15–16, 22, 152, 158, 164n64; pan-Arabism to, 158–59; PLO and, 129–30, 133–38; pressure on, 10; Rabin and, 28n20, 29n30; reputation of, 15, 106, 123–24, 138–43, 151; Rusk and, 162n33; Sadat and, xi, xiv–xvi, 3–4, 13, 25–26, 32n109, 111, 135; scholarship on, 61–68, 76–78, 81n19, 82n23, 166–67; shuttle diplomacy by, 106, 108, 135, 156; for U.S., 24–25; USSR and, 88n78, 90n85, 92n99, 101–2, 157–58; to WSAG, xvi, 155–57

Kuwait, 155–56

Lebanon, 95, 112–13, 116–17, 137, 164n64
Lebow, Richard Ned, 59–60

Maronite Christians, 116
Marwan, Ashraf, 7, 18–20
media, 39, 110
mediation, 18
Meir, Golda: Brezhnev and, 60; Dayan and, xiii, 11–12, 14–15, 17–18, 30n70; détente to, 156; diplomacy of, 1–2, 24, 29n49; on Egypt, 5; to Galili, 10–11; Ismail, H., and, 3; Kissinger and, xi, 6–8, 12, 14, 27, 28n26, 29n28, 62, 72–73, 87n77; leadership of, 23, 60, 63; Nixon and, xii–xiii, 3, 154; policy of, 7; Rabin and, ix, 9; Sadat and, vii–viii, x, 7; in speeches, 1; Syria to, 20; U.S., and, 9–10, 14–15, 29n32; Yariv and, 25

memorandum of agreement (MOA), 136–37, 139, 142
MENA. *See* Middle East and North Africa
Middle East: anarchy in, 97; Arabs in, 64; Arab Triangle in, 100–101; authority in, 133–34; to Brezhnev, 58; civil-military relations in, 38–39; diplomacy in, xi, 156; Egypt and, 75; geopolitics in, 164n64; history of, xvi, 37–38; international crises in, ix; Israel and, 66–67, 98–99; Kissinger and, 13–14, 127–28, 130–31; military in, 26; nationalism in, 96; to Nixon, x, 106, 127; oil in, 113; politics in, 137–38, 155; Rogers Plan for, 3; Sadat and, 1–2, 164n64; shuttle diplomacy in, 106, 108, 135, 156; Suez Canal and, ix, xiii, 41, 44–45; Syria and, 93–97; to UN, xi, 38; to U.S., 22, 59, 61–62, 168, xviin2; USSR in, xiv–xv, 77–78. *See also specific topics*
Middle East and North Africa (MENA), 93–94
military: Agranat Commission on, 31n85, 31n90; of Arabs, 98–99, 101–2; civil-military relations, 36, 38–41, 45–46; effectiveness, 36, 41–48, 52n21; of Egypt, 21, 35–41, 48–50, 51n11, 53n42, 54n56, 59, 74, 102–3; of Israel, 8–9, 16, 32n96, 36; Israel Defense Forces, 15–18, 20–21, 31n89, 32n96; in Middle East, 26; Nixon and, 153; personnel, 41–42, 46–48; Phantom jets, 3; political-military integration, 43–45; politics, xviin7; Sadiq for, 40, 43–44, 53n37; SAMs, 102–4; Skyhawk jets, 3; Suez Canal for, 22; of Syria, 15–16, 99–100, 103–5, 109–10; Tal for, 12–13; technological-military inferiority, 18–21; U.S., ix, xi, 18, 90n84
MOA. *See* memorandum of agreement

Morgenthau, Hans, 61
Morocco, 130, 156

NAM. *See* nonaligned movement
Nasser, Abdel, 35–41, 47–49, 53n37, 65, 100, 165
nationalism, 96, 99–100, 102
Netanyahu, Benjamin, 170n11
1967 War: geopolitics of, 96–102; history of, 35–40, 43, 46–47, 49–50; politics after, 3, 16, 19, 21–22, 24–27, 31n89
Nitze, Paul, 81n14
Nixon, Richard: Brezhnev and, xvi, 13, 57, 80n12, 86n71, 154; Egypt to, 4–5; energy to, 155–57; foreign policy of, 6, 32n104, 58, 163n48, 166, xviiin14; Ismail, H., and, 4, 67; Israel and, 25, 74; Kennedy and, viii; Kissinger and, viii, xiv, 2–3, 5, 7, 15–16, 22, 152, 158, 164n64; Meir and, xii–xiii, 3, 154; Middle East to, x, 106, 127; military and, 153; USSR to, xv, 64–66
nonaligned movement (NAM), 126–27
nuclear war, viii, xiii, 90n84

OAPEC. *See* Organization of Arab Petroleum Exporting Countries
Obama, Barack, 160
oil: from Arabs, xi, xv–xvi, 101, 129; Cold War and, 151–61, 163n48, 163nn60–61, 164n64; embargoes, 155–56, 159, 169; geopolitics of, 22–23, 111; in Middle East, 113; from Saudi Arabia, 22; in Syria, 104
operational planning, 42, 46–47
Organization of Arab Petroleum Exporting Countries (OAPEC), 155–56, 160
Oslo process, 117–18, 124, 140–41, 143

Palestine: Arabs in, 105, 169; Arafat for, 125–30, 132–40, 142–43, 146n51, 149n89, 168; at Camp David, 141–42; Christians in, 116; to CIA, 127, 136; DFLP, 124; foreign policy with, 5–6; in geopolitics, 123–24, 128–34, 143–44; history of, 124–26; Israel and, 22, 68, 97; Jordan and, x, 25, 69–70, 127; Lebanon and, 95; nationalism in, 99–100; in Oslo Accord, 117–18; Palestinian Authority, 141–42; PFLP, 124, 126, 132; sovereignty of, 26–27, 114; Syria and, 71, 95–96, 165; U.S., and, 138–42
Palestine Liberation Organization (PLO): diplomacy with, 126–34; history of, 112–13, 117; Kissinger and, 129–30, 133–38; politics of, 134–42; Syria and, 131; terrorism and, 168; U.S., and, 123–30; USSR and, 129
pan-Arabism, 95, 113–14, 158–59
PFLP. *See* Popular Front for the Liberation of Palestine
Phantom jets, 3
Plan Badr, 44
PLO. *See* Palestine Liberation Organization
political analysis: of diplomacy, 9–14, 25–27; of foreign policy, 7–9, 14–16; history and, 2–7, 29n31; of Israel, 17–18; of Sadat, 21–25; scholarship on, 1–2; technological-military inferiority and, 18–21
politics: of Cold War, 57, 100, 127, 131; of diplomacy, 12–13, 24–25; economics and, 48–49; in Egypt, 17–18, 23–24; of Fateh, 124–30, 138; of history, 61–68; in Israel, 24; in Middle East, 137–38, 155; military, xviin7; after 1967 War, 3, 16, 19, 21–22, 24–27, 31n89; of PLO, 134–42; political control, 40; political dominance, 49–50; political goals, 44–45; political-military integration, 43–45; of Suez Canal, 18; of U.S., 26–27, 61

Popular Front for the Liberation of Palestine (PFLP), 124, 126, 132
Portugal, 153
Powell, James, 47–48
pragmatism, 99–100
Pressman, Jeremy, xv
prisoners of war, 45, 108–9

al-Qadir, Hasan Abdel, 43
Quandt, William, 88n78, 90n84, 132, 152–53, 156–57, 166–67

Rabin, Yitzhak: Allon and, 9–10; Dayan and, 31n89; Dinitz after, 13–15; diplomacy of, 5; Ford and, 136; foreign policy of, 111; Kissinger and, 28n20, 29n30; Meir and, ix, 9; reports from, 3, 6, 8
radicalism, 97, 99–100, 131
Ramadan War. *See specific topics*
Reagan, Ronald, 140
recruitment, 41–42
responsiveness, 45–47
Rogers, William, 3, 18, 53n42
Rogers Plan, 3, 27n7
Rostow, Eugene V., 79n4
Rusk, Dean, 162n33
Russia. *See* Soviet Union

Sadat, Anwar: Arabs to, 101–2; al-Asad and, 100–101, 108; authority of, 53n37, 53n42; civil-military relations under, 39–41; demands of, 5–6; diplomacy with, 158; Dobrynin on, xviin7; for Egypt, 51n14, 100, 157, xviin5; Elazar and, 15; foreign policy of, 107–8; Ismail, H., to, 10; Israel to, 113–14; Kissinger and, xi, xiv–xvi, 3–4, 13, 25–26, 32n109, 111, 135; leadership of, 26–27, 39, 44–45, 49, 170n8; Meir and, vii–viii, x, 7; Middle East and, 1–2, 164n64; political analysis of, 21–25; reputation of, ix, xi, xiii, 17, 29n49, 39–40, 43–44; scholarship on, 35–36, 47–48; Suez Canal and, 37–38, 105; Syria to, xi, 54n57; USSR and, 3, 132
Sadiq, Mohamed, 40, 43–44, 53n37
SAMs. *See* surface-to-air missiles
Saudi Arabia: Egypt and, 100–101, 134; Faisal for, 107–8, 155; foreign policy of, 156; oil from, 22; Syria and, viii, 22–23
Saunders, Hal, 6–7, 135–36
SCAF. *See* Supreme Council of the Armed Forces
Schlesinger, James, xiii, 88n82
Seale, Patrick, 108
Sharon, Ariel, 38, 142
al-Shazly, Saad al-Din, 43–44, 54n56, 55n61
al-Shihabi, Hikmat, 109
shuttle diplomacy, 106, 108, 135, 156
Sinai II, 111, 113
Sisco, Joseph, 23
Six-Day War, 24
skills, of military personnel, 42, 46–48
Skyhawk jets, 3
sovereignty: authority and, 40–41; diplomacy and, 8; of Egypt, 4, 10, 13, 21–22; of Palestine, 26–27, 114; territory and, 6–7
Soviet Union (USSR): Arabs and, xiii, 72–76, 163nn60–61, 168; Begin and, 27; to CIA, 22; Dobrynin on, xi; Egypt and, xiii–xiv, 18, 32n100, 45–46, 63, 88n82, 131–32, 154; foreign policy of, ix, xiv, 47; Gromyko for, 63–64, 71; Israel to, 81n14, 82n23; Kissinger and, 88n78, 90n85, 92n99, 101–2, 157–58; in Middle East, xiv–xv, 77–78; NAM to, 126–27; to Nixon, xv, 64–66; PLO and, 129; Sadat and, 3, 132; U.S., and, vii, xi, 4, 22, 24, 37, 57–58, 68, 80n12, 127–28, 151–61, 161n11, 161n14, 166–67
State Department, 2–3
Stein, Janice Gross, 59–60

Stein, Kenneth, 82n23
strategic surprise, 45–46
Suez Canal: to Arabs, 46, 103; in diplomacy, 26; to Egypt, ix, 73, 107, 111, 167; to Israel, 8; Middle East and, ix, xiii, 41, 44–45; for military, 22; politics of, 18; Sadat and, 37–38, 105
Supreme Council of the Armed Forces (SCAF), 43
surface-to-air missiles (SAMs), 102–5
Syria: Arabs and, 24–25; to Dayan, 32n96; diplomacy with, 27, 106–12; Egypt and, ix, xv, 1, 12–14, 17, 19–20, 95, 116, 125, 165, 167; foreign policy of, 96–97; in geopolitics, 112–18; irredentism in, 95; Ismail, H., on, 5–6; Israel and, xiii, 21, 25, 31n89, 70, 96–97, 164n64, 169, 170n11; Jordan and, 5–6, 67–68, 97, 131–32; to Meir, 20; Middle East and, 93–97; military of, 15–16, 99–100, 103–5, 109–10; oil in, 104; Palestine and, 71, 95–96, 165; pan-Arabism in, 114; PLO and, 131; to Sadat, xi, 54n57; SAMs for, 105; Saudi Arabia and, viii, 22–23; scholarship on, 98–106

Tal, Yisrael, 12–13
technological-military inferiority, 18–21
terrorism, xv, 128, 168
Themido, Joao Hall, 153
Third World, 126–27
Trump, Donald, 142
Turkmani, Hasan, 109

UN. *See* United Nations
unilateralism, 159–60
United Arab Republic, 96
United Nations (UN): authority of, 73–74, 97, 109, 155; Dinitz and, 90n85; General Assembly, 133–34; Jarring for, 23; Middle East to, xi, 38; Resolution 242, 67, 98, 100, 102, 105, 106–7, 109–10, 125, 128–29; Resolution 338, xi–xii, 51n11, 105, 109–10, 128–29, 153–54; Security Council, xi; U.S., and, 109–10
United States (U.S.): to al-Asad, 105; Dayan and, 14, 31n87; détente to, xiv, 77–78; diplomacy by, x–xi, 51n14, 138–44, 170n7; Egypt and, xii, xiv–xv, 7, 94, 110, 112, 136; foreign policy of, viii, 71–76; in Gulf War, 115, 140–41; intelligence in, 132–33; Iraq to, 115; Israel and, xii–xiii, 14, 21–22, 29n31, 90n85, 98–99, 101–2, 107–11, 123–24; Kissinger for, 24; Lebanon and, 164n64; Meir and, 9–10, 14–15, 29n32; Middle East to, 22, 59, 61–62, 168, xvin2; military, ix, xi, 18, 90n84; in Oslo Accord, 124; Palestine and, 138–42; PLO and, 123–30; politics of, 26–27, 61; shuttle diplomacy by, 106, 108, 135, 156; State Department, 2–3; terrorism to, xv; UN and, 109–10; USSR and, vii, xi, 4, 22, 24, 37, 57–58, 68, 80n12, 127–28, 151–61, 161n11, 161n14, 166–67; in Vietnam War, 61, 73, 97, 152; WSAG in, xvi, xvin2
USSR. *See* Soviet Union

Vaïsse, Justin, 79n4
Venn, Fiona, 155–56
Vietnam War, 61, 73, 97, 152
Vitalis, Robert, 159

Walters, Vernon, 129–30
war. *See specific topics*
War of Attrition, 18, 37
Washington Special Actions Group (WSAG), xvi, 155–57, xvin2
Wohlstetter, Albert, 81n14
World War I, 93–94
WSAG. *See* Washington Special Actions Group

Ya'ari, Ehud, 53n37
Yamani, Ahmed Zaki, 155
Yariv, Aharon, 25, 32n108
Yom Kippur War. *See specific topics*

Zamir, Zvi, 10, 18–20
Zeira, Eli, 10, 16
Zionist project, 93–94

About the Authors

Galen Jackson, the editor of the volume, is an assistant professor of political science at Williams College, where he teaches courses in international relations, international security, American foreign policy, nuclear weapons, cybersecurity, the international relations of the Middle East, and the Arab-Israeli conflict. He is the author of *A Lost Peace: Great Power Politics and the Arab-Israeli Dispute, 1967–1979*.

Risa Brooks is the Allis Chalmers Professor of Political Science at Marquette University, a senior fellow at West Point's Modern War Institute, and a non-resident fellow in the International Security Program at New America in Washington, DC. She is the author of *Shaping Strategy: The Civil-Military Politics of Strategic Assessment* (2008). She is an expert on the Middle East and North Africa, and has written about Egyptian military reforms during the period that preceded the October 1973 Arab-Israeli War.

Khaled Elgindy is a senior fellow at the Middle East Institute, where he directs the Program on Palestine and Israeli-Palestinian Affairs. He is the author of *Blind Spot: America and the Palestinians, from Balfour to Trump* (2019). He previously served as a fellow in the Foreign Policy program at the Brookings Institution from 2010 through 2018. Prior to arriving at Brookings, he served as an adviser to the Palestinian leadership in Ramallah on permanent status negotiations with Israel from 2004 to 2009, and was a key participant in the Annapolis negotiations of 2007–2008. He is also an adjunct instructor in Arab studies at Georgetown University.

Raymond Hinnebusch is professor of international relations and Middle East politics at the University of St. Andrews and founder and director of the Centre for Syrian Studies. His works include *Authoritarian Power and State Formation in Ba'thist Syria* (1990) and *Syria: Revolution from Above* (2001). He is the coeditor of *Syria: From Reform to Revolt* (2014); *The Syria*

Uprising: Domestic Factors and Early Trajectory (2018); and *The War for Syria: Regional and International Factors in the Syrian Conflict* (2019) and the author of "The Foreign Policy of Syria" in *The Foreign Policies of Middle Eastern States* (2014).

Yigal Kipnis is an Israeli historian who researches the settlement geography and political history of Israel. He has written several books, including *The Mountain That Was as a Monster: The Golan between Syria and Israel* (Hebrew, 2009); *The Golan Heights: Political History, Settlement and Geography since 1949* (2013); and *1973: The Road to War* (2013).

Jeremy Pressman is a professor of political science at the University of Connecticut. He studies international relations, the Arab-Israeli conflict, Middle East politics, and American foreign policy. He is the author of numerous articles and books about international politics and the Middle East, including *Warring Friends: Alliance Restraint in International Politics* (2008) and *The Sword Is Not Enough: Arabs, Israelis, and the Limits of Military Force* (2020).

William Quandt is professor emeritus in the Department of Politics at the University of Virginia. He previously served as a senior fellow in the Foreign Policy program at the Brookings Institution and on the National Security Council staff in the Richard Nixon and Jimmy Carter administrations. He was actively involved in the negotiations that led to the Camp David Accords and the Egyptian-Israeli peace treaty, and was an adviser to Henry Kissinger during the October 1973 Arab-Israeli War. He has published many works on US Middle East policy and the Arab-Israeli dispute. His book *Peace Process: American Diplomacy and the Arab-Israeli Conflict Since 1967* (2005) is generally considered to be the most important, and most reliable, general work on the subject.

Jerome Slater is professor emeritus of political science at the State University of New York at Buffalo. He has published a number of books and many articles about the United States and the Arab-Israeli conflict, in outlets such as *International Security*, *Middle East Policy*, and *Political Science Quarterly*. His most recent book is *Mythologies Without End: The US, Israel, and the Arab-Israeli Conflict, 1917–2020* (2020).

Marc Trachtenberg is a research professor of political science at UCLA. A historian by training, he is the author of many scholarly works dealing mostly with twentieth-century international politics. A collection of his articles, *The Cold War and After: History, Theory, and the Logic of International Politics*, was published in 2012.